USA TODAY

LOGIC
SUPER CHALLENGE

Can't get enough of USA TODAY puzzles?

You can play:

- In the USA TODAY newspaper

- At puzzles.usatoday.com

- By downloading the FREE USA TODAY app (Get it on Google Play or iTunes)

- By downloading the FREE USA TODAY Crossword app (Get it on Google Play or iTunes)

USA TODAY

LOGIC
SUPER CHALLENGE
200 PUZZLES

Andrews McMeel
PUBLISHING®

Andrews McMeel Publishing
a division of Andrews McMeel Universal
1130 Walnut Street, Kansas City, Missouri 64106

www.andrewsmcmeel.com

19 20 21 22 23 PAH 10 9 8 7 6 5 4 3 2 1

ISBN: 978-1-5248-5110-1

Editor: Patty Rice
Art Director/Designer: Holly Swayne
Production Editor: Meg Daniels
Production Manager: Cliff Koehler

Solving Tips

The next few pages have all the instructions you'll need to tackle all the puzzles in this book. They may look a little complicated but you'll soon get the hang of things.

Logic Problems

With each standard problem we provide a chart that takes into account every possibility to be considered in the solution. First, you carefully read the statement of the problem in the introduction, and then consider the clues. Next, you enter in the chart all the information immediately apparent from the clues, using an **X** to show a definite **no** and a ✓ to show a definite **yes**. You'll find that this narrows down the possibilities and might even reveal some new definite information. So now you re-read the clues with these new facts in mind to discover further positive/negative relationships. Be sure to enter information in all the relevant places in the chart, and to transfer newly discovered information from one part of the chart to all the other relevant parts. The smaller grid at the end of each problem is simply a quick-reference chart for all your findings.

Now try your hand at working through the example below—you'll soon get the hang of it.

EXAMPLE

Three children live on the same street. From the two clues given below, can you discover each child's full name and age?

Clues

1. Miss Brown is three years older than Mary.
2. The child whose surname is White is 9 years old.

Solution

Miss Brown (clue 1) cannot be Brian, so you can place an **X** in the Brian/Brown box. Clue 1 tells us that she is not Mary either, so you can put an **X** in the Mary/Brown box. Miss Brown is therefore Anne, the only possibility remaining. Now place a ✓ in that box in the chart, with corresponding **X**'s against the other possible surnames for Anne.

If Anne Brown is three years older than Mary (clue 1), she must be 10 and Mary, 7. So place ✓'s in the Anne/10, Brown/10 and Mary/7 boxes, and **X**'s in all the empty boxes in each row and column containing these ✓'s. The chart now reveals Brian's age as 9, so you can place a ✓ in the Brian/9 box. Clue 2 tells us that White is 9 years old too, so he must be Brian. Place a ✓ in the White/9 box and X's in the remaining empty boxes in that row and column, then place a ✓ in the Brian/White box and X's in all the remaining empty boxes in that row and column. You can see now that the remaining unfilled boxes in the chart must contain ✓'s, since their rows and columns contain only X's, so they reveal Green as the surname of 7-year-old Mary.

Anne Brown, 10.
Brian White, 9.
Mary Green, 7.

The solving system for the puzzles that don't have grids is very similar. Read through the clues and insert any positive information onto the diagram. Then read through the clues again and use a process of elimination to start positioning the

	Brown	Green	White	7	9	10
Anne	✓	X	X	X	X	✓
Brian	X			X		X
Mary	X			✓	X	X
7	X					
9	X					
10	✓	X	X			

	Brown	Green	White	7	9	10
Anne	✓	X	X	X	X	✓
Brian	X	X	✓	X	✓	X
Mary	X		X	✓	X	X
7	X		X			
9	X	X	✓			
10	✓	X	X			

remaining elements of the puzzle. You may find it easier to make a few notes about which elements of the puzzle you know are linked but that cannot yet be entered on the diagram. These can be positioned once the other examples of those elements are positioned. If you find it difficult to know where to begin, use the starting tip printed upside down at the foot of the page.

Battleships

Before you look at the numbers around the grid, there are a number of squares you can fill in from the starter pieces given. If an end piece of a ship is given, then the square next to it, in the direction indicated by the end, must also be part of a ship. If a middle piece is given, then the pieces on either side must also be ship parts; in this instance, you need some more information before you can decide which way the ship runs. Also, any square that is adjacent to an end piece (apart from those squares in the direction of the rest of the ship), any square touching the corners of a middle piece, and all squares around destroyers (one-square ships) must be sea.

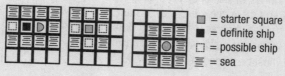

 = starter square
 = definite ship
 = possible ship
 = sea

Now, look at the numbers around the grid and eliminate rows and columns in which the large aircraft carrier might be. Either from this or by looking at the next consequences of the remaining possibilities, you should be able to position this ship. Now fill in the sea squares around the carrier and move on to the smaller ships.

Domino Search

Starting this puzzle is just a matter of finding one domino (number pair) that is unique in the grid. It is often easiest to look for the double numbers first (0 0; 6 6). When you have discovered one or more of these unique possibilities, you will find that their position in the grid forces you to place one or more dominoes in order to fill in the shape of the grid left. Cross off all these dominoes in the check-grid for future reference. Now, look at the dominoes you have managed to fill in and check around the grid, especially near the edge of the grid or next to dominoes already positioned, where the possibilities are reduced, to find other examples of those number pairs. Since you have already positioned that domino, you know that the second example you have found is not a pair and the domino must run in one of the other possible directions. Carry on in this vein, finding dominoes and then eliminating possibilities elsewhere in the grid until the puzzle is cracked.

Logi-5

Start by looking at the intersection of columns and rows that contain at least two starter letters, preferably more, and then use the "shapes" to further eliminate possible letters from that intersection square. You may well find that you can now position at least one letter exactly. There is one more "trick" to help: If, in your eliminating, you find two squares in a row or column, each of which must contain one of the same pair, then the other squares in the row or column cannot contain those letters and can be eliminated.

Sign In

When solving Sign In puzzles, the clues that aren't there are just as important as the ones that are. In the second row of our example puzzle, the 5 can only be positioned in column two, since placing it elsewhere in that row would mean that a 6 would have to be entered according to the signs. Following the 5, a 4 can now be written in below it. Now here's where the clues that aren't there come into play. If the 2 was placed in either of the shaded squares, either a 1 or 3 must be next to it. And there is no + or − sign linking these two squares. Therefore the 2 must be placed at the top.

Sudoku

The basic Sudoku puzzle is a 9 × 9 square grid, split into 9 square blocks, each containing 9 cells. Each puzzle starts off with roughly 20 to 35 of the cells filled in with any of the numbers 1 to 9. There is just one rule: The rest of the cells must be filled in with the missing numbers from 1 to 9 so that no number appears twice in any row, column, or 3 × 3 block. Use the numbers provided to eliminate places where the same number can't appear. For example, if there is already 1 in a cell, then 1 cannot appear again in that same row, column, or 3 × 3 block. By scanning all the cells that the various 1 values rule out, often you can find where the remaining 1s must go.

Killer Sudoku

This puzzle uses the solving skills of Sudoku, but in addition, the digits within each dotted-line shape imposed on top of the Sudoku grid must add up to the number in the top left corner of each shape. No digit may be repeated within a dotted-line shape. Look for the unique digit answers in the dotted-line shapes. For example, two squares totaling 17 must contain a 9 and an 8. Two squares totaling 4 must contain a 1 and a 3, as two 2s would not be allowed. Don't get so involved in the totals that you forget to use normal Sudoku solving methods as well.

USA TODAY

Martial Arts

Marshall Matthews spends his Saturday evenings in the bar of the Wallingfen Arms with his buddies, but keeps well clear for the rest of the week prefering to improve his body and mind instead. For his bodily well-being he chooses a selection of martial arts classes at the Leisure Center in Stonekeigh. From the clues, can you give the day and time of the class for each martial art and the color of belt Marshall currently holds in each?

Clues

1. Marshall needs to get to the Leisure Center on a Tuesday evening by 7:00 p.m.

2. Marshall has just begun learning karate and so is still a white belt; the outfit he dons on a Sunday is held together with a green belt.

3. The aikido class kicks off at 5:00 p.m.

4. At the 6:00 p.m. class Marshall wears his yellow belt.

	5:00 p.m.	6:00 p.m.	7:00 p.m.	Aikido	Karate	Taekwondo	Green	White	Yellow
Sunday									
Tuesday									
Thursday									
Green									
White									
Yellow									
Aikido									
Karate									
Taekwondo									

Day	Time	Martial art	Color

Stand and Deliver

The three residents of Webb Street were out when the item they had bought was delivered. From the clues, can you work out on what day each of the people received their package, which courier company delivered it, and where the courier left it after not getting an answer when ringing the doorbell?

Clues

1. Erica Schioppe returned home to find a note from the courier saying "Package left in the trash."

2. Fastline made their delivery the day after Elizabeth Perchess received her package.

3. On Tuesday, one package was left "under the car."

4. The Interswift courier, who wasn't delivering to Edwin Byer, left the note that said "Parcel is in the BBQ."

	E. Byer	E. Perchess	E. Schioppe	Fastline	Interswift	Speedway	In barbecue	In trash can	Under car
Monday									
Tuesday									
Wednesday									
In barbecue									
In trash can									
Under car									
Fastline									
Interswift									
Speedway									

Day	Person	Courier	Left where?

Battleships

Do you remember the old game of battleships? These puzzles are based on that idea. Your task is to find the vessels in the diagram. Some parts of boats or sea squares have already been filled in, and a number next to a row or column refers to the number of occupied squares in that row or column. The boats may be positioned horizontally or vertically, but no two boats or parts of boats are in adjacent squares— horizontally, vertically, or diagonally.

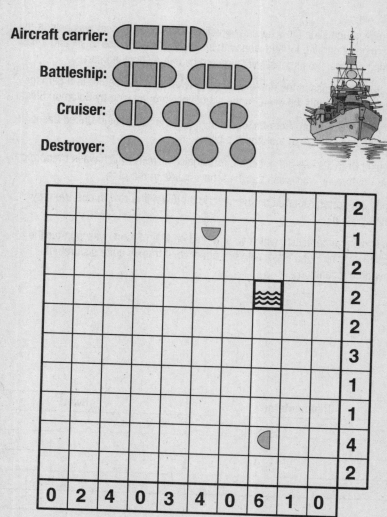

Aircraft carrier:

Battleship:

Cruiser:

Destroyer:

Winter Games

The sudden fall of snow across the state has spurred the Keighshire Winter Games Committee to organize the annual (if weather allows) event for this evening and SportRadio has hastily rearranged their schedule—dropping the regular baseball phone-in show *What Went Wrong* and replacing it with a special SportsWatch taking in all the frosty fun and games. From the clues, can you say who covered which sport from which location in Stonekeigh and who won?

Clues

1. The playground slide (how far can you slide in your best shoes) was held in the supermarket parking lot and won with an impressive distance of six and a half parking spaces, beating last year's record by half a shopping cart.

2. Rex Rabbit witnessed the no-sled sledding (won by a competitor in a garbage can) but this wasn't the event in the school playground won by Solomon Sleat.

3. Barry Babble reported from the center circle of the Stonekeigh United Baseball Club field where a man took the top prize.

4. Dominic Driffed's win did not come in the icicle javelin, which wasn't reported by Clive Chattaway, who wasn't at the tennis courts in the park.

5. Bobby Blatherton reported on the historic third win in a row in one event by Walter Wytout.

6. The snowman demolish, which wasn't held on Main Street, was won for the second year by Fiona Flayk with her effective, if frankly quite disturbing, blowtorch technique.

Commentator	Event

	Icicle javelin	No sled sledding	Playground slide	Snowball fight	Snowman demolish	Parking lot	Baseball field	Main Street	Playground	Tennis courts	Beatrice Blizzard	Dominic Driffed	Fiona Flayk	Solomon Sleat	Walter Wytout
Barry Babble															
Bobby Blatherton															
Clive Chattaway															
Perry Prattle															
Rex Rabbit															
Beatrice Blizzard															
Dominic Driffed															
Fiona Flayk															
Solomon Sleat															
Walter Wytout															
Parking lot															
Baseball field															
Main Street															
Playground															
Tennis courts															

Location	Winner

Knight Visions

You will be amazed to hear that five old friends, the knock-kneed knights, each pulled off a spectacularly brave rescue of a maiden in distress, assailed by a different adversary. Unfortunately, these incidents occurred only during the night, while the five worthies were asleep and dreaming, and on each occasion the knight in question awoke trembling and sweating. From the clues, can you sort out the full details of each knight's dream?

Clues

1. One knight's epic single-handed rescue of Joanne from a band of thieves took place two nights after Sir Poltroon à Ghaste's moment of glory.

2. Rosanna did not feature in the Wednesday night extravaganza, which did not have the ogre as its villain.

3. The wicked wizard was defeated by the fearless Sir Timid de Shayke of his own dreams.

4. The delectable, fragile, and surprisingly grateful Philomena played the leading role in the Thursday night dream.

5. Sir Coward de Custarde carried out the daring rescue of Lady Elaine.

6. Monday was the night on which Sir Sorely à Frayde reached the pinnacle of his Round Table career before his rude awakening; his opponent was not the evil knight, who was not Melanie's oppressor.

Day	Knight

	Sir Coward de Custarde	Sir Poltroon à Ghaste	Sir Sorely à Frayde	Sir Spyneless de Feete	Sir Timid de Shayke	Elaine	Joanne	Melanie	Philomena	Rosanna	Dragon	Evil knight	Band of thieves	Ogre	Wizard
Monday															
Tuesday															
Wednesday															
Thursday															
Friday															
Dragon															
Evil knight															
Band of thieves															
Ogre															
Wizard															
Elaine															
Joanne															
Melanie															
Philomena															
Rosanna															

Damsel	Villain

Mouse Sale

Pets'n'Stuff in Netherlipp Retail Park is, according to its advertising flyer, "your one-stop store for all your pet's needs." But stock isn't moving as fast as they would like and they are having weekly sales of specific items. This week, the focus is on white mice and each is being offered with a free computer mouse—Pets'n'Stuff's staff are a witty bunch. From the clues, can you name the mouse and mouse manufacturer for each of the pairs shown?

Clues

1. Jerry is immediately below the mouse from Microtek.

2. Philida is the next right on the same shelf as the mouse from the Poynter company.

3. The combination of Harvey mouse and the Logiput mouse is not pairing 1.

4. The Klikkit mouse is numbered two higher than the Mickey mouse; Dora is shown with an even number.

Mice: Dora; Harvey; Jerry; Mickey; Philida
Mouses: Kerser; Klikkit; Logiput; Microtek; Poynter

Starting tip: Name the animal mouse in place 1.

USA TODAY

Sporting Ladies

The picture below shows four of the founding members of the Eddsbury Sporting Ladies Group, which is celebrating its fiftieth anniversary this year. From the clues, can you work out each woman's name and age and the sport in which she still participates?

Clues

1. Beryl Owen is somewhere to the left from our point of view of the roller skater, who has been using the same pair of skates since 1968—though they have been repaired!

2. Position 2 is occupied by the lady who is now 73 years of age.

3. The table-tennis player is three years older than Emily Ross.

4. 76-year-old Maude Young is standing next to the fencer.

5. The golfer is older than the lady in position 1.

Names: Beryl Owen; Emily Ross; Joan White; Maude Young
Ages: 70; 73; 76; 79
Sports: fencing; golf; roller skating; table tennis

Starting tip: Work out the sport of lady No. 1.

Injured at the Gym

The resident first aider at the Gettfitt Gym in Storbury was busy last Friday; her services were called on by five of the lady patrons. (The males aren't more agile—just less adventurous.) From the clues, can you work out the full name of each injured exerciser, what part of her body she injured, and which piece of equipment she hurt herself on?

Clues

1. Edna managed to injure herself using the leg press, which involves using the legs to push yourself up a ramp on a sliding seat.

2. Ms. Hawse was hurt while working out on the exercise bike; the lady who injured her shoulder did so while using the shoulder lift machine—or, rather, by falling off it.

3. Irene, who injured her finger, doesn't have a surname beginning with the letter B.

4. The lady who injured her knee, who wasn't Ms. Beame, didn't sustain the damage while using the medicine ball or the pectorals machine known colloquially as a "pec deck."

5. The lady hurt while using the pec deck, which involves bringing two handles together at shoulder level in the chest, wasn't named Olive or Beame.

Move up Jim. The doctor's told me to join you.

6. Annie Flore has been using the Gettfitt Gym for the last eighteen months; Ursula isn't Ms. Rings, who hurt her elbow.

First name	Surname

	Barr	Beame	Flore	Hawse	Rings	Elbow	Finger	Knee	Nose	Shoulder	Bike	Leg press	Medicine ball	Pec deck	Shoulder lift
Annie															
Edna															
Irene															
Olive															
Ursula															
Bike															
Leg press															
Medicine ball															
Pec deck															
Shoulder lift															
Elbow															
Finger															
Knee															
Nose															
Shoulder															

Body part	Equipment

Looks Familiar

In the bad old days when superstition was rife, there were lots of witches and every one of them had a familiar—a spirit in the shape of an animal that acted as a servant. These days there are still people who purport to be witches—though not quite as many—and some of them still have familiars. For instance, there are the five women featured here; from the clues, can you work out each one's full name, the type of creature she claims as her familiar, and the name she has given it?

Clues

1. Mrs. Potter's familiar, known as Poor John, is not a hedgehog.

2. Mrs. Faust, whose name isn't Beryl, has chosen as her familiar a bat—and not even a decent American bat, but one of those big Transylvanian ones with the red eyes and long fangs.

3. For some reason, one of the witches—but not Fran O'Lochlainn—has named her familiar Cuddy Wifter.

4. Helen's familiar is named, a little unimaginatively, Tip.

5. Katy's familiar is a big white rabbit with long ears and a one-word name.

6. Drogo is a red squirrel with a particularly luxuriant tail.

7. Millie's familiar has a name beginning with a letter in the second half of the alphabet.

8. Ms. Merlyn—she insists that's the right way to spell it—has not named her familiar Smaug after the dragon in Tolkien's *The Hobbit*.

First name	Surname

● USA TODAY

	Daniels	Faust	Merlyn	O'Lochlainn	Potter	Bat	Hedgehog	Platypus	Rabbit	Squirrel	Cuddy Wifter	Drogo	Poor John	Smaug	Tip
Beryl															
Fran															
Helen															
Katy															
Millie															
Cuddy Wifter															
Drogo															
Poor John															
Smaug															
Tip															
Bat															
Hedgehog															
Platypus															
Rabbit															
Squirrel															

Familiar	Name

Models

After years of research, art historian Professor Dauber of Goatsferry University has identified the models who sat for the five most famous paintings by Sir Willard Pleydell, mid-Victorian baronet and painter—and discovered that they all worked on his family estate in Surrey. From the clues below, can you work out the full name and occupation of the person who modelled for each painting?

Clues

1. The model for *The Visitor* was actually a servant (a footman or a housemaid) employed in Sir Willard's home, Pleydell Towers.

2. Edgar Danvers was born in 1815, the year of Waterloo, and lived until 1879, the year of the Zulu War, though he took part in neither.

3. Simon didn't model for Pleydell's *The Pilgrim*, said to be based on a character from Chaucer's *Canterbury Tales*.

4. The model for *The Medium*—Pleydell, like many Victorians, was a keen Spiritualist—was named Price but was not employed as a gardener.

5. Hilyard, the cowman (meaning a man who looked after cows, not a bovine centaur!), was not Alfred.

6. Katie, Pleydell's model for *The Dreamer*, wasn't named Lester, nor was that the surname of the footman.

7. The lady's maid surname wasn't Digby.

Painting	First name

USA TODAY

	Alfred	Edgar	Katie	Simon	Vera	Danvers	Digby	Hilyard	Lester	Price	Cowman	Footman	Gardener	Housemaid	Lady's maid
The Artist															
The Dreamer															
The Medium															
The Pilgrim															
The Visitor															
Cowman															
Footman															
Gardener															
Housemaid															
Lady's maid															
Danvers															
Digby															
Hilyard															
Lester															
Price															

OK, so let's try it without the big smile

Surname	Occupation

Sable Ovines

The gossip column of today's *Daily Lantern*—which these days occupies a page and a half—includes items about five "reprobate" children of respectable and well-known fathers who have chosen careers of which their parents seriously do not approve. From the clues, can you work out the full names of each of the five, the occupation of his or her father, and what he or she does that is not approved?

Clues

1. Caroline Noble is not the artist whose oil paintings have been described by critics as "challenging" and "deeply meaningful" and by a parent as "a mess."

2. Fiona, whose father is the Archbishop of Northchester, is not named Bonar-Fydes.

3. Franklin, who says that he's a poet (though his output convinces few others), is not the son of the wealthy landowner Randolph Pridefull, whose offspring is not the artist.

4. The burglar (three convictions and currently on bail awaiting trial on two other charges) is named Bonar-Fydes, though known professionally as Sykes, but not Matthew.

5. The model's father is a State Court judge, though people are beginning to refer to him as "father of the well-known model."

6. Mr. Wellborn junior went to Eton like his father but—unlike him—was expelled.

7. Joseph's father is not the General commanding the British peace-keeping troops.

First name	Surname

	Bonar-Fydes	Loftey	Noble	Pridefull	Wellborn	Archbishop	Senator	General	Judge	Landowner	Artist	Burglar	Model	Poet	Social worker
Caroline															
Fiona															
Franklin															
Joseph															
Matthew															
Artist															
Burglar															
Model															
Poet															
Social worker															
Archbishop															
Senator															
General															
Judge															
Landowner															

Father's job	Career

Safe and Sound

The safe deposit room at Noke, Weston, and Asqued Securities contains a dozen boxes rented to whomever is prepared to pay the high price for their confidentiality. Currently, all the customers are people whose line of work involves liberating items from other secure locations but who would prefer that fact not to be spread far and wide. From the clues, can you work out who rents each numbered box and what it contains?

Clues

1. As you can see from the drawing, boxes 5, 9, and 10 are currently unused; until yesterday, they were rented by Phil the Fence but he boarded a plane for the Caribbean this morning with a heavy piece of hand luggage chained to his wrist—"Vacation reading," he told the check-in staff.

2. Jimmy the Jemmy, known for his skillful use of the pry bar and whose box contains wads of used and non-sequential $20 bills, rents the box immediately above the one containing a decent collection of gold coins.

3. Fingers Freddie, whose delicate finger pads can feel the tumblers of combinations locks tumbling, has the box immediately below the one containing $80,000 in bills.

4. Numbers Neville, whose keen mathematical mind has created a system of quickly narrowing down the combination numbers, has a velvet bag full of rubies in his box which has a number half that of the one rented by Terry the Torch, whose expertise with the oxyacetylene circumvents the combination locks altogether.

5. Jellyman Jake, who also never bothers with the lock except to blow it off with a decent wedge of gelignite, doesn't have exactly $50,000 in his box which is immediately left of the one containing a large number of gold watches, which isn't on the top row of safe deposit boxes.

6. Lugs Larry, whose exquisitely trained ears can hear the lock's tumblers falling into place, has an odd-numbered box in the same column of boxes as the one containing a silk purse full of cut diamonds.

7. Box 8, which isn't rented by Percy the Picker, who can pick any lock anywhere with anything, contains gold of some sort; box 6 is full of valuable gemstones.

8. Box 7, rented by Don the Drill, who swears by the old-fashioned system of drilling through the lock, doesn't contain gold; box 11 is not the current home of the satin purse of glittering emeralds.

Box renters: Claude the Cracker; Don the Drill; Fingers Freddie; Jellyman Jake; Jimmy the Jemmy; Lugs Larry; Numbers Neville; Percy the Picker; Terry the Torch
Contents: $50,000; $80,000; $100,000; diamonds; emeralds; gold bars; gold coins; gold watches; rubies

1	2	3
4	5	6
7	8	9
10	11	12

Starting tip: Begin by locating the gold coins.

Winter Warmers

Five women decided to have a break from the seemingly unending winter weather besieging the streets of Stonekeigh by visiting a friend or relative in the Antipodes. From the clues, can you say who is visiting whom, what the connection is, and identify the city where each visitor is staying? (NB: For the sake of clarity, Auckland and Wellington are in New Zealand; Adelaide, Perth, and Sydney are in Australia.)

Clues

1. The woman who had been a bridesmaid at Kelly's wedding suddenly moved to Australia not long after the wedding, although rumors that it was because of events at the reception have never been proven; Virginia, who is not the old school friend of one of our travelers, is now in New Zealand.

2. Gloria is taking a vacation with Carol.

3. Samantha's antipodean home is not in Perth and no one is visiting a cousin in Wellington.

4. One visitor has traveled to Adelaide to spend some time with her daughter and son-in-law, whether they like it or not.

5. Angie's sister, who is paying her a visit, is not Maxine, who is spending a few weeks in Sydney, while Bernice is not staying in Auckland.

Visitor	Visitee

	Angie	Bronwen	Carol	Samantha	Virginia	Bridesmaid	Cousin	Daughter	School friend	Sister	Adelaide	Auckland	Perth	Sydney	Wellington
Bernice															
Gloria															
Kelly															
Maxine															
Stella															
Adelaide															
Auckland															
Perth															
Sydney															
Wellington															
Bridesmaid															
Cousin															
Daughter															
School friend															
Sister															

DISPOSABLE BOOMERANG

ONE TIME USE ONLY

Connection	City

Stake-Out

The five Private Eyes in the Southern Californian town of San Angelo are each spending an uncomfortable night on a stake-out for their current case. From the clues, can you say what sort of location each detective is watching, what sort of person arrives at the stroke of midnight, and what happened next?

Clues

1. Spike Spanner looked up from his position overlooking the San Angelo docks and saw a woman arrive on the scene; across town at the offices of Fleecem and Runne Attorneys, another woman entered the case of another detective.

2. A car pulled up at one location, and out stepped a senior officer. "I wasn't expecting that," said Mike Mallet to himself from the car parked nearby.

3. One detective watched as a man arrived at the door of a depot and a fist fight broke out.

4. Dick Drill shrunk further back into the shadows as he watched a new character enter the scene; this wasn't outside the Excelsior Hotel, which wasn't where the man in the hat made his appearance.

5. Ricky Wrench watched as a diminutive figure arrived and, with fingers pointing and much anger, indulged in a loud quarrel; Nicky Nail couldn't see the identity of the short person who had arrived under the hat they were wearing.

6. The tall man reached into his pocket and pulled out a large bundle of bills. He handed it over and left without saying another word.

7. Neither woman handed over the leather holdall.

Private eye	Location

	Docks	Hotel	House	Office	Depot	Man in hat	Officer	Tall man	Tall woman	Woman in hat	Fist fight	Hand over cash	Hand over bag	Kidnap	Querrel
Dick Drill															
Mike Mallet															
Nicky Nail															
Ricky Wrench															
Spike Spanner															
Fist fight															
Hand over cash															
Hand over bag															
Kidnap															
Quarrel															
Man in hat															
Officer															
Tall man															
Tall woman															
Woman in hat															

Person	Event

Adventurous Addifields

Last year, Bernard Addifield began writing a history of his family's life in the USA since 1839, when the first of them emigrated from England. He quickly discovered that, despite the fact that they settled in Samville, Utah, in 1849—a town that's as small today as it was then—and have mostly lived there ever since, some of his ancestors still managed to have adventurous experiences. From the clues, can you work out when each of the listed Addifields was born, what occupation he took up and what adventure he had?

Clues

1. The sailor—one of the few Addifields to desert the family home—was shipwrecked off the coast of Central America.

2. The farmer, who was born in 1917, wasn't Virgil Addifield; Joseph Addifield was born in 1942.

3. It was the Addifield born in 1842 in Nauvoo, Illinois, who found a buried treasure of old Spanish gold.

4. Moroni Addifield single-handedly (he only had one arm) and more by accident than intent, captured the man who had robbed Samville's one and only bank.

5. John Addifield made a career as a soldier, eventually retiring with the rank of Major and a chest full of decorations.

6. Edward Addifield was born in the second half of the nineteenth century.

7. The man who was kidnapped by Indians was born twenty-five years before the Addifield who became a schoolteacher; the Addifield who became a printer wasn't the one born in 1867.

First name	Birth date

	1842	1867	1892	1917	1942	Farmer	Printer	Sailor	Soldier	Teacher	Built land yacht	Captured robber	Found treasure	Kidnapped	Shipwrecked
Edward															
John															
Joseph															
Moroni															
Virgil															
Built land yacht															
Captured robber															
Found treasure															
Kidnapped															
Shipwrecked															
Farmer															
Printer															
Sailor															
Soldier															
Teacher															

Occupation	Adventure

Stamps of Approval

At a recent auction of postage stamps, Russian multibillionaire Igor Talotomuni purchased five spectacularly rare examples at spectacularly high prices. From the clues, can you work out the nationality, value, and color of the tiny pieces of paper for which he paid the immense prices listed?

Clues

1. The green stamp—it's a repellent shade of verdigris green, actually—cost $125,000 more than the one with a face value of twelve konang, but $125,000 less than the Adari stamp, which came from the Duchy of Adar, now part of—er, somewhere else.

2. The Holirran stamp didn't cost Igor exactly $625,000 and is not the sepia stamp—which, being printed in brown ink, is easily mistaken for a small, blank square of dirty paper.

3. The Lustrian stamp cost Igor $875,000, which he thought was quite a bargain.

4. The Ciwalian stamp, a sickly lilac in color, was not the one for which Igor paid a mere $500,000.

5. The Minean stamp was cheaper, or perhaps that should be less extortionately expensive, than the ten quiral example.

6. Igor paid $750,000 for the stamp with a face value of one mirj, which in today's money is about 0.1 cent.

7. One of the stamps Igor acquired was the sole surviving example of the triangular thirty galter orange.

Price	Nationality

	Adari	Ciwalian	Holirran	Lustrian	Minean	1 mirj	5 buzat	10 quiral	12 konang	30 galter	Green	Lilac	Orange	Pink	Sepia
$500,000															
$625,000															
$750,000															
$875,000															
$1 million															
Green															
Lilac															
Orange															
Pink															
Sepia															
1 mirj															
5 buzat															
10 quiral															
12 konang															
30 galter															

Going, going where's it gone?

Value	Color

Date Nights

Marc and Cleo Paramor have been married for years so they try to make every Tuesday night their date-night, when they get a babysitter to look after the kids, the dog and the goldfish and go out for a meal and to take in a show or a movie. From the clues, can you work out the details of each of this January's Tuesday evenings—the restaurant at which they ate, the theater or movie theater they patronized, and the entertainment they enjoyed there?

Clues

1. On January 29th, Marc and Cleo went to see a stage performance of the musical *West Side Story*.

2. Marc and Cleo didn't visit the Eldorado on the Tuesday they dined at the Taj Mahal Indian restaurant, which was earlier in the month than their meal at Le Provençal.

3. The Paramors' trip to the Regent took place two weeks earlier than their visit to the Empire; their dinner at the Riverside Bar and Grill was the week after they visited the Pavilion.

4. The visit to the Coronet came the week before the dinner at Maison Marcel but the week after the trip to the "Sixties Superstars" concert.

5. Marc and Cleo didn't go to see a musical on either of the Tuesdays on which they ate at a restaurant with a French name (Le Provençal or Maison Marcel); the dinner at Gordon's Highland Steak House and the visits to the stage thriller *Wait Until Dark* and the special showing of the classic movie comedy *The Sting* took place on successive Tuesdays in that order.

Date	Restaurant

	Gordon's	Le Provençal	Maison Marcel	Riverside	Taj Mahal	Coronet	Eldorado	Empire	Pavilion	Regent	Movie comedy	Movie musical	'60s concert	Stage musical	Stage thriller
1st															
8th															
15th															
22nd															
29th															
Movie comedy															
Movie musical															
'60s concert															
Stage musical															
Stage thriller															
Coronet															
Eldorado															
Empire															
Pavilion															
Regent															

Venue	Entertainment

Miss Attributed

Quite often, the activities of Miss Raffles—the more professional criminal sister of the famous Amateur Cracksman—were blamed on other people, but sometimes she and her gang were blamed for other people's felonious jobs. From the clues, can you work out the details of five of these—victim, city, and year—and say who really did it? (To avoid helping too much, we've translated all the victims' names into English—e.g., Star House might really have been Dom Gwiazda if it had been in Warsaw.)

Clues

1. The Grand Hotel jewel robbery, carried out by a political organization called the Anarchist Liberators, took place later than the Pike Gang's crime in Lisbon, a quite clever theft which Miss Raffles was happy to take credit for.

2. The robbery of Franco Brothers' jewelry store in Paris wasn't carried out by the notorious Irish criminal Ivan Lenkov—and no, that wasn't his real name.

3. The crime in Berlin took place before—but not immediately before—the one in Rome.

4. The robbery that took place in the summer of 1896 was the work of Billy Boyle, who, strangely enough, was Ivan Lenkov's brother—and also operated under a false name.

5. The Capital Bank was robbed of a quantity of gold bullion just before Christmas 1900.

6. It was in 1894 that Miss Raffles was blamed for the crime in Moscow.

7. The robbery at Hart & Lukas took place later than the one carried out by the infamous Green Skull Gang.

Victim	City

USA TODAY

	Berlin	Lisbon	Moscow	Paris	Rome	1894	1896	1899	1900	1903	Anarchist Liberators	Billy Boyle	Green Skull Gang	Ivan Lenkov	Pike Gang
Capital Bank															
Franco Brothers															
Grand Hotel															
Hart & Lukas															
Star House															
Anarchist Liberators															
Billy Boyle															
Green Skull Gang															
Ivan Lenkov															
Pike Gang															
1894															
1896															
1899															
1900															
1903															

Date	Culprit(s)

Trubble at Mills

Granville Trubble, general manager of T. Mills and Son in Netherlipp, is an understanding supervisor but was forced to call five of the company's employees into his office for reprimands last week, one on each day. From the clues, can you work out the name of the employee called in each day, in which department they work, and what they had done to earn a reprimand?

Clues

1. Mr. Trubble had words with the person from the Advertising Department—who had returned to work tipsy after lunch with a client—two days after reprimanding the Research worker; these two people are of the same gender.

2. It was on Thursday that Granville Trubble took the rep from Sales to one side; the sales rep had not been caught breaking the strict no-eating-at-desks rule that applies in the company's offices.

3. The person found playing computer games at their desk, who wasn't Ann Gellick, was called into Trubble's office the day after the employee who had been very rude to a major customer on the phone, thinking it was a cold caller.

4. The person who felt the rough side of Trubble's tongue on Tuesday wasn't from the Transportation Department.

5. Sue Dann was reprimanded by Granville on Monday.

6. Barry Dock from Accounts, who fell afoul of Trubble the day before Don Key, hadn't been misusing the computers.

Day	Name

	Ann Gellick	Barry Dock	Don Key	George Cross	Sue Dann	Accounts	Advertising	Research	Sales	Transportation	Bad timekeeping	Computer games	Eating	Rude on phone	Tipsy
Monday															
Tuesday															
Wednesday															
Thursday															
Friday															
Bad timekeeping															
Computer games															
Eating															
Rude on phone															
Tipsy															
Accounts															
Advertising															
Research															
Sales															
Transportation															

Department	Offense

Bernards All

These five St. Bernard dogs patrol mountain passes helping vacationers and locals who get into trouble in the snow and ice. From the clues, can you name each dog and say which mountain pass is his patch?

Clues

1. The dog called Matthews is left of the one who patrols the Under Pass, who is right of the one who looks after Tres Pass, who is left of the dog called Shaw, who is right of the one who works on the Over Pass, who is left of the dog called Cribbins, who is right of the one called Montgomery, who is shown in the diagram with an even number lower than the number of the dog called Herman.

2. The dog called Matthews is immediately next to the one who guards the Encom Pass, who is not next to the one who watches over the Sur Pass, who is next right to Cribbins, who isn't the guardian of the Tres Pass and who isn't next to the one who looks after Over Pass.

Dogs: Cribbins; Herman; Matthews; Montgomery; Shaw
Passes: Encom; Over; Sur; Tres; Under

Starting tip: Begin by naming dog 1.

Battleships

Do you remember the old game of battleships? These puzzles are based on that idea. Your task is to find the vessels in the diagram. Some parts of boats or sea squares have already been filled in, and a number next to a row or column refers to the number of occupied squares in that row or column. The boats may be positioned horizontally or vertically, but no two boats or parts of boats are in adjacent squares—horizontally, vertically, or diagonally.

Aircraft carrier:

Battleship:

Cruiser:

Destroyer:

										0
										0
										1
							◖			**5**
										2
										2
	●			≈						**2**
							◡			**3**
										3
										2
0	**4**	**1**	**1**	**4**	**2**	**2**	**2**	**3**	**1**	

Crew Room

The picture below shows the crew room of the interplanetary freighter *Firefly*, preparing to transfer from the ship to the Terran settlement on the planet of Dolarma with a cargo of machine tools. The transfer from the ship to the hermetically sealed "bubble city" involves a short walk across the surface of Dolarma whose atmosphere, as I'm sure you know, contains a high proportion of cyanide and sulfuric acid and so requires full spacesuits. The people shown are ship's officers, including the master, the term for the captain of a civilian ship of either sex, heading for a spot of R and R. From the clues, can you fill in the role of each officer and his or her name?

Clues

1. Marc Polo is the *Firefly's* helm—not the steering mechanism itself, of course, but the officer responsible for controlling it—his deputy is on duty at the moment.

2. The so-called sysso (it's short for "systems officer" and refers to the person responsible for the ship's computer systems) is immediately to the left of Toby Roche (as we look at the picture).

3. Liz Mond is two places left of *Firefly's* engineer, who looks after—well, the engines, of course.

4. Gus Hill is three places left of Zia Welzl, who was born on the planet Isis, out in the Kraken Sector.

5. The woman in position 7 is the ship's surgeon, and also functions as life support engineer and chief caterer; her immediate neighbor is also female.

6. The purser, who is the ship's financial controller and business manager, is two places left of Kate Luce and two places right of the comms, which is the traditional and universal nickname for the communications officer.

7. The crew member in position 3 is Ella Beit, a Terran—meaning she was born on the planet once known as Earth.

Names: Ella Beit; Gus Hill; Kate Luce; Liz Mond; Marc Polo; Toby Roche; Zia Welzl
(For the sake of clarity, Ella, Kate, Liz, and Zia are female.)

Starting tip: Work out which crew member is Gus Hill.

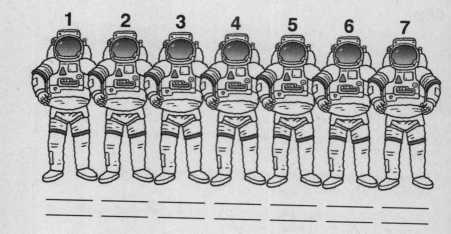

1   2   3   4   5   6   7

——— ——— ——— ——— ——— ——— ———
——— ——— ——— ——— ——— ——— ———

Clarion Calls

Several pages of this week's *Netherlipp Clarion* have been filled with Valentine messages, most of them of singular uninventiveness and banality. This problem gives five examples, with the printer's reference numbers. From the clues, can you work out who devised what message for whom?

Clues

1. Neither the originators nor the addressees are listed in their alphabetical positions, nor, in any instance, does the alphabetical order of the former match that of the latter (e.g. Bonzo did not create message 1411 or the Valentine for Apollo).

2. Tiger's Valentine appears next after the one addressed to Tankman; the one addressed to Gorjus appears next after the one created by Flossie.

3. Cattikins's Valentine is lower down the list than the one addressed to Peachy-Pie; the latter's is not for "My chocolate soldier."

4. "IOU4 Evva" immediately precedes the plea for a loved one's return and immediately follows one originated by a female.

5. The Valentine for Apollo comes immediately after Bonzo's effort; neither contains a would-be cryptic and coded message.

6. Neither Snazzy's message for his would-be girlfriend nor the one for The It Girl is 1412; neither the recipient of 1411 nor Tankman is promised "Huggies and kissies."

Reference	Originator

	Bonzo	Cattikins	Flossie	Snazzy	Tiger	Apollo	Gorjus	Peachy-Pie	Tankman	The It Girl	Come back darling	Huggies and kissies	My chocolate soldier	IOU4 Evva	UR4Me
1411															
1412															
1413															
1414															
1415															
Come back darling															
Huggies and kissies															
My chocolate soldier															
IOU4 Evva															
UR4Me															
Apollo															
Gorjus															
Peachy-Pie															
Tankman															
The It Girl															

Addressee	Message

Lawn Order

With spring not too far away (hopefully), three residents from Gardner's Drive turned their attention to perennial problems with their lawns and ordered new liquid products to cure them this year before they started. From the clues, can you name the resident of each house, the company from whom he ordered his chemical problem solver, and the name of the new product?

Clues

1. Jeremy Jade, who doesn't live at 6 Gardner's Drive, has ordered five liters of Daisyways.

2. Lucas Lime has become a new customer of Sod Supplies.

3. Turf Nuts, Ltd., sells Cloverover in a handy spray container.

4. Half a gallon of Mossloss has just been delivered to 2 Gardner's Drive.

	Ellis Emerald	Jeremy Jade	Lucas Lime	Grass Routes	Sod Supplies	Turf Nuts	Cloverover	Daisyways	Mossloss
No. 2									
No. 4									
No. 6									
Cloverover									
Daisyways									
Mossloss									
Grass Routes									
Sod Supplies									
Turf Nuts									

House	Resident	Company	Product

Law'n'Order

In the mid-1880s, the pioneers of the Wild West relied heavily on their local sheriffs to keep some semblance of law and order. From the clues, can you name the sheriff of each of the small towns, the one person he currently has locked up in his jail, and the reason he's there?

Clues

1. Rowdy Raynes spent last night asleep in Doomstone's jail.

2. Walter Slurp is the sheriff of Leadwood; Wally Burp wasn't the lawman who jailed Punk Petersen.

3. Bruiser Baker, who didn't get his nickname for nothing, was thrown in jail for fighting in the saloon; he doesn't live in Smudge City.

4. Wallis Chirp's jail contains a man who was cheating at poker in the saloon and was lucky to escape with his life.

	Wallis Chirp	Wally Burp	Walter Slurp	Bruiser Baker	Punk Petersen	Rowdy Raynes	Cheating	Drunk	Fighting
Doomstone									
Leadwood									
Smudge City									
Cheating									
Drunk									
Fighting									
Bruiser Baker									
Punk Petersen									
Rowdy Raynes									

Town	Sheriff	Jailbird	Crime

Pop the Question

On Monday to Thursday, Radio Keighshire's afternoon show hosted by Owen Tilfore includes their very popular quiz show section where the music knowledge of a couple of listeners is put to the test. From the clues, can you work out the names of the winning and losing competitors each day, and say what prizes the winners were awarded?

Clues

1. "Let's say good afternoon to Wetherby Wise," said Owen at the start of one quiz. "That's an unusual name." "Well, I was named after my father," replied Wetherby. "He was called Mr. Wise too." "Err . . . right," said Owen. "And your opponent this afternoon is Coralie Clutts. So where does your name come from?" "It was on my birth certificate," replied Ms. Clutts.

2. "This afternoon's prize," said Owen on Wednesday, "is a year's supply of second class stamps—if you send only one letter a month."

3. Dominic Dimm-Witte missed out on winning the calendar (a free one downloaded from the internet) the day after Craig Canny ran off with the spoils.

4. Norma Nowell won the pen that could be used for labeling CDs (so long as you don't mind it rubbing off soon after labeling); Stephanie Smart wasn't on the radio on Tuesday.

5. The photo of Owen Tilfore was won by someone of the same sex as the competitor who lost on Tuesday.

Day	Winner

	Craig Canny	Norma Nowell	Stephanie Smart	Wetherby Wise	Chester Chump	Coralie Clutts	Dominic Dimm-Witte	Sophie Sapp	Calendar	CD pen	Photo	Stamps for year
Monday												
Tuesday												
Wednesday												
Thursday												
Calendar												
CD pen												
Photo												
Stamps for year												
Chester Chump												
Coralie Clutts												
Dominic Dimm-Witte												
Sophie Sapp												

Loser	Prize

Question the Pop

The new carbonated beverage FizzUp advertises itself as: "The fizziest pop ever made—it'll take your head off." Unfortunately, on the first day of sale, some of the supermarkets haven't read the instructions from the manufacturer: "keep chilled, keep very chilled;" and the slogan is proving all too true. As the FizzUp has warmed up, the tops have begun to pop, shooting the bottles across the store like jet-propelled missiles, leaving customers diving for cover behind the broccoli. From the clues, can you say which person is organizing the anti-FizzUp actions in each store, their job, and the number of bottles that have gone "pop" so far?

Clues

1. Cashlow's store manager took control the moment the bottles started going "bang" and is busy organizing countermeasures.

2. Lucas Lynart found himself in Pricedeels supermarket when the tops started to pop and the bottles started to fly; he isn't the police sergeant who is battling the display of FizzUp where twelve bottles had so far gone off.

3. Douglas Doughty, who doesn't shop in Savelot, is a teacher and unwisely decided that if he can cope with thirty excitable seven-year-olds, he could deal with a few excitable bottles.

4. Vicky Valiant, who isn't a firefighter, is counting, and so far, sixteen bottles have become jet-propelled.

5. The location where so far only eight bottles had broken free of their display stand isn't Kostov's Money Saving Supermarket.

Supermarket	Organizer

	Belinda Brayve	Douglas Doughty	Lucas Lynart	Vicky Valiant	Firefighter	Police sergeant	Store manager	Teacher	8	12	16	20
Cashlow												
Kostov												
Pricedeels												
Savelot												
8												
12												
16												
20												
Firefighter												
Police sergeant												
Store manager												
Teacher												

Job	Popped so far

Earwigging

Abigail Armstrong has held the post of Matron at St. Keigh's boarding school for four years, and she is held in high esteem by the staff and even higher esteem by the boys. She always has a bandage for a grazed knee, a pill for a headache, and a sympathetic ear for other troubles. And so when the four boys from dormitory B4 overheard a few snippets of conversation—"older on Friday," "another year," "many returns," and "need candles," they naturally concluded that Matron's birthday was at the end of the week. From the clues, can you say at what time and to whom Matron was heard speaking by each boy and which snippet he overheard?

Clues

1. One lad overheard Matron talking to a delivery boy, telling him that he'd brought all the wrong things and there would be many returns, but caught only the last two words.

2. Hamish Hazel overheard the snippet of conversation immediately before the boy who overheard, "My mother shouldn't have expected me for tea on Sunday, she knew I couldn't make it, I told her on Friday," and grabbed with both hands the wrong end of the stick offered by the last five syllables.

3. Chris Cockroft heard Matron discussing her choir's Spring Equinox evening performance on the town green and mentioning the need for many candles; this was earlier in the day than one boy earwigged a conversation with a visiting parent, but later than one lad heard the last two words of the sentence, "I'm getting fed up with my car, but it's going to have to last me another year."

4. Martin Masters earwigged a conversation in the middle of the afternoon, on his way from Geography to Latin.

5. Matron's conversation with Math teacher Mr. Stern ("Fuller" to the boys) at the breakfast table was overheard, misunderstood, and misinterpreted before the toast was cold.

Boy	Time

	Breakfast	Mid-morning	Lunchtime	Midafternoon	Delivery boy	On phone	Parent	Teacher	Another year	Many returns	Need candles	Older on Friday
Ben Barton												
Chris Cockroft												
Hamish Hazel												
Martin Masters												
Another year												
Many returns												
Need candles												
Older on Friday												
Delivery boy												
On phone												
Parent												
Teacher												

Talking to	Snippet overheard

Present Day

Having concluded that Matron's birthday was imminent, our four school friends decided that they must mark the day by giving her presents. Abigail Armstrong turned thirty-two last November, and while for some of us she is a mere slip of a lass barely out of her teens, for an eleven-year-old, she's ancient. So each boy enrolled a member of his family as an accomplice to help choose (and buy) the present. From the clues, can you work out who each boy contacted, by what means, and what gift they supplied?

Clues

1. "So how old is she, dear?" said the voice on the phone. "She's archaic, Grandma, prehistoric—must be at least a hundred," replied her grandson.

2. Uncle Godfrey thought hard and concluded that if the venerable lady was anything like him, her teeth would be a little dodgy and marshmallows would be all she could manage.

3. "I need to get an elderly lady a present—she tries walking sometimes," wrote one boy in a letter. The return mail brought him a walking stick.

4. Ben Barton's accomplice supplied a bottle of sweet sherry—but only because there was one in the cupboard; Chris Cockroft contacted Aunt Petunia—she's good at presents and she's about ninety herself.

5. Martin Masters wrote the text message "Pls send gft 4 matron bday, She vry old"; his accomplice didn't decide that thermal slips would be perfect for a lady in her dotage; it wasn't Hamish Hazel who recruited his grandad.

Boy	Accomplice

	Aunt Petunia	Grandfather	Grandmother	Uncle Godfrey	Email	Letter	Phone	Text	Marshmallows	Sherry	Thermal slippers	Walking stick
Ben Barton												
Chris Cockroft												
Hamish Hazel												
Martin Masters												
Marshmallows												
Sherry												
Thermal slippers												
Walking stick												
Email												
Letter												
Phone												
Text												

Contact Method	Gift

Long Time in Store

Gross Brothers department store in the West London suburb of Waxlow is holding a celebration to honor four of its lady assistants who have worked there for twenty years or more. From the clues below, can you fill in each one's full name and the year in which she joined the company?

Clues

1. Ruth Candy is standing directly right, from our point of view, of the woman who began working at Gross Brothers in 1991.

2. Mrs. Chayne was the next to get a job in the store after Susie.

3. The lady in position A has served the longest of the four.

4. Mrs. Dime joined the company in 1989—but she was Miss Booke in those days.

5. It wasn't the lady standing in position D who first went to work for Gross Brothers in 1994.

6. Martha's surname isn't Seegar.

First names: Grace; Martha; Ruth; Susie
Surnames: Candy; Chayne; Dime; Seegar
Start years: 1980; 1989; 1991; 1994

Starting tip: Work out when Ruth joined the staff of Gross Brothers.

Disaster Area

The Movie Store in Netherlipp Market Place is a small store that sells DVDs, posters, memorabilia, and all things "moving pictures." In one corner, they have a "Disaster Area"—a couple of shelves that hold disaster movies. Today, it had eight DVDs, each of which has a single word title. From the clues, can you place each movie?

Clues

1. The DVD of *Flood* (It's getting wetter all the time) is somewhere to the right of *Avalanche* (There's snow business like it) and somewhere to the left of *Asteroid* (The crater and the good); these three DVDs are not all on the same shelf.

2. The copy of *Landslide* (Mud is thicker than water) is somewhere to the right of *Eruption* (No lava lost between us) and somewhere to the left of *Hurricane* (The answer, my friend, is . . .).

3. *Blaze* (It's the flame of the game) is immediately to the right of *Hurricane*, and *Earthquake* (Scary to a fault) is numbered two lower than *Eruption*.

Titles: *Asteroid*; *Avalanche*; *Blaze*; *Earthquake*; *Eruption*; *Flood*; *Hurricane*; *Landslide*

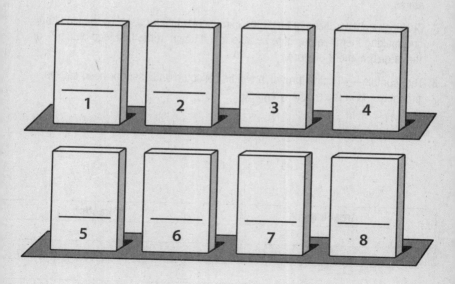

Starting tip: Begin by naming movie No. 1.

Mall Teaser

A new shopping mall has just opened on the outskirts of Netherlipp, hoping to pull in customers from across Keighshire. The Castle Center is cross-shaped and, from its central atrium, four arms radiate outwards north, south, east, and west, each boasting stores to please everyone and an attractive added feature. From the clues, can you work out the names given to the five areas (four arcades and central atrium) and the feature to be found in each, as well as the number of stores?

Clues

1. The central area contains a large castellated sign that reads "Castle Square" and is known as Castle Keep.

2. The easterly arcade contains nine stores but has neither the most nor the fewest number of letters in its name; the first word in the name of the area with the French-style open diner offering croissants and coffee, which is the area with the fewest stores, is one letter shorter than that of the westerly arcade.

3. There are seven stores in Leather Lane, while the indoor trees—no dogs allowed—grow in Brook Lane.

4. The sculpture of the dolphin is not in Dolphin Walk or in the arcade with six stores.

5. Buckingham Way does not boast the carousel—ideal for keeping the kids happy and making them feel too ill to be able to eat lunch at the fast food outlets—or the largest number of stores.

6. The fountain—all coins thrown in will be collected and used for good causes, probably—is in the northerly arcade.

Arcade name	Direction

	Center	East	North	South	West	5 stores	6 stores	7 stores	9 stores	10 stores	Carousel	Fountain	Open diner	Sculpture	Trees
Brook Lane															
Buckingham Way															
Castle Keep															
Dolphin Walk															
Leather Lane															
Carousel															
Fountain															
Open diner															
Sculpture															
Trees															
5 stores															
6 stores															
7 stores															
9 stores															
10 stores															

Store	Feature

Logi-5

Each line, across and down, is to have each of the letters A, B, C, D, and E, appearing once. Also, every shape—shown by the thick lines—must also have each of the letters in it. Can you fill in the grid?

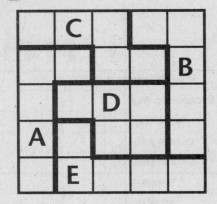

Killer Sudoku

The normal rules of Sudoku apply. In addition, the digits in each inner shape (marked by dots) must add up to the number in the top corner of that box.

20		10			18			21
	12		11		10			
	19	23			12			9
8			12			22		
		23	11		14			
19					20		12	
			13					17
8			5	9	17			
22						8		

Domino Search

A standard set of dominoes has been laid out, using numbers instead of dots for clarity. Using a sharp pencil and a keen brain, can you draw in the lines to show where each domino has been placed? You may find the check grid useful—crossing off each domino as you find it.

0	4	6	2	3	4	3	3
6	5	5	2	2	5	1	1
1	5	0	4	1	5	0	4
5	4	3	1	3	6	5	3
6	6	4	3	1	6	4	2
0	1	4	0	6	6	1	0
0	2	0	2	3	5	2	2

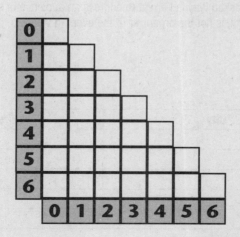

Wayne in Spain

Ecologist and green campaigner Wayne Forrest is in Spain, working on his latest book, and while he's there, he has been invited to participate in five different events in different cities. From the clues, can you work out where each invitation came from, the full name of the person who issued the invitation, and the nature of the event?

Clues

1. The letter from Málaga concerns an award which local conservationists want to give him to recognize his work—and to attract more attention to their own work.

2. None of the invitations are signed by an individual with name and surname of the same length.

3. It's the person named Palmero who wants Wayne Forrest to lead a demonstration against local abuse of the environment to gain international attention and, hopefully, get the police to go easy.

4. Eduardo is the leader of Bilbao Verde, an extreme ecology group in that city; Joaquin isn't involved with the plan to have Wayne address a group of politicians on conservation issues.

5. Ferreira's signature was on the invitation from Pamplona, a city best known for its annual running of the bulls through the streets.

6. Maria Valladaros is a millionaire's daughter who could have spent her life being one of the "beautiful people," but has instead devoted her life to saving the planet.

7. Jose, who has asked Wayne Forrest to address an audience of students about his life and work, is not the organizer of the event in Valencia.

City	First name

	Eduardo	Francesca	Joaquin	Jose	Maria	Ferreira	Garcia	Palmero	Quiroga	Valladaros	Address politicians	Address students	Lead demonstration	Receive award	Train activists
Bilbao															
Granada															
Málaga															
Pamplona															
Valencia															
Address politicians															
Address students															
Lead demonstration															
Receive award															
Train activists															
Ferreira															
Garcia															
Palmero															
Quiroga															
Valladaros															

Surname	Event

Knuckle Dusters

The five Regency Beaux who often grace these pages were all interested in the pugilistic art—or, to be more precise, gambling on the outcomes of pugilistic encounters—and each went to watch a different bare-knuckle fight at about the same time. From the clues, can you name the winner and the loser in the match each watched, and say how many rounds it lasted?

Clues

1. The fight which Beau Tighe attended, and which cost him two guineas, lasted twenty-two rounds.

2. The fight won by Tom Allen, at which Beau Nydel lost a pretty penny (and quite a number of attractive shillings too), lasted for more rounds than the one in which Beau Belles saw Esau Creasey beaten and his wager go down the drain.

3. Ben Keyes's fight was the next longer one than the bout won by Adam Fell.

4. Jake Smith fought Zach Murphy for a small purse and the enjoyment of the clamorous audience.

5. Ezra Mason was the winner of the eighteen-round prize fight.

6. Toby Swift, whose opponent was not Jem Pendle, failed to come up to the scratch for the seventh round of his contest, much to the disgust of the Beau who had backed him, who was not Beau Legges.

Beau	Winner

	Winners					Losers									
	Adam Fell	Ezra Mason	Jake Smith	Jem Pendle	Tom Allen	Ben Keyes	Esau Creasey	Kit Tanner	Toby Swift	Zach Murphy	6 rounds	18 rounds	22 rounds	27 rounds	31 rounds
Beau Belles															
Beau Legges															
Beau Nydel															
Beau Streate															
Beau Tighe															
6 rounds															
18 rounds															
22 rounds															
27 rounds															
31 rounds															
Ben Keyes															
Esau Creasey															
Kit Tanner															
Toby Swift															
Zach Murphy															

Losers

How's the other guy?

He says his hands are sore

Loser	Rounds

Punishing Schedule

It's the year 2214, and many things have changed in the last two centuries, but some are still the same; youngsters still go to school, even if the school's on or, as the locals say, *in* Luna, known as "the Moon" before colonization. And pupils still break rules and are punished when caught. From the clues, can you work out the names of each of these errant students at The Neil Armstrong School, the names of their teachers, what they've done wrong, and how they were punished?

Clues

1. Suzan Thom, who's not in Mr. Louva's class, wasn't the pupil punished by having to clean the school's emergency airlock, who wasn't caught playing games (minicomputer games, of course) in class.

2. Miro Nothar is in the class of Daneel-41, one of the school's robot teachers (you recognize them by their numbers); he wasn't the youngster who was heard speaking Terran (the language of Terra, formerly known as Earth) when the rules decreed that pupils should be speaking Universal, the synthetic language used throughout the Confederation of Planets.

3. The pupil who was caught pre-programming exam answers onto a personal minicomputer, and was punished by having to use an old-fashioned keyboard instead of verbal programming for one week, has a human teacher.

4. Helen Ivarson was banned from going onto the surface of Luna (the school is underground, like almost all of Luna's structures) for her transgression; Jan Kalli was punished for simple disobedience.

5. It was Ms. Sladek's pupil who had to write (actually *handwrite*, without using a computer!) an essay about the historic figure for whom the school is named.

6. Captain Boland, who is a retired StarForce officer, punished one of his class members for wasting water—a serious offense on notoriously arid Luna.

Pupil	Teacher

	Captain Boland	Daneel-41	Mr. Louva	Ms. Sladek	Ubik-16	Disobedience	Playing games in class	Pre-programming	Speaking Terran	Wasting water	Banned from surface	Clean airlock	Sent to principal	Use keyboard	Write essay
Charli Bodel															
Helen Ivarson															
Jan Kalli															
Miro Nothar															
Suzan Thom															
Banned from surface															
Clean airlock															
Sent to principal															
Use keyboard															
Write essay															
Disobedience															
Playing games in class															
Pre-programming															
Speaking Terran															
Wasting water															

Offense	Punishment

Having a Break

Five women who earn their crusts at the international GloboCorp headquarters in Netherlipp like to take a short break away from the office to clear their heads and prepare for the rest of the day. They drop into the Singing Kettle Diner at different but regular times for a regular order of a cup of something and something nice to eat. From the clues, can you work out the full details?

Clues

1. Madge, who works in Incoming Exports, is an afternoon customer but does not drink coffee with her regular order of fruitcake.

2. The pot of tea is always accompanied by a toasted tea cake.

3. Ella, who works in Post-Human Resources, comes into the Singing Kettle sometime later than the mineral water drinker, but earlier than the person who orders gingerbread.

4. The cookies are not ordered by the customer who always comes in at half past eleven.

5. Nancy always orders a cup of hot chocolate when she's having a quick break from her work in the Inverse Recruitment department.

6. Lucy, who works in the Underpurchasing department, is the next regular visitor after Ethel, the company's deputy assistant Illegal Advisor; neither of these two drink black coffee.

7. The person who always drinks white coffee does not order a scone to go with it.

Time	Name

	Ella	Ethel	Lucy	Madge	Nancy	Black coffee	Hot chocolate	Mineral water	Pot of tea	White coffee	Cookies	Fruitcake	Gingerbread	Scone	Tea cake
10:00															
11:30															
2:00															
3:10															
4:15															
Cookies															
Fruitcake															
Gingerbread															
Scone															
Tea cake															
Black coffee															
Hot chocolate															
Mineral water															
Pot of tea															
White coffee															

Drink	Food

Ollie Wood's Bowl

Ollie Wood runs the music venue in Netherlipp known as the Bowl and he has just finished lining up the acts that will grace the stage during March. From the clues, can you name the singing group in each illustration on the poster that he hopes will persuade thousands of screaming teenagers to part with their pocket money, and the date on which they will perform?

Clues

1. Take What?—a group of boys from Netherlipp College—will appear three days after Boyztwo (described, mainly by themselves, as the pride of Lower Crispin), and appear on the poster in the row below them.

2. One Correction, the latest teen sensation from Stonekeigh High School, will appear at the Bowl on Saturday the 8th.

3. The Wasted, a group of refuse collectors from Wallingfen looking to earn a little extra beer money, are shown in an even-numbered position on the poster, and will appear immediately before the boy band shown in position 7 and sometime after the band who call themselves 6ix (but only because of a typing error by one of their mothers), who are shown in a position numbered half that of the one with the picture of Westwife.

4. The picture of McWhy is shown immediately to the left of the band who will strut their stuff on Wednesday the 12th.

5. Buckled, who will appear at the bowl on a Saturday, are shown directly above, in the row above, the picture of the band who will begin the month-long gig list.

6. The band in position 5 will do their thing on Wednesday the 19th, but the band in position 1 is not the one that will bring the curtain down on March's entertainment at the Bowl.

Groups: Boyztwo; Buckled; McWhy; One Correction; 6ix; Take What?; The Wasted; Westwife
Dates: Wednesday the 5th; Saturday the 8th; Wednesday the 12th; Saturday the 15th; Wednesday the 19th; Saturday the 22nd; Wednesday the 26th; Saturday the 29th

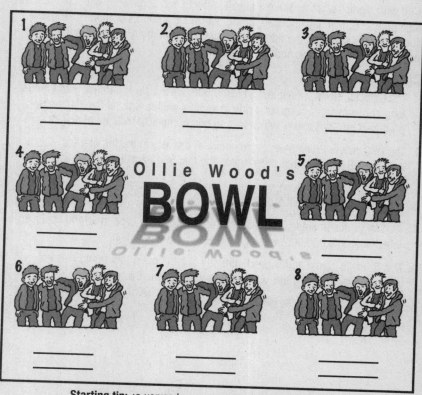

Ollie Wood's
BOWL

Starting tip: Begin by naming the band shown in position 5.

Flipp Flops

Over the past few years, Franz Flipp, the great but eccentric movie director, has made five movies for various producers in America's Ivywood movie center, each filled with biggish stars and minor special effects and confidently expected to make huge profits. But all have flopped, losing enormous amounts of money. From the clues, can you work out the title of each movie, the name of the studio that made it, the name of the producer, and the amount it lost?

Clues

1. The Galactic movie, which lost $18,000,000, wasn't *Dark Carnival* (eight hours long and showing a fairground ride at various angles with all the lights off), produced by Sol Rubitch, which lost an odd number of millions of dollars.

2. The QKQ movie *Prime Number* (the story of one day in the life of a top anesthetist) lost less than *Interceptor* (the tale of a parallel line that wants to branch out).

3. Al Garbidge's movie lost $23,000,000.

4. *Warstar* (a documentary about how bitumen has been used in armed conflicts), which lost $15,000,000, wasn't the Buena Sera production.

5. *The Tower* (a gentle and, indeed, unfunny short about a tow truck) was not produced by Jess Torrible, who doesn't work for the Dixon studios.

6. Pat Hettick is Summit Studios' top producer.

Movie	Studio

	Buena Sera	Dixon	Galactic	QKQ	Summit	Adam Leuser	Al Garbidge	Jess Torrible	Pat Hettick	Sol Rubitch	$15,000,000	$18,000,000	$19,000,000	$23,000,000	$26,000,000
Dark Carnival															
Interceptor															
Prime Number															
The Tower															
Warstar															
$15,000,000															
$18,000,000															
$19,000,000															
$23,000,000															
$26,000,000															
Adam Leuser															
Al Garbidge															
Jess Torrible															
Pat Hettick															
Sol Rubitch															

Producer	Loss

Attacks Evasion

It is an occupational hazard for Private Eyes that, once in a while, they will incur the wrath of people whose wrath is best left unincurred. Our five friends who work as investigators in the Southern California town of San Angelo have each recently brought some illegal scheme to the attention of the local police while helping one of their clients. In return, five crime bigwigs have sent a number of henchmen to deliver messages of disapproval. From the clues, can you work out which gang leader is annoyed with which Private Eye, the number of men he sent to settle the score, and the location the P.I. needed to rapidly vacate to avoid unpleasantness?

Clues

1. Mike Mallet dodged one more thug than Sugsy Stokes dispatched to settle a score, and one fewer than arrived at the railway station just as one Private Eye made a quick exit through the mail door.

2. Nicky Nail made a hasty exit, half-shaved, from the Kwiksnip Barber Shop.

3. Spike Spanner, who had annoyed Rugsy Ricks by breaking his smuggling ring at the docks, wasn't the P.I. who left O'Malley's Bar via a restroom window when five large and determined-looking young men walked through the door.

4. Lugsy Locks sent fewer men to make his point to one Private Eye than almost caught another P.I. at the park.

5. Bugsy Brakes's best men—Knuckles and Duster—always work as a pair and were sent to deliver his message of disapproval.

6. Dick Drill dodged a larger group of thugs than were sent to have a quiet word with Ricky Wrench.

Private eye	Gang boss

	Bugsy Brakes	Lugsy Locks	Mugsy Maker	Rugsy Ricks	Sugsy Stokes	1	2	3	4	5	Bar	Barber's	Diner	Park	Station
Dick Drill															
Mike Mallet															
Nicky Nail															
Ricky Wrench															
Spike Spanner															
Bar															
Barber's															
Diner															
Park															
Station															
1															
2															
3															
4															
5															

Number	Location

My Grandfather's . . .

When their late grandfather's will was read, his five grandchildren found that he had left each of them an antique item of furniture from a different room in his house. From the clues, can you say who was left which item, work out its approximate date of manufacture, and name the room in which it was to be found?

Clues

1. Grandfather's mirror was too tall for the sitting room, so it hung for many years in the main bedroom; the item left to grandson Roger dates from the same century.

2. Eileen's item did not come from a bedroom.

3. The item made around 1870 was not the sideboard, and its place was not in Grandad's drawing room.

4. Owen's bequest had pride of place in his grandfather's living room; it was more modern than the item in the hallway, which was made about 1770.

5. Grandfather's table was too tall for the porch but it dated from around 1720.

6. Neil was left the object dated circa 1820.

7. Grandfather's clock was too tall for the shelf and was bequeathed to Stella, who doesn't have many, in his will.

Legatee	Item

	Chest	Clock	Mirror	Sideboard	Table	1720	1770	1820	1870	1920	Back bedroom	Drawing room	Hallway	Living room	Main bedroom
Eileen															
Neil															
Owen															
Roger															
Stella															
Back bedroom															
Drawing room															
Hallway															
Living room															
Main bedroom															
1720															
1770															
1820															
1870															
1920															

Date	Room

Quick Getaway

I've made a last-minute decision to take a vacation away from the snow and the rain, and our local travel agent has a number of low-priced getaways available for departure next week. From the clues, can you discover the leaving date of each vacation, the destination, the number of nights, and the cost per person?

Clues

1. The departure on the 4th is not the package offering fifteen nights of sea, sand, and sunburn for $378.

2. The departure on the 5th is the cheapest, while that on the 6th is for Minorcash.

3. The flight to Costa Poco is the day before the fourteen-night vacation; the latter costs more than the vacation in Fuquid.

4. The departure on the 8th is for seven nights (some of them in a hotel!), but is not to Fuquid.

5. The cost of five nights in Nodeira is less than $420 (the days, on the other hand . . .).

6. The vacation in the Bargin Islands is priced at $420.

Date	Destination

	Bargin Islands	Costa Poco	Fuquid	Minorcash	Nodeira	5 nights	7 nights	10 nights	14 nights	15 nights	$294	$336	$378	$420	$462
4th															
5th															
6th															
7th															
8th															
$294															
$336															
$378															
$420															
$462															
5 nights															
7 nights															
10 nights															
14 nights															
15 nights															

Nights	Cost

Ghost Writer

Meredith Rawden Jonas is a writer of modern ghost stories who has discovered a best-selling formula to which all his five novels adhere—a ghost haunting a famous London landmark appears to an American visitor who becomes involved in investigating the phenomenon and ultimately exorcises the ghost. From the clues, can you work out the name of each book, and the landmark, ghost, and tourist it involves?

Clues

1. The ghostly clergyman, the Reverend Runcible Bunthorne, imprisoned in this world after the unjust verdict of a corrupt witch-hunting magistrate, contacts and is ultimately freed from his plight by Officer Joe Sheppard of the New York Police Department, visiting London to research his family history.

2. Both *Inheritance* and the book in which the haunted landmark is the Royal Opera House feature one of the two ghosts who once commanded ships.

3. *The Call,* in which the American visitor is a physician from Baltimore, Maryland, does not involve the haunting of Kew Gardens.

4. It's artist Ray Maggio from San Francisco, California, who encounters an apparition in the British Museum; *Full Circle* is not the book in which the ghost is that of Victorian novelist Crispin Winston.

5. The ghost of Captain Dudley Bishop of the Royal Navy features in *Beneath the Surface*—though his ship was not a submarine!

6. In *On the Way Home*, the ghost appears on platform 1 at London Bridge Station.

7. *Full Circle* does not involve the ghost of seventeenth-century poet and dramatist Ranulph Crauford, nor did the poet contact Philadelphia-born student Lyle Kaufman or physician Boyd Dempster.

Title	Landmark

	British Museum	Highgate Cemetery	Kew Gardens	London Bridge Station	Royal Opera House	Clergyman	Naval officer	Novelist	Pirate captain	Poet	Artist	Cop	Physician	Student	Teacher
Beneath the Surface															
Full Circle															
Inheritance															
On the Way Home															
The Call															
Artist															
Cop															
Physician															
Student															
Teacher															
Clergyman															
Naval officer															
Novelist															
Pirate captain															
Poet															

Ghost	Investigator

Pirates

The pirate ship *Sea Devil* is at anchor in Santa Maria Bay on the Mexican coast, and, as it's late at night, most of the crew are asleep below decks. From the clues, can you fill in the nickname and surname of each of the four men still on deck and say what he does aboard the *Sea Devil*?

Clues

1. The scrawny pirate nicknamed "Bones" is on the same deck level as the Royal Navy deserter surnamed Watkins.

2. Figure 1 is known as "Bristol Bill," having been born in that city and christened William.

3. Red Jack, the *Sea Devil's* sadistic first mate, is not Jarvis.

4. The man whose scarred face has earned him the highly original nickname "Scar" is immediately left of Craddock, the *Sea Devil's* gunner; the gunner is somewhere further to the right than Fisher.

5. Figure 3 is the *Sea Devil's* bosun, and, as usual at this time of day, is drunk—if it was a moving picture, you'd see him staggering.

Nicknames: Bones; Bristol Bill; Red Jack; Scar
Surnames: Craddock; Fisher; Jarvis; Watkins
Roles: bosun; first mate; gunner; seaman

Starting tip: Work out the role of Pirate 1.

Salad Days

GloboCorp's staff breakroom at their Netherlipp headquarters features a new Saladomatic machine from which workers can grab a quick snack during the day. Pressing a button on the keypad will deposit a portion of a salad ingredient in the corresponding tray below. From the clues, can you work out what ingredient pops out of which chute?

Clues

1. The cucumber spears are in an even-numbered chute, which isn't numbered two lower than the shredded iceberg lettuce.

2. The celery sticks are kept in the chute numbered two lower than the one with the grated carrots.

3. To order a celery, lettuce, and tomato salad, GloboCorp staff need to press buttons that total 13.

Salad Ingredients: celery sticks; cucumber spears; grated carrots; onion rings; shredded lettuce; sliced tomatoes

Starting tip: Work out what ingredient is in chute 1.

Sign In

Each row and column is to contain the digits 1-5. The given signs tell you if a digit in a cell is plus 1 (+) or minus 1 (-) the digit next to it. Signs between consecutive digits always work from left to right or top to bottom.
Examples: 3 + 4 or 2 ALL occurences of consecutive digits have been marked by a sign.

Sudoku

Complete this grid so that each column, each row, and each marked 3 X 3 square contains each of the numbers 1 to 9.

					6			5
			7	5				
			1			3		
	7	2			8		5	6
	3				5	4		
6			2	1			8	3
		8		2				
			6		3			1
3			8		9		4	

Battleships

Do you remember the old game of battleships? These puzzles are based on that idea. Your task is to find the vessels in the diagram. Some parts of boats or sea squares have already been filled in, and a number next to a row or column refers to the number of occupied squares in that row or column. The boats may be positioned horizontally or vertically, but no two boats or parts of boats are in adjacent squares—horizontally, vertically, or diagonally.

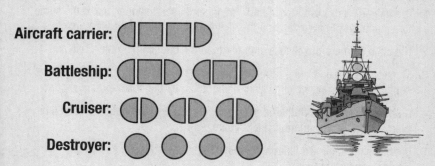

Aircraft carrier:

Battleship:

Cruiser:

Destroyer:

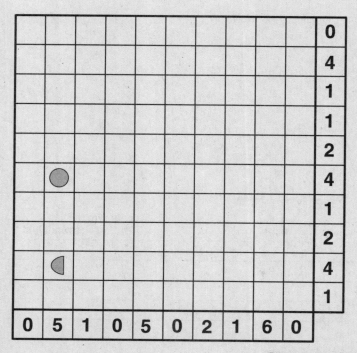

Mini Maestros

Five doting grandparents were determined that their only grandchild (so far) should be given the opportunity and encouragement to develop the musical genius they obviously must contain, and so they each paid for private lessons on a different instrument. From the clues, can you match the grandparents with their grandchildren and their ages, and say which instrument each was learning?

Clues

1. The ages of Vera's grandchild and Tim, when added together, make the same total as those of Lawrence and the violinist, these being four different children.

2. The child learning the cello is younger than the one learning the violin.

3. Much to the despair of her daughter and son-in-law, Olive is paying for the euphonium lessons, which are not being taken by the child aged nine.

4. Graham, whose grandfather is paying for his lessons, but not on a bowed or plucked string instrument, is eight years old.

5. Rachel is not the child learning to play the harp, who is ten and whose grandparent is not Rita.

6. Norman's grandchild is twelve.

Name	Grandchild

	Graham	Lawrence	Rebecca	Rachel	Tim	8	9	10	11	12	Cello	Euphonium	Harp	Piano	Violin
Martin															
Norman															
Olive															
Rita															
Vera															
Cello															
Euphonium															
Harp															
Piano															
Violin															
8															
9															
10															
11															
12															

Grandchildren

Grandparents

Age	Instrument

The Cactus Kid

The western outlaw Frederick Franklin Fitzgerald, known as "the Cactus Kid," was finally captured by US Marshal Kirk Luther just outside Rio Portillo, New Mexico, on May 7, 1880. The map below (which isn't to scale) shows his route to Rio Portillo over the previous six days. From the clues given, can you fill in the name of the town he visited on each date, the saloon where he spent the night, and how far it was from his previous stop?

Clues

1. After the night he spent at the Range Rider Saloon in the little town of Covenant, the Cactus Kid had a 22-mile ride to his next stop, which wasn't in Rio Portillo.

2. The Kid was in Harmony the night before he stayed at the Wagon Wheel Saloon in a little town 20 miles further on, which wasn't where he stayed on the night of May 6th.

3. The Cactus Kid had only an 8-mile ride to reach the town where he spent the night of May 4th; his 24-mile ride didn't end at the Star of Arizona Saloon, which wasn't where he was accommodated on the second night in May.

4. On May 1, the Cactus Kid was in Santa Isabel, a small town even by Wild West standards; the day's ride that ended there was longer than both his ride to Fort Barrow, which wasn't where he arrived on May 3rd, and his day's journey to the town where he took a room at the Bucket of Blood Saloon (which wasn't as bad as it sounds—not quite).

5. Apache Butte, which wasn't where the Kid spent the night of May 5th, was a full 16 miles from his next stop, which was before Rio Portillo.

6. The Fremont House saloon was in a town which the Kid reached after riding two miles fewer than he did to reach the community where he stayed at Texas Annie's, the Cactus Kid didn't enjoy the hospitality of these two establishments on successive nights.

Towns: Apache Butte; Covenant; Fort Barrow; Harmony; Russell's Wells; Santa Isabel

Saloons: Bucket of Blood; Fremont House; Range Rider; Star of Arizona; Texas Annie's; Wagon Wheel

Distances covered that day: 8 miles; 14 miles; 16 miles; 20 miles; 22 miles; 24 miles

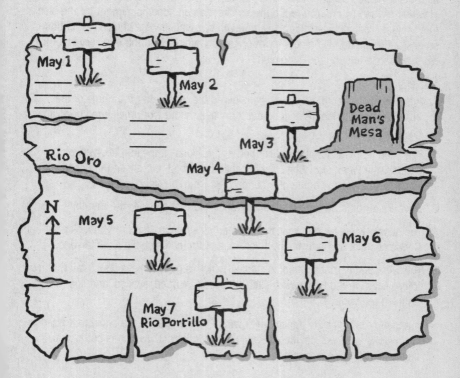

May 1

May 2

May 3

Dead Man's Mesa

Rio Oro

May 4

N ↑

May 5

May 6

May 7
Rio Portillo

Starting tip: Work out how far the Kid rode to get to Santa Isabel.

Wining On

NetherlippTV's "cooking and all things gastronomic" show *Weekend Scullery* features a weekly section where wine expert Ivor Pallet gives his considered opinion of wines chosen by one of the program's chefs as an accompaniment for the dish they've just created. From the clues, can you say whose wine choice Ivor critiques on each of these dates, its country of origin (and color), and the one very helpful word he chose to sum up his opinion?

Clues

1. Rita Boyle's choice of wine was considered the week after the bottle of the French white Chateau Plonque, and the week before Ivor proclaimed one wine to be "noisy."

2. The wine that was helpfully described as "nervous" appeared on *Weekend Scullery* the week after Steve Grille cooked the food and chose the booze, and the week before the bottle of American red from the Nappy Valley.

3. Dave Baker didn't demonstrate his dish on the first show of the month.

4. The Aussie wine—a red from the Boomer Valley—was featured a week after Jeff Cooke cooked, and a fortnight before one of the chefs chose a white wine.

5. The wine that Ivor described as "tall"—which is good, unless it's so tall that it's lofty—was served two weeks after he sipped, slurped, swilled, and spat the Spanish red wine.

6. Joanne Fry brought the Italian white wine Pinot Grogue to the show that aired two weeks after Ivor decided one wine was "abstract" (which is better than being Cubist, but not much).

Date	Chef

	Dave Baker	Jeff Cooke	Joanne Fry	Rita Boyle	Steve Grille	American red	Australian red	French white	Italian white	Spanish red	Abstract	Distracted	Noisy	Nervous	Tall
2nd															
9th															
16th															
23rd															
30th															
Abstract															
Distracted															
Noisy															
Nervous															
Tall															
American red																
Australian red																
French white																
Italian white																
Spanish red																

Country	Opinion

Officer Material

Five young American actresses have all achieved fame and fortune playing police officers of different sorts in different series. From the clues, can you work out the name of each actress, the name of the police officer she plays, and the squad and police department in which she serves?

Clues

1. The actress who plays an officer of the Dallas, Texas, police department (DPD) has an even number of letters in her surname.

2. Nancy Oriano's character is a member of one police force's K9 Squad—a dog-handler.

3. Ella Fremont's character, who isn't Sergeant Samantha "Sam" Thatcher, is neither the Cold Case Squad member, who has been assigned there because of her tendency to disobey orders, nor the officer from the Robbery Squad whose father used to be a notorious jewel thief.

4. One of the five officers is a young New York Police Department (NYPD) cop who has just joined the Homicide Squad and doesn't always see eye to eye with the Squad's veteran commander.

5. Liz Marlowe is a member of the Maine State Police (MSP), up in New England on the Canadian border.

6. Kate Lockhart's character, who is a member of the United States Air Force Police (USAFP), is not Robbery Squad member Lucy McGee.

7. Erica Fell, played by Cleo Diaz, is not the officer from the Special Investigations Squad; either the actress playing the special investigator or the one who appears as the officer from the Los Angeles Police Department (LAPD) has a first name beginning with a vowel—but not both of them.

Actress	Character

	Erica Fell	Fran Grant	Liz Marlowe	Lucy McGee	Sam Thatcher	Cold Case	Homicide	K9	Robbery	Special Investigations	DPD	LAPD	MSP	NYPD	USAFP
Ali Booth															
Cleo Diaz															
Ella Fremont															
Kate Lockhart															
Nancy Oriano															
DPD															
LAPD															
MSP															
NYPD															
USAFP															
Cold Case															
Homicide															
K9															
Robbery															
Special Investigations															

Characters

Actresses

Squad	Force

Fishing Poll

Judy Side is employed by the Straw in the Wind, Ltd., market research bureau and has been dispatched into the streets of Netherlipp to ask unsuspecting members of the public how they would respond to a new type of solidified yogurt—perfect, apparently, for sandwiches. So far, she has approached five people, all of whom were unresponsive. From the clues, can you work out where she was when she stopped each person, her opening line hoping to get their attention, and the excuse they gave for not giving an opinion on Yog Slices?

Clues

1. The woman with the baby in a stroller, who wasn't in the seating area in the mall center, brushed off Judy with a hurried "Feeding time!"

2. Judy laid her cards on the table for the large Russian hat, and said, "I'm asking about yogurt;" this wasn't the person on Main Street who responded with, "No comment," nor was the Main Street target the lady who was approached with the polite "Excuse me, madam."

3. "Do you have a minute or two?" Judy asked, as one person walked through the mall entrance.

4. "Excuse me, sir," said Judy to a man who rushed away saying, "I have to catch a bus."

5. The man in the baseball cap was approached as he neared the diner.

6. "Could I have a moment of your time?" Judy asked one of her female targets; the person who mistook Judy for a collector, and replied, "I've already given," wasn't the tall man.

Location	Person

	Elderly lady	Man in baseball cap	Tall man	Woman in fur hat	Woman with baby	Could I have…?	Do you have…?	Excuse me, madam…	Excuse me, sir…	I'm asking about…	Already given	Catch bus	Catch train	Feeding time!	No comment!
High Street															
Mall entrance															
Mall diner															
Mall center															
Town Square															
Already given															
Catch bus															
Catch train															
Feeding time!															
No comment!															
Could I have…?															
Do you have…?															
Excuse me, madam…															
Excuse me, sir…															
I'm asking about…															

So, as you can see, 62% of the 36% of the people who completed the survey in less than 43% of the allotted time didn't understand the question

SURVEY RESULTS

Approach	Excuse

Aliens

Yes, four aliens from worlds far beyond the Solar System have landed on our planet—but don't worry; this is the year 2418, and the four have just disembarked from the star liner *Cinruss* at John Lennon Intergalactic Spaceport (formerly known as Merseyside). From the clues, can you work out each visitor's name, planet of origin, and reason for coming here?

Clues

1. As the aliens line up to have their passports scanned, Xan Balu from Durdane is immediately behind the visitor who has come here for a shopping trip.

2. The alien on a sightseeing trip (you can see a lot of sights with six eyes and X-ray vision!) is somewhere ahead of the traveler from Worlorn.

3. The Helliconian, a businessman (or business creature, anyway) on a sales trip and concerned that his sample case may have been sent to Gethen, on the other side of the Milky Way, occupies an even-numbered position in the line; he (she? it?) is not Toarn Tumika.

4. Q'inshav Bek, who is not from Poloda, is here to spend a year studying at Hawking College in the mega-city of Goatsferry.

Names: Q'inshav Bek; Rovedah; Toarn Tumika; Xan Balu
Planets: Durdane; Helliconia; Poloda; Worlorn
Reasons: going to college; sales trip; shopping; sightseeing

Starting tip: Begin by working out why Xan Balu is visiting us.

Casino Royale

The Royale Casino in Netherlipp contains a room for novice casino-goers, and three newcomers to the world of gambling have been trying their hands. From the clues, can you say which game each new gambler played, the name of the croupier or dealer, and how much each newcomer lost before vowing, "Never again?"

Clues

1. The new gambler who played blackjack for a while lost the most of these three and stormed out, vowing never to return.

2. Stephanie Stake tried her hand at the game run by Henry Heinz; she lost less than the gambler at Yolanda Yankee's table but still left the premises in a bit of a huff.

3. Percy Punt took a shot at roulette; he isn't the gambler who lost exactly $7.50.

	Blackjack	Poker	Roulette	Henry Heinz	Thomas Trixie	Yolanda Yankee	$5	$7.50	$10
Percy Punt									
Stephanie Stake									
Walter Wager									
$5									
$7.50									
$10									
Henry Heinz									
Thomas Trixie									
Yolanda Yankee									

Gambler	Game	Croupier/Dealer	Loss

For Your Eyes Only

Three customers are scheduled for eyesight tests at the Eye Spy Opticians on Netherlipp's Main Street. From the clues, can you give the name of each customer with each time's appointment, the name of his or her optician, and the response they gave when asked to read the chart?

Clues

1. "Can you read the chart, please?" said the optician. Saul Blurd, who wasn't the 10 a.m. appointment holder, squinted and looked around the room. "Yes," he said, "E, X, I, T."

2. Justin Haze has an appointment with Len Sella.

3. Iris Scanne's first appointment of the morning was at 10:20; it wasn't Luke Strate's patient who responded, "Chart? What chart?"

4. The customer with the 10:40 appointment looked aghast at the optician, and said, "Well, not from here, obviously."

	Donna Seyitt	Justin Haze	Saul Blurd	Iris Scanne	Len Sella	Luke Strate	E, X, I, T	Not from here	What chart?
10:00									
10:20									
10:40									
E, X, I, T									
Not from here									
What chart?									
Iris Scanne									
Len Sella									
Luke Strate									

Appointment	Customer	Optician	Response

Battleships

Do you remember the old game of battleships? These puzzles are based on that idea. Your task is to find the vessels in the diagram. Some parts of boats or sea squares have already been filled in, and a number next to a row or column refers to the number of occupied squares in that row or column. The boats may be positioned horizontally or vertically, but no two boats or parts of boats are in adjacent squares—horizontally, vertically, or diagonally.

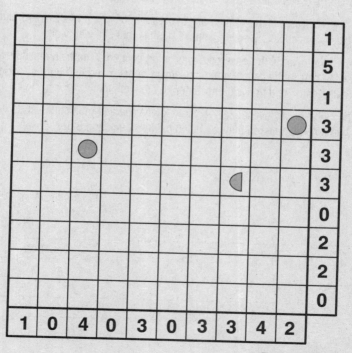

Aircraft carrier:

Battleship:

Cruiser:

Destroyer:

										1
										5
										1
									●	**3**
		●								**3**
							◗			**3**
										0
										2
										2
										0
1	**0**	**4**	**0**	**3**	**0**	**3**	**3**	**4**	**2**	

Paint

The headmaster of St. Keigh's Boarding School, Mr. Archibald Barrington-Carstairs, has made a bit of a blunder with his dates and has booked a local firm to spruce up some areas of the school with a lick of paint during term time rather than during the vacations. "Never mind," he thought, "if we rope off each area as it's done, the boys can be trusted to be careful." So, from the clues, can you say where each of our eleven-year-old friends from dormitory B4 encountered the wet paint, and which part of their body they painted with which color?

Clues

1. Chris Cockroft's exuberant stair-descending style resulted in an encounter with wet paint on the landing; he wasn't the boy who spent most of the day with hair of an unexpected color.

2. Hamish Hazel, who wasn't the boy whose playful tussle in the school's main entrance resulted in a collision with a freshly painted wall, spent most of the day with part of his body in a warming shade of Sunrise Yellow.

3. One boy spent the day with Titanium White hands, transferring quite a lot of it to his uniform, desks, and anyone within a ten-foot radius.

4. One boy received a shove in the back in the rush to get out of Gym, and found one side of his cheek pressed against a pristine, but still wet, wall.

5. The corridor towards the classroom was being painted a soothing Meadow Green when one boy, to the delight and amusement of his friend Ben Barton, skidded to a halt just too late to avoid encountering the wet paint.

6. The boy whose unconventionally-colored knees sparked much interest during the day had not encountered the wall being painted Duck Egg Blue.

Boy	Location

	Gym	Corridor	Landing	Main entrance	Face	Hair	Hands	Knees	Blue	Green	White	Yellow
Ben Barton												
Chris Cockroft												
Hamish Hazel												
Martin Masters												
Blue												
Green												
White												
Yellow												
Face												
Hair												
Hands												
Knees												

Body part	Color

Back in the Swim

The week before school restarts, the boys who attend St Keigh's Boarding School assemble for a few days to get back into the swing of the routine. Included in those days is an informal swimming gala to engender the spirit of competition and to spot any younger boy whose skills need improving. Our four friends from dormitory B4 are good swimmers and, while on vacation during the summer, each developed a new stroke that he's sure will take the swimming world by storm. From the clues, can you name each boy's new style, where they developed it, and how they plan to breathe while employing it?

Clues

1. Chris Cockroft developed the "Scythe," in which both arms swing from side to side in concert, but it isn't the stroke in which the swimmer has to stand up every few strokes to catch their breath.

2. Martin Masters hopes to aid breathing by taping an old piece of hose pipe to the side of his head; the inventor of the "Windmill," a wild revolving motion of both arms and body, has taped together a few drinking straws as a breathing tube.

3. Hamish Hazel developed his new stroke while vacationing on the island of Pilchardia; the "Periscope" stroke, which involves holding one arm straight up in the air at all times and for no discernible reason, is the offspring of a week on the neighboring island of Crudica.

4. The boy who vacationed on the Linnet Islands has blown up a balloon which he holds under the water as a sort of scuba tank.

5. The "Eel," a stroke that includes no arm motion at all, was not the one developed in the coastal resort of Costa del Buoy.

Boy	Stroke

	Eel	Periscope	Scythe	Windmill	Costa del Buoy	Crudica	Linnet Islands	Pilchardia	Balloon	Hose pipe	Stand up	Straws
Ben Barton												
Chris Cockroft												
Hamish Hazel												
Martin Masters												
Balloon												
Hose pipe												
Stand up												
Straws												
Costa del Buoy												
Crudica												
Linnet Islands												
Pilchardia												

Vacation spot	Breathing

Behind the Man

Back in 1930, five young women, almost completely unknown to history, were the mistresses of the rulers of five lesser-known countries of Central Europe. These women were dutiful, caring, wise, ruthless, and the real site of power in each realm. From the clues, can you work out the title and the country of each of the five rulers, name each man's mistress, and say for how long she had been with him, guiding his reign?

Clues

1. The mistress of the Margrave of Kukuklokz had held her semi-official position two years longer than Eva had been in hers.

2. Karen was the mistress of the official ruler of Frankenstein (although, truth be told, he was the lover of the real ruler); she had not been around as long as the Prince's lady friend.

3. It was in Vulgaria that one woman had held sway at court for a four-year period.

4. The Grand-Duke's mistress had been in situ and had held the reins of power for the longest period of time.

5. The Regent, who had usurped power from his under-age nephew, had chosen Heidi to share power with him (share being her word for it, not his); he was not the ruler of Urdigurdi.

6. Greta had been at the side of her man for six years.

Title	Country

	Frankenstein	Kukuklokz	Schlossenberg	Urdigurdi	Vulgaria	Eva	Greta	Heidi	Karen	Mitzi	2 years	4 years	6 years	8 years	10 years
Count															
Grand-Duke															
Margrave															
Prince															
Regent															
2 years															
4 years															
6 years															
8 years															
10 years															
Eva															
Greta															
Heidi															
Karen															
Mitzi															

The trouble with you is you can only ever do one step at a time, without me you're nothing.

Mistress	Time

The Paragon and . . .

Peter Galahad, the vigilante/crook/detective known as "the Paragon," featured in numerous books and short stories by Charles Litoris, published from the 1930s onward. *The Paragon and the Malefactors*, published in 1936, featured five of The Paragon's adventures in different US cities. From the clues, can you work out the second element in the title, the first part always being *The Paragon and . . .*, the city in which it's set, the crime involved, and the identity of the main criminal?

Clues

1. Both *The Paragon and the Bull's Eye*—which is set in Washington, DC—and the espionage case featured male malefactors.

2. In *The Paragon and the Copycat*, Peter Galahad investigates a brutal murder for which an old friend has been framed.

3. The story about the kidnapping of a famous movie star is set not in Hollywood, but in an American city whose name immediately precedes (in the alphabetical list) that of the place where the Paragon brings Lola Crocetti to justice.

4. The man who steals a historic diamond, once part of the Lotharingian crown jewels, and tries to put the blame on Peter Galahad is a veteran criminal named Roddy Keeler.

5. Zack Rovin is the Paragon's opponent in the story set in San Diego, California.

6. In one of the stories, the Paragon takes on—and, of course, breaks up—a crime ring operating in New York City.

7. *The Paragon and the Gymnast* is not the case in which Peter Galahad sends Kitty Jason and her associates to jail—or, at least, those of them who survive to the end of the story.

8. *The Paragon and the Jailbird* ends with the death of villain Joe Bickel in a car accident as he flees from the police after Peter Galahad has revealed his villainy.

9. *The Paragon and the Loup Garou*—a *loup garou* is a French or Canadian vampire, though that's totally irrelevant to this problem—isn't set in Dallas, Texas.

Title	City

	Dallas	Hollywood	New York City	San Diego	Washington, DC	Espionage	Jewel theft	Kidnapping	Murder	Crime ring	Joe Bickel	Kitty Jason	Lola Crocetti	Roddy Keeler	Zack Rovin
...the Bull's Eye															
...the Copycat															
...the Gymnast															
...the Jailbird															
...the Loup Garou															
Joe Bickel															
Kitty Jason															
Lola Crocetti															
Roddy Keeler															
Zack Rovin															
Espionage															
Jewel theft															
Kidnapping															
Murder															
Crime ring															

Crime	Malefactor

The Webster

The Webster Building, on New York City's East 13th Street, is just another city office block these days, but back in the 1920s, five of its offices were used by private detectives of various degrees of competence and honesty. From the clues, can you work out the full name of the Private Eye who occupied each of the listed offices, and say what he did for a living before taking up that occupation?

Clues

1. Office 7 was used by the private investigator named Homer, who was the oldest of the five, but by no means the tallest.

2. Mr. Crispin rented office 5 from January 1921 to March 1929, when he moved to the West Coast—meaning, in this instance, Los Angeles, California.

3. Richard had been an attorney in New Jersey before giving up that career—well, being let go, actually—to move to New York and become a detective.

4. Ex-Sergeant Goulet, formerly a member of the New York Police Department, had an office numbered two higher than that rented by the man surnamed Wilhelm, but with a lower number than the one used by Mr. Spurlock.

5. The detective who worked out of office 10, whose first name wasn't Oliver, had actually been a successful jewel thief in the Boston area before undergoing a change of heart and deciding to work for the law—more or less.

6. Valentine Keyes wasn't the man who had been an employee of the famous Pinkerton's Detective Agency before deciding to go into business for himself—or, rather, being forced to when they fired him.

Office	First name

	Eddie	Homer	Oliver	Richard	Valentine	Crispin	Goulet	Keyes	Spurlock	Wilhelm	Attorney	Jewel thief	Military policeman	Pinkerton's	Police sergeant
5															
7															
8															
9															
10															
Attorney															
Jewel thief															
Military policeman															
Pinkerton's															
Police sergeant															
Crispin															
Goulet															
Keyes															
Spurlock															
Wilhelm															

Surname	Previous job

Quiet Monday

The life of a private detective comprises periods of boredom and inaction interspersed with moments of adrenaline-filled peril. And so it was that one week for our five Private Eye acquaintances from the Southern Californian town of San Angelo began with a very dull Monday—no work, no clients, no calls—until late in the afternoon. From the clues, can you say at what time and by which method each detective was contacted, and by whom?

Clues

1. The male client who made contact with Mike Mallet did so earlier in the afternoon than a San Angelo Police officer walked through the door of one private detective needing to engage his particular, often less than legal, methods on behalf of the Police Department.

2. Cesar Lopez—the much-feared Cesar Lopez—made contact with a Private Eye as the clock in the Town Square struck five.

3. One detective snoozed, stared out of the window, and practiced throwing crumpled sheets of paper into his wastepaper basket until 4:15, when his phone rang.

4. Nicky Nail looked up from his newspaper to see a client, in person, hesitantly stepping through his door; this was earlier in the afternoon than San Angelo society high-roller Conrad Sanders made contact with a gumshoe.

5. Ricky Wrench was woken from a fitful snooze at 4:45 but not by the messenger boy who had been sent to engage a Private Eye on behalf of a male client.

6. Dick Drill's first contact with his client—the sultry nightclub singer Sandra Andersen—was not by text message.

Detective	Time

	4:15 p.m.	4:30 p.m.	4:45 p.m.	5:00 p.m.	5:15 p.m.	Client visit	Messenger	Phone call	Policeman	Text	Amanda Jonson	Cesar Lopez	Conrad Sanders	San Angelo Police	Sandra Andersen
Dick Drill															
Mike Mallet															
Nicky Nail															
Ricky Wrench															
Spike Spanner															
Amanda Jonson															
Cesar Lopez															
Conrad Sanders															
San Angelo Police															
Sandra Andersen															
Client visit															
Messenger															
Phone call															
Policeman															
Text															

Contact	Client

Welcome Break

Among the drinks lined up on the shelf at the back of the theater bar at the end of Act 1 of *Pupation*, a new experimental drama at the Netherlipp Hexagon, are these five, ordered by patrons before the show. From the clues, can you discover under which name each was ordered, the seats in the auditorium on which each couple are numbing their nether portions, and the long drink and spirit making up each order?

Clues

1. The order for the Twichers—who have seldom looked forward to a drink as much—includes a port and lemon; they are sitting in a pair of seats, of which the lower-numbered is an odd number.

2. The couple who ordered the draft lager is not sitting in row E; the patrons in E8/9 ordered the vermouth and may well have another before the second half begins.

3. Mr. Riggle drove to the theater this evening and has ordered the alcohol-free shandy, but is now considering having something a lot stronger and a taxi; the Riggles didn't also order the vodka and tonic, and they are not sitting in seats E5/6.

4. Mr. and Mrs. Skwurm, sitting in row C but seriously considering leaving their seats empty for the remaining parts of the play, have not ordered a cola; the cola was ordered by a couple in higher-numbered seats than those occupied by the Fijettes, who didn't order draft lager.

5. The Schuffles are not sitting in row J; the couple in row M have ordered draft beer.

6. One of the interval drinks orders comprises a bottle of lager and a whiskey—better make that a large whiskey.

Seats	Name

	Fijette	Riggle	Schuffle	Skwurm	Twicher	Bottled lager	Cola	Draft beer	Draft lager	Shandy	Gin and tonic	Port and lemon	Vermouth	Vodka and tonic	Whiskey
C21/22															
E5/6															
E8/9															
J16/17															
M13/14															
Gin and tonic															
Port and lemon															
Vermouth															
Vodka and tonic															
Whiskey															
Bottled lager															
Cola															
Draft beer															
Draft lager															
Shandy															

Drink	Spirit

Sporting Writers

Five very successful sportsmen whose competing careers have been brought to an end by injury, age or, to be frank, interest have embarked on new careers boosted by their famous name and have written whodunit novels. From the clues, can you work out each man's full name, his sporting credentials, and the title of his book?

Clues

1. Donald's surname isn't Lynch.

2. Brian, the author of *Dead Letter* (featuring the murder of a house leasing agent), isn't Mr. Goodyear.

3. Mr. Campion, the Olympic yachtsman, isn't Gregory.

4. The first name and surname of the author of *Full Tilt* (a historical whodunit set in Henry VIII's jousting arena) are the same length as each other.

5. Alan was one of the world's top showjumpers for more than a decade; the former high jumper isn't Donald.

6. The man surnamed Lynch wrote *Party Piece* (a murder mystery set at a political party's annual conference in which the number of suspects is one of the highest ever recorded).

7. Jonathan Tanner's book is not called *Scapegoat*. (Was it the goat who done it? You'll have to read it to find out. And if you do, perhaps you could tell the rest of us who couldn't make it to the end of the book.)

8. *In the Bag* (murder, mystery, and mayhem at the airport carry-on X-ray machine) is the work of the former professional golfer.

First name	Surname

USA TODAY

	Campion	Goodyear	Lynch	Tanner	Wolf	Basketball player	Golfer	High jumper	Showjumper	Yachtsman	Dead Letter	Full Tilt	In the Bag	Party Piece	Scapegoat
Alan															
Brian															
Donald															
Gregory															
Jonathan															
Dead Letter															
Full Tilt															
In the Bag															
Party Piece															
Scapegoat															
Basketball player															
Golfer															
High jumper															
Showjumper															
Yachtsman															

	Sporting role	Book title

Logi-5

Each line, across and down, is to have each of the letters A, B, C, D, and E, appearing once. Also, every shape—shown by the thick lines—must also have each of the letters in it. Can you fill in the grid?

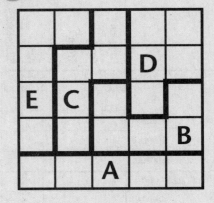

Killer Sudoku

The normal rules of Sudoku apply. In addition, the digits in each inner shape (marked by dots) must add up to the number in the top corner of that box.

10	29			26			4	
		7			7	23		14
	18		21			8		
		15				13		
28			20	11	17			24
		12						
						8		
16		8			12		12	10
12			12		8			

Domino Search

A standard set of dominoes has been laid out, using numbers instead of dots for clarity. Using a sharp pencil and a keen brain, can you draw in the lines to show where each domino has been placed? You may find the check grid useful—crossing off each domino as you find it.

1	3	6	1	2	5	5	4
2	2	0	2	1	4	6	6
4	3	1	1	0	0	0	5
6	6	6	5	4	4	3	6
3	2	0	3	3	2	4	6
4	3	5	3	1	1	0	0
0	5	5	5	2	4	2	1

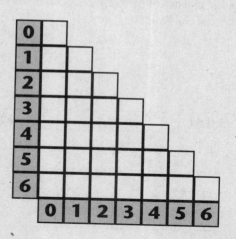

Can't Wait

The Rusty Service restaurant in Wallingfen is famed across Keighshire and rarely has a table spare. The food is good but customers come not to be delighted gastronomically but to witness the inept waiting of owner and chief waiter Algernon Amsfist. Diners cheer as plates go flying and salad is served with ice cream. From the clues, can you name the five lucky customers who were the subject of last night's bungles, what happened, what Algernon blamed, and the tip they left as appreciation of a great night's entertainment?

Clues

1. The overcharging was blamed on a power surge at the cash register, and the diner was so delighted they left a larger tip than the diner whose mishap Algernon blamed on a sudden localized earthquake, which wasn't the excuse for the spilt soup.

2. According to Algernon, Wilbur Wolf was to blame because he was waving his arm about—Wilbur agreed and so didn't leave the smallest tip.

3. Tiffany Tuckin left a $25 tip; the diner who went home with pants covered in spilt red wine left $15.

4. Brian Bolt's bread rolls were dropped but it certainly wasn't Algernon's fault; Brian left a tip $10 lower than the one whose accident was blamed on the resident poltergeist.

5. Sylvia Swallow wasn't the customer whose cutlery was thrown on the floor and cursorily wiped on Algernon's towel, to general applause.

6. The diner who, apparently, moved his feet in a suggestive manner, causing Algernon to fumble, left $20 as a tip.

Customer	Accident

	Dropped cutlery	Dropped rolls	Overcharged	Spilt soup	Spilt wine	Diner's arm	Diner's feet	Earthquake	Poltergeist	Power surge	$10	$15	$20	$25	$30
Brian Bolt															
Charles Chew															
Sylvia Swallow															
Tiffany Tuckin															
Wilbur Wolf															
$10															
$15															
$20															
$25															
$30															
Diner's arm															
Diner's feet															
Earthquake															
Poltergeist															
Power surge															

No, not the food sir. Just the menu.

Vegetarian MENU

steak
Sausages
Roasts
chicken
Lamb
Fish

Blame	Tip

San Guinari Romance

Romance is not the first thing that people associate with the little South American republic of San Guinari, but nevertheless five female British nurses, working in the country for the United Nations, have all managed to fall in love with San Guinarian men. From the clues, can you work out each nurse's name, the English county she comes from, and the name and occupation of her Latin American lover? (NB: For those of us unsure, the county list on the grid is in order from north to south.)

Clues

1. Mel Bourne, who isn't the nurse from Walmer in Kent, has fallen in love with the musician, a violinist regarded as South America's equivalent of Sarah Chang—by some people, anyway.

2. Connie Mara has found romance with Diego Mateos, who is not the journalist who works on El Presidente's favorite newspaper, *El Periodico*, nor the doctor from the Hospital Central, who has fallen in love with the nurse from a town in Essex; the doctor's name isn't Manuel Garza, and the nurse from Essex isn't called Sarah Jevo.

3. Eduardo Huerta is a politician; his beloved doesn't come from Durham.

4. Antonio Rubio's girlfriend is the nurse from Derbyshire; she is not Beverley Hills, whose home county is somewhere north of Mel Bourne's.

5. Eduardo Huerta's girlfriend was born and bred in an English county further south than the home of the Army officer's beloved.

Nurse	County

	Durham	Derbyshire	Suffolk	Essex	Kent	Antonio Rubio	Diego Mateos	Eduardo Huerta	Manuel Garza	Ricardo Obregon	Army officer	Doctor	Journalist	Musician	Politician
Beverley Hills															
Connie Mara															
Mel Bourne															
Pam Plona															
Sarah Jevo															
Army officer															
Doctor															
Journalist															
Musician															
Politician															
Antonio Rubio															
Diego Mateos															
Eduardo Huerta															
Manuel Garza															
Ricardo Obregon															

In order N to S

Boyfriend	Job

Writer's Block

Writer's block is when a writer suddenly finds that he or she is suddenly devoid of any ideas; it can happen to the best of writers. The five penmen we're looking at here reacted to it in rather drastic ways. From the clues, can you work out each man's name, into what genre his output falls, how many books he had written before the dreaded "block" struck, and how he tried to deal with it?

Clues

1. Barry Fabler, who has written more books than Jason Hack, tried to deal with his problem by plagiarizing previously-published works.

2. Jason Hack has never written a whodunit; neither the whodunit writer nor the science fiction author are the person who, after writing two books, developed writer's block and gave up to become a journalist.

3. The man who was a science fiction writer, hailed (by his publisher) as "the next Isaac Asimov," is neither the author of three books nor the writer who tried to fake his death in a yachting accident.

4. The writer of horror novels produced two more books before becoming "blocked" than the man who dealt with his problem by hiring well-known hack Bob Wheel as a "ghost."

5. One of the novelists produced six books of historical fiction before the block set in.

6. Perry Scribe produced four books before becoming blocked; Hugh Bookwright's output consisted of World War II novels about a fictional Royal Marines officer.

Writer	Genre

	Historical fiction	Horror novels	Science fiction	War novels	Whodunits	2 books	3 books	4 books	5 books	6 books	Became editor	Became journalist	Faked death	Hired ghost	Plagiarized
Barry Fabler															
Hugh Bookwright															
Jason Hack															
Mark Besseller															
Perry Scribe															
Became editor															
Became journalist															
Faked death															
Hired ghost															
Plagiarized															
2 books															
3 books															
4 books															
5 books															
6 books															

STORBURY
AUTHORS'
GROUP

TONIGHT—
WRITER'S
BLOCK

How to handle
...cope with...
deal with...
oh never mind!

Books	Remedy

Riding the Rales

The Southern Californian town of San Angelo is served by the Rales Tram Company, which provides regular, if a little uncomfortable, transportation into the center of town. By coincidence, all of the Private Eyes in the city, into whose lives we often peer, have found themselves on the same tram running from the train station to the tram station. From the clues, can you name each man "riding the Rales" in the picture (it's nice to be able to put the back of a hat to a name at last, don't you agree?), say at which destination he intends to alight, who he will meet there, and the number of days his current case has so far lasted?

Clues

1. Dick Drill is sitting on a seat behind the one occupied by the Private Eye who will alight the tram at Scotch Square and drop into O'Malley's bar to have a word with its owner, Earl O'Malley.

2. This is the second day that Nicky Nail has been working on his current case, the detective in seat 4 has been working his case for four days, and the man whose investigations have stalled after six days is meeting his friend Sgt. Stanley Hansell of the San Angelo Police Department to see if he can help.

3. The Private Eye in seat 3 has an appointment with a person of the same sex as that of the person the detective in seat 5 is riding the Rales to Pernod Place to see.

4. Mike Mallet has arranged a meeting in a coffee bar on Bourbon Boulevard.

5. Ricky Wrench, who hasn't been working on his current case for exactly five days, has been employed one day longer than the man who is riding the Rales to see nightclub singer Countess Von Stefl (real name Gertrude Brown), but for not as long as the man who will hop off the tram as it trundles through Tequila Terrace.

6. The nervous detective who is putting his well-being in danger by meeting mobster boss Bugsy Brakes is sitting on the opposite side of the central aisle from, but on the same row of seats as, the man who is on his third day of investigations.

7. The man riding the Rales to meet his client Petula Rigger, socialite and sole heiress to the Rigger family's oil business, isn't sharing a double seat.

Private eyes: Dick Drill; Mike Mallet; Nicky Nail; Ricky Wrench; Spike Spanner
Destinations: Bourbon Boulevard; Pernod Place; Schnapps Street; Scotch Square; Tequila Terrace
Contacts: Bugsy Brakes; Countess Von Stefl; Earl O'Malley; Petula Rigger; Sgt. Stanley Hansell
Times: 2 days; 3 days; 4 days; 5 days; 6 days

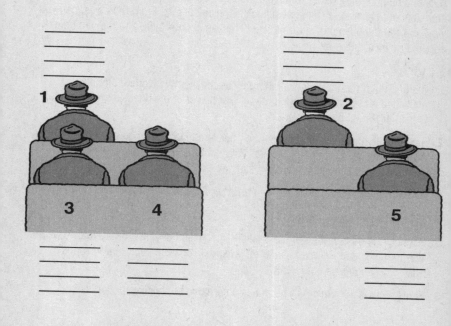

Starting tip: Work out who the man in seat 4 is meeting.

Bandwagon Books

Following the ending of a famous and extraordinarily successful series of children's books, a number of other writers have tried to fill the gap (and their pockets) with stories about children studying at schools for magical folk. From the clues, can you work out the full titles of five of the least creative counterfeits, and the pen names adopted by their authors?

Clues

1. The book that has . . . *Egyptian Mummy* as the last two words in its title is published as by J.K. Rapping; its hero, star player of his House's swappitch team, is neither Harold nor Pulman.

2. Heidi Pibble has a star-shaped scar on her forehead and studies at Hogwild's Academy for the Children of Magical Folk; the title of the book in which she features doesn't mention a shape-changer.

3. One of the book titles includes . . . *Parker and the Imitation Witch.*

4. J.K. Rybling's hero is named Peters.

5. Possibly the best-written of the books—which isn't saying a great deal—has the title that includes *Horace . . . and the Magic Sword;* the book that includes . . . *and the Flying Pig* is not by J.K. Ribbing.

6. Henry, who is J.K. Rusting's hero, has a surname containing the letter K.

First name	Surname

	Parker	Peters	Pibble	Pulman	Pyckle	...Egyptian Mummy	...Flying Pig	...Imitation Witch	...Magic Sword	...Shape-Changer	J.K. Rapping	J.K. Redding	J.K. Ribbing	J.K. Rusting	J.K. Rybling
Hamish															
Harold															
Heidi															
Henry															
Horace															
J.K. Rapping															
J.K. Redding															
J.K. Ribbing															
J.K. Rusting															
J.K. Rybling															
...Egyptian Mummy															
...Flying Pig															
...Imitation Witch															
...Magic Sword															
...Shape-Changer															

Title	Writer

Model Tea

The four finalists at the All-Keighshire Tea-Making Contest sat nervously as the judges sniffed, slurped, and spat as they tasted the teas. From the clues, can you work out the type of tea each competitor chose for their final offering, the individual action that they hope sets them apart from the rest, and the position they achieved?

Clues

1. The brew based on Darjeeling tea placed lower than the tea whose production system included a one and a half swirls of the tea in the pot, but beat the tea made from Nilgiri.

2. Prunella Potter used a high pour technique (usually by standing on a chair) that aerated the tea and splashed the carpet and the judge's pants.

3. The Ceylon tea was helped along the way by stirring it for exactly 4.7 seconds with an egg whisk.

4. The double brewing technique was frowned upon and its output placed fourth.

5. Brian Brewer chose Assam tea for his final push for the summit.

6. Betty Boyle took home the bronze strainer for third place.

Competitor	Tea

	Assam	Ceylon	Darjeeling	Nilgiri	Double brew	Pot swirl	High pour	Whisk stir	First	Second	Third	Fourth
Betty Boyle												
Brian Brewer												
Prunella Potter												
Stewart Steepe												
First												
Second												
Third												
Fourth												
Double brew												
Pot swirl												
High pour												
Whisk stir												

Action	Position

Student Models

Netherlipp College runs lessons for aspiring models—locally known as the Catwalk Course—and as part of the course students are taught how to react when "caught" in compromising situations by the paparazzi. This morning, four students are taking their Expression practical exams. From the clues, can you name each student's examiner, the expression they are currently adopting, and the grade they have received?

Clues

1. Examiner Charlie Tann awarded a higher grade than Samantha received, but the next grade lower in the list than was given to the student who was asked to pout.

2. Pamela's grade was lower than the one awarded by Beau Guss, but higher than that given to the student attempting to look surprised.

3. Arty Fisher said, "Imagine you're coming out of a night club to be confronted by the photographers you've asked to be there. Now—give me 'anger.'"

4. Ricardo's attempt at a "coy" expression was met with a non-committal "hmm" and given one of the B grades.

Student	Examiner

	Arty Fisher	Beau Guss	Charlie Tann	Fay Kitt	Angry	Coy	Pouting	Surprised	A	B+	B-	C
Pamela												
Quentin												
Ricardo												
Samantha												
A												
B+												
B-												
C												
Angry												
Coy												
Pouting												
Surprised												

Please do not feed the models

Expression	Grade

Five Sisters

Among the members of the Ackland family who attended a recent family reunion in Eddsbury, Suffolk, were five sisters, the daughters of Martin and Freda Ackland, and each was accompanied by her husband. From the clues, can you work out the name and occupation of each sister's husband, and where the couple now make their home?

Clues

1. Margaret, oldest of the five sisters, is married to a successful dentist.

2. Jean Lebas is the man from Monaco who met and married one of the Ackland girls while she was working as a nurse in Monte Carlo—where they both now live.

3. The first name of the man from Auckland, New Zealand, begins with a consonant.

4. Otis Morgan, who was born in New York but left the "Big Apple" in 1985 to live elsewhere with his wife, the former Jane Ackland, is not the used car dealer who flew in from Vancouver with his wife for the reunion.

5. The couple who only had to drive to Eddsbury from their home in North London weren't the police officer and his wife, whose surname differed in length by two letters from Georgina's married name.

6. Ian Dugdale is a publisher, specializing in cookbooks.

7. Amanda and her husband have lived in Dublin for the last fifteen years.

Sister	Husband

	Ian Dugdale	Jean Lebas	Leo Cox	Nick Dunn	Otis Morgan	Car dealer	Dentist	Movie producer	Police officer	Publisher	Auckland	Dublin	Monaco	North London	Vancouver
Amanda															
Georgina															
Jane															
Margaret															
Susan															
Auckland															
Dublin															
Monaco															
North London															
Vancouver															
Car dealer															
Dentist															
Movie producer															
Police officer															
Publisher															

Job	Hometown

Cherry Tree Radio

The Cherry Tree Hospital in Storbury has its own hospital radio system, Cherry Tree Radio, run by volunteers, which operates from 7 a.m. to 7 p.m., Monday to Saturday every week. From the clues below, can you identify the presenter who handles each time slot, what he or she did before retiring, and the style of music he or she plays between the interviews and news items?

Clues

1. The presenter whose musical taste tends toward traditional jazz handles the next program after the one presented by the retired bus driver.

2. Hazel Roberts is in charge of the lunchtime program, which runs from 12 noon to 2 p.m.

3. The 2 p.m. to 4 p.m. presenter is not the person who used to work as a cashier for a local brewery.

4. Colin Bush is on the air later in the day than the ex-decorator, but earlier than the presenter who plays 1960s pop music between the spoken parts of the show.

5. The presenter who plays country music and who is in charge for the final show of the day, from 4 p.m. to 7 p.m., isn't Roy Ferguson.

6. The retired librarian loves folk music and has been known to perform it on their Cherry Tree Radio show.

7. Jerry Pye intersperses the news and interviews on his shows with modern pop records—which is interpreted as anything from the last ten years.

Time slot	Presenter

	Colin Bush	Hazel Roberts	Jerry Pye	Lucy Murphy	Roy Ferguson	Bus driver	Cashier	Decorator	Firefighter	Librarian	Country	Folk	Jazz	Modern pop	1960s pop
7 a.m. to 10 a.m.															
10 a.m. to 12 noon															
12 noon to 2 p.m.															
2 p.m. to 4 p.m.															
4 a.m. to 7 p.m.															
Country															
Folk															
Jazz															
Modern pop															
1960s pop															
Bus driver															
Cashier															
Decorator															
Firefighter															
Librarian															

Welcome to HELL

Kidnappers   murderers

Evil Dictators

DJ's who speak over the records

Occupation	Music

USA TODAY 129

Battleships

Do you remember the old game of battleships? These puzzles are based on that idea. Your task is to find the vessels in the diagram. Some parts of boats or sea squares have already been filled in, and a number next to a row or column refers to the number of occupied squares in that row or column. The boats may be positioned horizontally or vertically, but no two boats or parts of boats are in adjacent squares—horizontally, vertically, or diagonally.

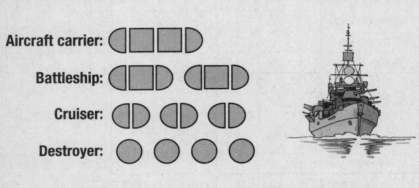

Aircraft carrier:

Battleship:

Cruiser:

Destroyer:

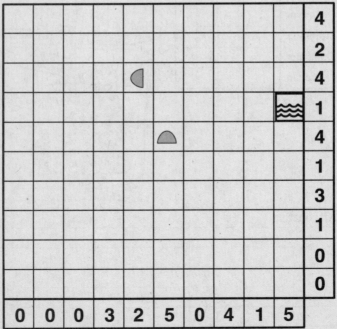

										4
										2
										4
										1
										4
										1
										3
										1
										0
										0
0	**0**	**0**	**3**	**2**	**5**	**0**	**4**	**1**	**5**	

Sign In

Each row and column is to contain the digits 1-5. The given signs tell you if a digit in a cell is plus 1 (+) or minus 1 (-) the digit next to it. Signs between consecutive digits always work from left to right or top to bottom.
Examples: $\boxed{3}$ + $\boxed{4}$ or $\boxed{2}$ ALL occurences of consecutive digits have been marked by a sign.

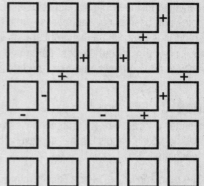

Sudoku

Complete this grid so that each column, each row, and each marked 3 X 3 square contains each of the numbers 1 to 9.

						3		
				9			4	8
5				8	4			
	2		6				5	1
		9			5			
	1		3				7	4
6				5	7			
				1			6	3
					2			

Fearsome Five

Fantasyland includes villains and villainesses of many kinds, from ape-men to zombies and basilisks to wampuses—and there are also human baddies, like the notorious gang of highway robbers known as the Fearsome Five. From the clues, can you work out the first name and nickname of each of the quintet, which Fantasyland town they come from, and what they did before they became one of the Five?

Clues

1. Neither Gortrach nor Khirpon, who was previously a gold miner, is the man nicknamed "Cudgels" from—in case you hadn't guessed—his choice of weapons.

2. The man known as "Stone Face" from his expressive visage, whose hometown, which isn't Kamanton, has an initial from the first half of the alphabet, was formerly a mercenary soldier in the service of the Optimate of Kroprom.

3. The name of Rampik's hometown—well, it's more of a village really, or even a hamlet—begins with a letter in the latter half of the alphabet.

4. The former horse-thief from the little town of Lhistz was not the man nicknamed "The Sausage-Maker"—who, confusingly, has never made a sausage in his life.

5. The man nicknamed "Umbrolus"—which can't really be translated into English (and just as well, too!)—was born and bred in Psephrok.

6. Neither Champley "The Sausage-Maker" nor the ex-embalmer has ever lived in, or even near, Wolframberg.

First name	Nickname

	Cudgels	Umbrolus	Stone Face	The Rodent	The Sausage-Maker	Chakitl	Kamanton	Lhistz	Psephrok	Wolframberg	Embalmer	Farmer	Gold miner	Horse thief	Soldier
Champley															
Gortrach															
Khirpon															
Rampik															
Vulport															
Embalmer															
Farmer															
Gold miner															
Horse thief															
Soldier															
Chakitl															
Kamanton															
Lhistz															
Psephrok															
Wolframberg															

Home	Job

Brewing Up

"When shall we five meet again? How about Tuesday, half past ten?" Huddled over their respective cauldrons, five hard-working witches are busy cooking up magic potions. From the following incantation, can you discover which part of which animal each are adding to their pots, and the purpose of each bubbling brew?

Clues

Tail of newt goes in the pot;
A bit of frog has Aggie got.
Ears are not in Helga's stew,
And wart removal's not her brew.

Warts aren't shifted by a vole;
To fly, put legs into the bowl.
Sibyl has prepared a liver,
A rat did not the organ give 'er.

Wanda wants to see the future.
To change your form, a shrew'll suit yer;
But not the liver of the shrew,
Nor its nose put in your stew.

Hubble bubble, toil and trouble,
Now work out this logic muddle!

Witch	Part

	Ears	Legs	Liver	Nose	Tail	Frog	Newt	Rat	Shrew	Vole	Cause earthquakes	Change form	Flying potion	See the future	Wart removal
Aggie															
Helga															
Sybil															
Wanda															
Winnie															
Cause earthquakes															
Change form															
Flying potion															
See the future															
Wart removal															
Frog															
Newt															
Rat															
Shrew															
Vole															

Hmm, this is lacking something

I know, I'm having difficulty adding hops

BROOMSTICK BEER

Animal	Purpose

Drones on Charge

None of our five friends from the Drones Club are strangers at the Arrow Street courthouse, all having attended on more than one occasion for various misdemeanors. But last week was a particularly busy time as each one was up before a judge on a different day of the week for committing an offense connected to the same local cop. From the clues, can you work out the day on which each Drone stood trial, the name of the presiding judge, and the offense for which each Drone had been called to answer?

Clues

1. Archie Fotheringhay cursed his luck. He might have got away with "borrowing" a bike (he'd meant to bring it back but it "fell" into a canal) if the bike he'd "borrowed" didn't belong to Sergeant Stanley Sucker.

2. Edward Tanqueray stood before the judge the day after one Drone was charged with concealing a suspect under the table when Sergeant Sucker visited the Drones Club, and the day before Judge Royston Robe presided.

3. Montague Folliott's pleas of innocence to Judge Simeon Silk resulted only in his fine being doubled; Montague's attendance at the court was later in the week than that of the Drone charged with sending Sergeant Sucker on a wild goose chase by supplying false information that some angry geese had escaped down by the river.

4. Judge Wynford Wigge looked up from his notes and said, "Young man, when a policeman is directing traffic, it is incumbent upon automobile owners to follow his instructions. Driving 'round and 'round him shouting 'Which way, Sucker?' just will not do."

5. Rupert de Grey was forced to get up early on Thursday to attend the Arrow Street court at noon.

6. The week began with Judge Barrington Beak sitting; he didn't preside over the case involving Gerald Huntingdon.

Day	Drone

	Archie Fotheringhay	Edward Tanqueray	Gerald Huntingdon	Montague Ffolliott	Rupert de Grey	Barrington Beak	Benedict Bench	Wynford Wigge	Royston Robe	Simeon Silk	Concealing suspect	Dislodging helmet	Driving offense	False information	Stealing bike
Monday															
Tuesday															
Wednesday															
Thursday															
Friday															
Concealing suspect															
Dislodging helmet															
Driving offense															
False information															
Stealing bike															
Barrington Beak															
Benedict Bench															
Wynford Wigge															
Royston Robe															
Simeon Silk															

Judge	Offense

Plays for Today

Five plays, each the first work by a young writer eager to make his mark in the business and move to Hollywood, have just opened in Netherlipp's Wideway theaterland. From the clues, can you work out who wrote each play, at which theater it is being produced, and the opinion of it given by Walter Loader-Twaddle, the highly-respected drama critic of the *Netherlipp Courier*?

Clues

1. It wasn't the play at the Capital Theater that was described as "total trash—and that was just the prologue!"

2. Ross Lord's play at the Hanover Theater was not the one which the critic referred to as "garbage, a heap of garbage, a pile of garbage, a veritable landfill of the stuff—just garbage!"

3. The play at the St. Denis Theater, which wasn't by Henry Prince and was not called *Watershed*, was deemed by the critic to be unspeakable (although he did find a few choice words which we won't print here for fear of prosecution), both from a moral and a dramatic point of view.

4. The play at the Imperial Theater, the merits of which the critic did not sum up as garbage or unspeakable, wasn't *Watershed*.

5. *Airtight*, which is being performed at Rowse's Theater, is not the John King play described as "extremely funny—I haven't laughed so much in years, the tears were rolling down my face." Unfortunately, Mr. King's play is advertised as a poignant, moving tragedy.

6. *Geneva* was not written by Siward Young.

7. *Stooge*, the first play by new writer Antony Mark, which isn't at the Imperial, wasn't called unspeakable or garbage.

Play	Playwright

	Antony Mark	Henry Prince	John King	Ross Lord	Siward Young	Capital	Hanover	Imperial	Rowse's	St. Denis	Extremely funny	Garbage	Total trash	Unspeakable	Very poor
Airtight															
Geneva															
Lockyer															
Stooge															
Watershed															
Extremely funny															
Garbage															
Total trash															
Unspeakable															
Very poor															
Capital															
Hanover															
Imperial															
Rowse's															
St. Denis															

Theater	Critic's opinion

Highway Robbery

Infamous eighteenth-century highwayman Mick Turnip had had a busy but successful week on the Great East Road from Stonekeigh to Netherlipp. On each day, he managed to waylay a member of the aristocracy and relieve them of a precious item and some cash. From the clues, can you discover on which day he robbed which victim, and what was stolen?

Clues

1. On Monday, Mick rode away from the scene of his hold-up with a gold pendant, but the victim was not Earl Richies and the money taken with it was not $8.

2. On Tuesday, it was Sir Hugo Cashe's turn to hear the terrifying cry of "Stand and deliver!", and on Thursday, Mick got away with $15 belonging to a noble couple.

3. Lord Fullbank dropped his watch into Turnip's swag bag, together with a sum of money in excess of $10.

4. Mick stole the silver-cased clock two days after he made his largest cash haul.

5. The jeweled bracelet did not belong to Lady Bundell . . . or, indeed, Lord Bundell.

6. Mick returned from one of his days working on the road with a diamond ring and $11 in cash.

Day	Victim

	Earl Richies	Lord and Lady Bundell	Lord and Lady Tidisome	Lord Fullbank	Sir Hugo Cashe	Bracelet	Clock	Pendant	Ring	Watch	$5	$8	$11	$15	$18
Monday															
Tuesday															
Wednesday															
Thursday															
Friday															
$5															
$8															
$11															
$15															
$18															
Bracelet															
Clock															
Pendant															
Ring															
Watch															

Stand and deliver

INFORMATION SUPERHIGHWAYMAN

Object stolen	Money stolen

Delivery Duty

The life of a Private Eye sometimes involves doing things with "no questions asked," and each of our five detective acquaintances from the Southern Californian town of San Angelo have recently been employed to make a delivery under such circumstances. From the clues, can you work out the name of each detective's client, the object they were given to deliver, and the exact time at which they had to make the delivery?

Clues

1. Dick Drill looked across his office at the bald head of his client glinting in the sunlight. "That's unusual," he thought, "you don't often see a bald-headed woman."

2. "Mr. Wrench," said Ricky's client, "this needs to be delivered at exactly two o'clock, but whatever you do, don't look inside. Can you do that?"; the item he was handed was not the leather pouch.

3. "Take this envelope," said one client sharply, "and deliver it at 1 p.m. on the dot. Do not open it. Understand?" "The delivery has to be made when the big hand is on the twelve and the little hand is on the eleven, you can manage that, can't you?" said Amanda Anderson in the most patronizing voice she could manage.

4. "It's a wallet," said one detective as he looked at the item on his desk, "what's in it?" "That's none of your business," replied the client, "don't look, just deliver at the time I said—before noon, OK?"

5. It wasn't Esther Erikson who instructed a detective to make the delivery at 3 p.m., which wasn't the delivery time that Spike Spanner was given; It wasn't Donald Davis who wanted a small, brown briefcase delivered, no questions asked.

6. Mike Mallet took the cigar box and fingered the lid. "Don't open it," said his client. "If you know what's good for you, you won't open it." His delivery time wasn't the latest one, but was later in the day that that prescribed by Carl Cooper.

Private eye	Client

	Amanda Anderson	Boris Bailey	Carl Cooper	Donald Davis	Esther Erikson	Briefcase	Cigar box	Envelope	Leather pouch	Wallet	10 a.m.	11 a.m.	1 p.m.	2 p.m.	3 p.m.
Dick Drill															
Mike Mallet															
Nicky Nail															
Ricky Wrench															
Spike Spanner															
10 a.m.															
11 a.m.															
1 p.m.															
2 p.m.															
3 p.m.															
Briefcase															
Cigar box															
Envelope															
Leather pouch															
Wallet															

Item	Time

Return Message

The five Private Eyes set out on their "no questions asked" delivery jobs with two final instructions from each client still running in their ears: "Don't look inside," and "You'll be given a short message to return. Remember it exactly and I'll pay you on return." From the clues, can you say what the Private Eyes found inside their delivery items—you didn't think they would resist looking, surely—the location of the delivery, and the message they were given to return?

Clues

1. One detective walked toward the meeting, pondering why anyone should pay him to deliver a wallet that contains nothing, absolutely nothing.

2. As he handed over the item that he by then knew contained only a small and unremarkable rock, one detective said to the seven-foot-tall gorilla of a henchman, "I'm told you have a message for me to return to my client." "Yeah," grunted the "ape," "tell him 'I love you.'" This was not the incident at the news stand.

3. One detective handed over his item and received the following, rather worrying message in return: "Tell Mr. Bailey, 'the morgue.' Got that?"

4. The cigar box, which wasn't the item containing a photograph of an elk, was handed over in a quiet booth in the Honolulu Bar.

5. The recipient of the item waiting at the train station said, "I'm only gonna say this once: 'Humph,'" and left; the detective sent to the meeting at the bus station scrutinized the contents of his delivery for some time but could only conclude that it was a dollar bill, a normal, everyday dollar bill.

6. Esther Erikson, who didn't send her detective to any kind of station, wasn't the client who was given the rather cryptic message, "Tuesday," on his return.

Private eye	Contents

	Key blank	Nothing	One dollar	Photograph	Small rock	Honolulu Bar	Bus station	News stand	McGinty's Bar	Train station	"Hmmph"	"I love you"	"It's on"	"The morgue"	"Tuesday"
Dick Drill															
Mike Mallet															
Nicky Nail															
Ricky Wrench															
Spike Spanner															
"Hmmph"															
"I love you"															
"It's on"															
"The morgue"															
"Tuesday"															
Honolulu Bar															
Bus station															
News stand															
McGinty's Bar															
Train station															

Location	Message

Sickies

There's a football game on this afternoon, so the staff at the Upper Crispin Health Center are not surprised to finds the surgery waiting room full of fit men trying to look ill or in pain on the hunt for a doctor's note. From the clues, can you work out the order in which the doctor saw the first five, their jobs, and the spurious ailment of which each was complaining?

Clues

1. The window cleaner explained to the doctor that unfortunately he had contracted a nasty case of drinker's elbow and would require a doctor's note for the day.

2. Guy Slacking was seen immediately after the builder explained why working that afternoon, specifically at about 3 p.m., would be dangerous to his health, and was followed immediately by the man with the case of tweeter's thumb.

3. Colin Ilmore was seen fourth; he's not the factory worker, who wasn't the patient complaining of an unflattened foot.

4. The road worker was the doctor's third patient of the morning.

5. The doctor's first patient of the day was a particularly nasty case of outgrowing hair; it wasn't Ed Downe's complaint.

6. Norm Shirker is a truck driver, when he's not laid up in his sick bed with only the TV and a football game to keep his spirits up.

Order	Patient

	Colin Ilmore	Ed Downe	Guy Slacking	Ivor Dodge	Norm Shirker	Builder	Factory worker	Truck driver	Road worker	Window cleaner	Drinker's elbow	Outgrowing hair	Sleeper's shoulder	Tweeter's thumb	Unflattened foot
First															
Second															
Third															
Fourth															
Fifth															
Drinker's elbow															
Outgrowing hair															
Sleeper's shoulder															
Tweeter's thumb															
Unflattened foot															
Builder															
Factory worker															
Truck driver															
Road worker															
Window cleaner															

HYPOCHONDRIACS'
SOCIETY
AGM
TONIC
canceled owing
to illness
7.30 pm

Job	Ailment

Blind Dates

Carinthia, an attractive lady in her thirties, registered with Stonekeigh's Fish A-Plenty dating agency (formed from the merger of On-The-Bounce.com and Soulmates.net) and was offered five dates in successive months. From the clues, can you work out the name of the man she met on each occasion, in what type of restaurant they had a meal, and what characteristic about the man she particularly disliked?

Clues

1. Carinthia met Timothy more than a month after the Indian meal but earlier than the tryst with the man who talked incessantly about sports.

2. It was sometime after her date with Martin that her companion displayed poor table manners; the latter date was not in July or August.

3. Her date with David was the month after the Italian meal, at which her companion was not the one whose egocentricity was overpowering, who was neither her first nor last date.

4. She met Hugh immediately after the man who had no conversation; the Thai meal was later than both these meetings.

5. The Chinese meal was the month before the date with a man whose sartorial standards were lacking, but the date with Monty was later.

6. The appointment with David was for an earlier day in a month than the ones on which she met the badly-dressed man and when she sampled Thai cuisine.

Date	Man

	David	Hugh	Martin	Monty	Timothy	Chinese	Greek	Indian	Italian	Thai	Badly-dressed	Egocentric	No conversation	Obsessed with sports	Poor table manners
April 16															
May 23															
June 4															
July 3															
August 19															
Badly-dressed															
Egocentric															
No conversation															
Obsessed with sports															
Poor table manners															
Chinese															
Greek															
Indian															
Italian															
Thai															

You're not quite what I was expecting

Restaurant	Characteristic

Logi-5

Each line, across and down, is to have each of the letters A, B, C, D, and E, appearing once. Also, every shape—shown by the thick lines—must also have each of the letters in it. Can you fill in the grid?

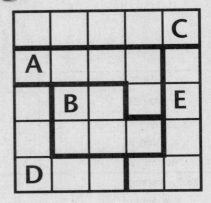

Killer Sudoku

The normal rules of Sudoku apply. In addition, the digits in each inner shape (marked by dots) must add up to the number in the top corner of that box.

16		8			14		7	
9		9	20				8	16
14			20	14		21		
5								12
13		19			11		11	
7			10	19				3
19				14			20	
7		15	7		15	11		11

Battleships

Do you remember the old game of battleships? These puzzles are based on that idea. Your task is to find the vessels in the diagram. Some parts of boats or sea squares have already been filled in, and a number next to a row or column refers to the number of occupied squares in that row or column. The boats may be positioned horizontally or vertically, but no two boats or parts of boats are in adjacent squares—horizontally, vertically, or diagonally.

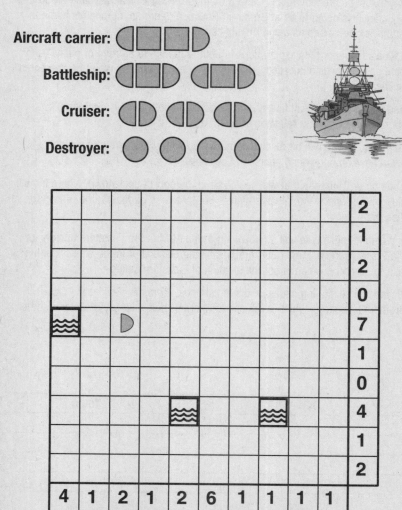

Aircraft carrier:

Battleship:

Cruiser:

Destroyer:

Wayne in the East

Next week, ecologist and green campaigner Wayne Forrest is visiting Eastshire, traveling to a different town for a different event every day. From the clues, can you work out which town he'll be visiting on each day, the venue where his meeting will take place, and what sort of meeting it will be?

Clues

1. Wayne will be presenting a prize to the organizers of a local recycling group the day after he's going to be at Grummitt House, a Georgian merchant's home in Gippswick now used as a community center.

2. Wayne's talk about his explorations in South America to a group of pupils from local schools (which is called "The Amazon Wayne Forrest") won't be presented on Tuesday.

3. Wednesday evening will find Wayne in the eighteenth-century St. Martin's Church—but not for a religious service.

4. On Friday, Wayne will be receiving an award for his work promoting green awareness among young people in Eastshire.

5. It will be on Thursday that Wayne will be in the port of Luckstowe, where he will stay with his sister Virginia overnight—but that isn't, of course, the reason for his visit.

6. In Woolmarket, Wayne will be speaking at the AGM of the Eastshire Society for the Preservation of Planet Earth; this will take place later in the week than his visit to Storbury, which is not the location of Eastshire College.

7. Wayne will be signing copies of his latest book, *Planet in Peril,* at the Elzevir Brothers bookstore, which is housed in a former public library of Victorian date.

Day	Town

	Gippswick	Luckstowe	Redewich	Storbury	Woolmarket	Eastshire College	Elzevir Brothers	Grummitt House	St. Martin's Church	Windmill Hall	AGM	Book signing	Present award	Receive award	Schools talk
Monday															
Tuesday															
Wednesday															
Thursday															
Friday															
AGM															
Book signing															
Present award															
Receive award															
Schools talk															
Eastshire College															
Elzevir Brothers															
Grummitt House															
St. Martin's Church															
Windmill Hall															

Venue	Event

Terminally Terminal

Terminal 2 at Stanwick Airport is for flights to European destinations, and on a cold and misty morning, five hopeful travelers have risen well before dawn and arrived hoping to board early flights. But they are disappointed to find that, for various reasons, they will be spending the rest of the morning at least in departures. From the clues, can you work out to which city each passenger was hoping to jet, for what reason, and the cause of their delay?

Clues

1. None of the passengers were traveling to the destination of their surname.

2. Emily Edinburgh was traveling for a job interview; Rebecca Rome listened carefully to the announcement about her flight: "We apologize for the delay, which is due to the late arrival of the aircraft,"—in other words, "we are running late because we are running late."

3. An unexpected snowfall in Berlin has temporarily closed the airport.

4. The surname of the person hoping to fly to Rome to attend a wedding is the same as Bartholomew Berlin's destination.

5. The woman traveling to a sales conference has been delayed because of a crash—luckily, it's just a crash of the plane's navigational computer, but worrying nonetheless; a man is hoping to depart for a week's vacation.

6. The surname of the person going on a weekend shopping trip is not the destination where the airport has been closed owing to a thick blanket of fog.

Passenger	Destination

This doesn't look like you

I was clean shaven when I arrived

PASSPORT CONTROL

	Berlin	Edinburgh	Lisbon	Paris	Rome	Vacation	Job interview	Sales conference	Shopping	Wedding	Baggage mix-up	Computer crash	Fog at destination	Late arrival	Snow at destination
Bartholomew Berlin															
Emily Edinburgh															
Lawrence Lisbon															
Pauline Paris															
Rebecca Rome															
Baggage mix-up															
Computer crash															
Fog at destination															
Late arrival															
Snow at destination															
Vacation															
Job interview															
Sales conference															
Shopping															
Wedding															

Travel reason	Delay cause

Native Germans

The picture below might be straight out of the old Wild West, with four Comanche warriors sitting around their campfire smoking peace-pipes and discussing tribal affairs—except that this is a backyard in Augsburg, and these four men are not Native Americans, they're Germans who reenact Comanche life as a hobby. From the clues, can you fill in each man's Comanche name and his real name and occupation?

Clues

1. Karl Brandt, who goes by the name Blue Cloud when he is being a Comanche, is seated next counterclockwise to the TV cameraman.

2. Fire Hawk's real name isn't Wilhelm Klein.

3. The auto mechanic—he works on, and indeed for, BMW—is seated clockwise next to Erich Spitz.

4. The man in position 1 is Ludwig Haber when he's not pretending to be a Comanche.

5. Red Owl is seated across the campfire from the airline pilot.

6. The man in position 3 is a computer programmer employed by one of Munich's biggest software companies.

Comanche names: Blue Cloud; Fire Hawk; Red Owl; Running Elk
Real names: Erich Spitz; Karl Brandt; Ludwig Haber; Wilhelm Klein
Jobs: airline pilot; auto mechanic; computer programmer; TV cameraman

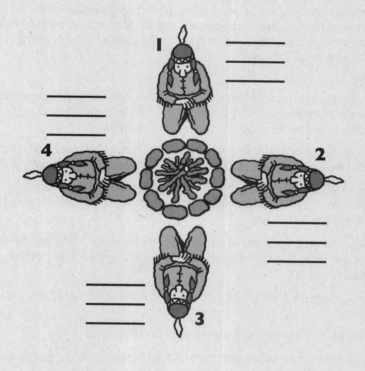

Starting tip: Begin by working out the occupation of Comanche 2.

Variations on a Raid

Desmond Whateley's novel *The Raid* was published in 1906, and has been filmed five times—though each time, the director has made changes in character names and settings. Originally, the hero was British infantry officer Arthur Price, his fiancée was Mary Ellis, and the background was the Boer War; but from the clues, can you work out their names and what the backgrounds were in the versions made in each of the listed years?

Clues

1. The heroine was renamed Barbara Adams in the movie that was made nineteen years after the version that featured heroic Confederate cavalry captain Tom Walker in an American Civil War adaptation of *The Raid*.

2. The movie that had as its British-but-heavily-American-accented hero Gavin Hart came out earlier than the one set during the Normandy campaign of World War II.

3. The 1938 version of *The Raid* is set during World War I, but does not feature Sarah Ryder as its leading female character; the 1957 movie wasn't given a Crimean War background.

4. Mary Liston is the girlfriend in the version of the movie set during the Spanish Civil War, which was released nineteen years after the one that has its hero called Brian Croft.

5. In one version of *The Raid*, the hero and heroine are called David Ellery and Jane Irwell.

6. Greta Fermi is the name of the girlfriend in the 1995 movie.

7. In the 2014 version of *The Raid*, the hero has changed name *and* gender, and is called Nadia Oswald.

Year	Hero

	Brian Croft	David Ellery	Gavin Hart	Nadia Oswald	Tom Walker	Barbara Adams	Greta Fermi	Jane Irwell	Mary Liston	Sarah Ryder	American Civil War	Crimean War	Spanish Civil War	World War I	World War II
1938															
1957															
1976															
1995															
2014															
American Civil War															
Crimean War															
Spanish Civil War															
World War I															
World War II															
Barbara Adams															
Greta Fermi															
Jane Irwell															
Mary Liston															
Sarah Ryder															

Heroine	Background

Way Downstream

It was a warm, sunny day last Saturday, and four young couples from Storbury took the chance to go out on the River Stor, which flows through the town, in various types of vessel. From the clues, can you work out the full names of the couple in each boat, and what sort of boat it was? (We've drawn each craft as a rowboat so as not to give the game away.)

Clues

1. Seventeen-year-old Penny and her boyfriend, who went out in a punt (and managed to complete their trip without either of them falling overboard), were somewhere upstream of the boat used by Miss Hanson and her companion.

2. Nick Dale's boat (well, actually, it belongs to his dad) was one place further upstream than the inflatable with the outboard motor, which wasn't the vessel in which Sandra took to the river.

3. Paul was in boat 2, while Miss Smith was in a boat further downstream than Bruce's vessel, which he had rented from a local boatyard called, amazingly, the Storbury Boatyard.

4. Mr. Moody's boat is shown further upstream than Lloyd's; neither of them were accompanied by Miss Gray, who was not in boat 4.

5. Anne shared Mr. Kirby's vessel, which was further downstream than the canoe—which, technically, was actually a kayak—that is, an Inuit design.

6. Mr. Graves's boat was one place higher upstream than the rowboat.

7. Lucy, who isn't Miss Lee, was in boat 3.

Male first names: Bruce; Lloyd; Nick; Paul
Male surnames: Dale; Graves; Kirby; Moody
Female first names: Anne; Lucy; Penny; Sandra
Female surnames: Gray; Hanson; Lee; Smith
Boats: canoe; inflatable; punt; rowboat

Downstream

2

3

Upstream

1

4

_____ _____ _____ _____
_____ _____ _____ _____
_____ _____ _____ _____
_____ _____ _____ _____

Starting tip: Begin by determining the type of boat used by couple 1.

The Eighth

Thanks to General Custer, most people have heard of the 7th US Cavalry and its unhappy end, but they weren't the only horse soldiers in the old Wild West. For instance, in the years between 1868 and 1880, the 8th Cavalry built and manned five forts in Arizona. From the clues, can you work out the name of each fort, when and where it was built, and the name of the modern town that now occupies its site?

Clues

1. The town of Los Pinons stands on the site of the fort built in 1877, which wasn't Fort Dohenny; Fort Dohenny, named for the man who commanded the 8th US Cavalry during the American Civil War, wasn't sited at a ford of the Arrow River.

2. The fort at Silver Butte, which has developed into the town of Swainson, was built six years after Fort Nelson.

3. Fort Bullen was built some years before the 8th Cavalry's stronghold in the Redstone Pass.

4. In 1874, the 8th Cavalry set up a fort in the Rodelo Hills.

5. The town of San Bernardo stands on the site of the fort built three years after the one that stood in Dyer's Canyon, which is not where the town of Guthrie now stands.

6. The town that has replaced Fort Lowell, built in 1871 and burned down accidentally in 1925 after being left derelict for thirty years, has a one-word name.

Fort	Date

	1868	1871	1874	1877	1880	Arrow River	Dyer's Canyon	Redstone Pass	Rodelo Hills	Silver Butte	Guthrie	Los Pinons	San Bernardo	Swainson	Tornillo
Fort Bullen															
Fort Dohenny															
Fort Hutton															
Fort Lowell															
Fort Nelson															
Guthrie															
Los Pinons															
San Bernardo															
Swainson															
Tornillo															
Arrow River															
Dyer's Canyon															
Redstone Pass															
Rodelo Hills															
Silver Butte															

Location	Modern town

Around Lyonesse

The diagram below shows five space freighters in orbit around the planet Lyonesse, waiting to land at Lyonesse Spaceport to deliver their cargo. (It's only a small spaceport, and the two bays are already occupied.) From the clues, can you fill in the name of each ship and its captain, the planet where it is registered, and the nature of its cargo?

Clues

One of the two ships carrying types of food is immediately counterclockwise of one whose captain has a surname initial in the second half of the alphabet; the *Argosy* is immediately counterclockwise of the ship registered on the planet Terra Nova; the *Wotan*'s captain has a surname initial in the second half of the alphabet.

1. Ship B is the only one with a single-word name that is registered on either Luna or Terra Nova, and ship D is the only one with a two-word name that *isn't* registered on either of those planets; neither of the ships orbiting adjacent to *Nomad* are registered on either Terra Nova or Luna.

2. Ship C is registered on Rubicon Prime; Captain Shamoun's ship has a two-word name, as does ship E.

3. Captain Kimball's ship, which doesn't have a two-word name or an edible cargo, is immediately counterclockwise of the vessel commanded by Captain Garlock; the ship carrying emergency ration packs to see the colonists on Lyonesse through the expected severe winter is immediately clockwise of the *Silver Fox*.

4. The *Black Opal*, whose captain's name is one of the first three in the alphabetical list, is immediately clockwise of the freighter registered in New Georgia and immediately counterclockwise of the one carrying farming equipment; the name of the ship loaded with mining equipment appears either first or last in the alphabetical list.

Ships: *Argosy; Black Opal; Nomad; Silver Fox; Wotan*
Captains: Garlock; Kimball; Kirk; Shamoun; Tarl
Registration planets: Cingraik; Luna; New Georgia; Rubicon Prime; Terra Nova
Cargo: emergency ration packs; farming equipment; industrial equipment; luxury foods; mining equipment

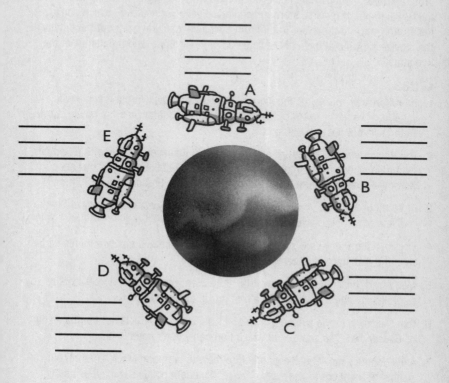

Starting tip: Begin by identifying ship C.

Lifestory

The Lifestory Channel is a TV channel that specializes in life stories—which probably doesn't altogether shock you. Tomorrow evening, it's showing five made-for-TV biographical movies, starring people you've never heard of, which don't necessarily stick to the exact truth. From the clues, can you work out the details of the movies showing at each of the listed times, their titles, and the names of the two stars?

Clues

1. *Your Money or Your Wife!*, the story of highwayman Dick Turpin and his wife, Jane (no, I've never heard of her either), is showing later than the movie starring Ruth Less, but not at 11:30 p.m.

2. *The Roman and the Rebel*—the story of Queen Boadicea's affair with a Roman centurion whose name might as well be Marcus Fictitious, played by Lance Korpral—doesn't feature Kerry Blue and isn't being broadcast at 8:30 p.m.

3. At 10:00 p.m., you'll be able to watch *Mr. and Mrs. Chaplin*, the story of Charlie and one of his four wives—I'm not sure which.

4. English actor Percy Vere stars in the movie that will begin ninety minutes earlier than the one starring Hazel Nutt.

5. Meg Awatt, described as "a powerful actress with an electrifying personality" (by her publicity agent), will be in the first movie transmitted.

6. Tom Morrow's movie will be shown at 11:30; Guy Sospittle is not the male star of *Caesar and Cleo*, the plot of which I probably don't need to describe.

7. Annie Moore's movie is showing before the one featuring Mack Numbre, but neither of them are in *Tony and Cherie*, "a modern political romance" that is being broadcast sometime between Annie's movie and Mack's.

Time	Male star

	Guy Sospittle	Lance Korpral	Mack Numbre	Percy Vere	Tom Morrow	Annie Moore	Hazel Nutt	Kerry Blue	Meg Awatt	Ruth Less	Caesar and Cleo	Mr. and Mrs. Chaplin	The Roman and the Rebel	Tony and Cherie	Your Money or Your Wife!
7:00 p.m.															
8:30 p.m.															
10:00 p.m.															
11:30 p.m.															
1:00 a.m.															
Caesar and Cleo															
Mr. and Mrs. Chaplin															
The Roman and the Rebel															
Tony and Cherie															
Your Money or Your Wife!															
Annie Moore															
Hazel Nutt															
Kerry Blue															
Meg Awatt															
Ruth Less															

Female star	Movie

Crème de la . . .

In Good Spirits is a small store on Stonekeigh's Main Street that stocks every spirit and liqueur you've ever heard of, and quite a number you haven't. One small section toward the back holds six bottles of viscous liquids for those who like their alcohol gloopy. From the clues, can you name the brand on each bottle, the type of crème it contains, and the price?

Clues

1. The bottle of crème de cucumber is immediately to the right of the Haskill's brew and immediately behind a bottle that costs $3 more.

2. Tingle's liqueur will set you back $2 less per bottle than the crème de cheese, which is not the most expensive drink.

3. The crème de carrot is the cheapest of these drinks; a bottle of Danebury's costs a nice, round twenty dollars.

4. The total cost of the two circular bottles is more than the total cost of the two triangular bottles.

5. Bartlet's crème de peanut costs $2 less than bottle 3 and is immediately left of the bottle that is priced at $23.

6. Bottle 1 contains crème de olive and is $2 cheaper than the liqueur made by Warton's in their Churchminster distillery.

	Bartlet's	Danebury's	Haskill's	Jasper's	Tingle's	Warton's	Crème de carrot	Crème de cheese	Crème de cucumber	Crème de olive	Crème de peanut	Crème de rice	$15	$18	$20	$21	$23	$25
Bottle 1																		
Bottle 2																		
Bottle 3																		
Bottle 4																		
Bottle 5																		
Bottle 6																		
$15																		
$18																		
$20																		
$21																		
$23																		
$25																		
Crème de carrot																		
Crème de cheese																		
Crème de cucumber																		
Crème de olive																		
Crème de peanut																		
Crème de rice																		

1 2 3
4 5 6

Domino Search

A standard set of dominoes has been laid out, using numbers instead of dots for clarity. Using a sharp pencil and a keen brain, can you draw in the lines to show where each domino has been placed? You may find the check grid useful—crossing off each domino as you find it.

1	3	0	6	5	5	1	5
6	1	3	3	6	2	5	0
3	2	5	0	0	1	1	2
3	4	6	0	3	4	5	4
5	6	4	4	4	2	2	1
0	1	2	1	3	5	6	6
2	3	6	4	0	0	2	4

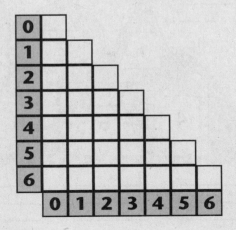

Sign In

Each row and column is to contain the digits 1-5. The given signs tell you if a digit in a cell is plus 1 (+) or minus 1 (-) the digit next to it. Signs between consecutive digits always work from left to right or top to bottom.

Examples: $\boxed{3}+\boxed{4}$ or $\boxed{2}$ $\underset{\boxed{1}}{-}$

ALL occurences of consecutive digits have been marked by a sign.

Sudoku

Complete this grid so that each column, each row, and each marked 3 X 3 square contains each of the numbers 1 to 9.

		7			4			
				2		3	7	
		1		5			4	
		2						5
7	4		3			2	1	
6				1				
5	6				9	7		3
		4		7				
		9	6	3				

Cooped Up

Henrietta Fowler keeps chickens in a large run in her backyard and, although they provide her and her neighbors with a regular supply of eggs, she considers them pets rather than employees. She knows their likes and dislikes and makes sure that each get their favorite food once in a while. From the clues, can you fill in (on the diagram of the six hens in the coop) each one's name, her favorite type of grub, and the number of eggs she produced last week?

Clues

1. Loretta is roosting directly opposite (on the same level) the hen whose favorite food is a nice mound of millet.

2. Shania is nestling down directly opposite (on the same level) the hen whose output last week was a very creditable 5 eggs.

3. Tammy, who is partial to a nice pile of corn, is numbered two lower than the hen who laid 3 eggs last week.

4. The hen in position 4 laid 6eggs last week; the hen in roost 2 is Dolly, who laid one more egg last week than did the chicken who prefers a meal of wheat.

5. Emmylou is roosting further from the door than the hen who likes to eat rice, but is on the same level (upper or lower).

6. Hen 1 loves a handful of mealworms; she laid two more eggs last week than did the hen spending a cozy night on roost 3.

	Dolly	Emmylou	Loretta	Shania	Tammy	Tanya	Barley	Corn	Mealworms	Millet	Rice	Wheat	2 eggs	3 eggs	4 eggs	5 eggs	6 eggs	7 eggs
Hen 1																		
Hen 2																		
Hen 3																		
Hen 4																		
Hen 5																		
Hen 6																		
2 eggs																		
3 eggs																		
4 eggs																		
5 eggs																		
6 eggs																		
7 eggs																		
Barley																		
Corn																		
Mealworms																		
Millet																		
Rice																		
Wheat																		

Chortle's Weekly

In the 1960s, Charlie Chortle was a very popular comedian whose weekly half-hour TV program *Chortle's Weekly* was a must-watch for most families. Charlie's comic adventures in a variety of adopted characters were the water-cooler talk of the next day in offices across the country, or would have been if water-coolers had been prevalent then. From the clues, can you identify the various characters, discover the order in which they appeared in one night's show, and which other comic actor appeared in each sketch with Charlie?

Clues

1. Pete Brennan appeared with Charlie in the first item, which was not a sketch about Dennis Digby.

2. Lucy Marsh appeared in the sketch immediately after the one featuring the Hugo character, and immediately before the one with Charlie as a spoof TV gardening program presenter.

3. The trendy schoolteacher character was in the third sketch.

4. E.R. Girles, Charlie's Bronx boy character, was in the sketch immediately after the one also featuring Dave Cooke.

5. Kate Franklin appeared with Charlie in the typewriter-repairman sketch.

6. Charlie played Graham in the sketch also featuring actor Ian Palmer.

Order	Character name

	Dennis Digby	E.R. Girles	Graham	Hugo	Toby	Bronx boy	Gardening presenter	High school student	Trendy schoolteacher	Typewriter repairman	Dave Cooke	Ian Palmer	Kate Franklin	Lucy Marsh	Pete Brennan
First															
Second															
Third															
Fourth															
Fifth															
Dave Cooke															
Ian Palmer															
Kate Franklin															
Lucy Marsh															
Pete Brennan															
Bronx boy															
Gardening presenter															
High school student															
Trendy schoolteacher															
Typewriter repairman															

Character type	Other actor

What's In the Trash?

It is a little-known fact that Larry Ledd's cartoon strip in the *Stonekeigh Planet, What's in the Trash?* is based on his own experiences of emptying garbage cans as a summer job while studying art at Netherlipp College back in the '70s, and his character Larry the Garbage Man is a mixture of all his coworkers and himself. This week's strips show Larry being asked by locals to cart away stuff he really shouldn't after they'd cleared out their yard. From the clues, can you say in which street each daily strip was set and work out which resident somehow persuaded Larry to take away which item?

Clues

1. Larry the Garbage Man was in Detritus Drive in the strip printed the day after Barry Bakander greased his palm to take away a large item, and the day before a small tip secured the disposal of a garden rain barrel.

2. Briony Brybe handed Larry an envelope with a wink and said in her most helpless voice, "You couldn't take this lawn chair away, could you?" in a strip printed sometime before the one set in Litter Lane.

3. Thursday's strip showed Larry's garbage truck trundling down Junk Junction.

4. Graham Grease, who owns a large house in Pulp Parade, was featured later in the week than the resident who backhanded Larry a few dollars to take away an old lawn mower.

5. Sophie Sweetener is not the character that Larry Ledd drew bribing Larry the Garbage Man to take away an old cold frame, which wasn't the item that Larry carted off on Monday.

6. The strip based in Waste Way featured on the day before readers watched Caroline Carrott sweeten the deal.

Day	Street

	Detritus Drive	Junk Junction	Litter Lane	Pulp Parade	Waste Way	Barry Bakander	Briony Brybe	Caroline Carrott	Graham Grease	Sophie Sweetener	Chair	Cold frame	Lawn mower	Roller	Rain barrel
Monday															
Tuesday															
Wednesday															
Thursday															
Friday															
Chair															
Cold frame															
Lawn mower															
Roller															
Rain barrel															
Barry Bakander															
Briony Brybe															
Caroline Carrott															
Graham Grease															
Sophie Sweetener															

Resident	Item

Takeout Cena

Being fed up (a particularly inapt phrase) with the third-rate fare their sloppy slaves serve up, the five masters have splurged and sent the clumsy cooks to collect a takeout meal from one of the city's taverns. From the clues, can you say to which tavern each slave was sent, the name of its owner, and the innovative dish developed there that is currently all the rage but will probably not last?

Clues

1. Cluelus was sent to collect a new-fangled dish comprising a piece of fish with some fried root vegetable and tentatively called "fish 'n' turnips."

2. The celebrity chef Pruus has created a new dish in which some game bird or fowl is served in the bottom half of an amphora, she calls it "chicken in a bucket;" her restaurant isn't Quindecim, which was where Euselus was sent to buy some edible food.

3. The new restaurant, The Fat Dormouse, wasn't the place that developed the stretched dough disk with tomato and cheese topping—"I'll have a pizza that"—nor was this meal invented by chef Fanius.

4. The chef at the IV Seasons, which wasn't the tavern to which Hopelus was sent, has created a sourdough meat package containing sliced meat, salad, and a piquant sauce (a favorite with people who have had too much wine); this isn't Nigelus's tavern, which was visited by Branelus but isn't the Labyrinth.

5. Celebrity chef Delius runs the new Tiberside Inn, by the side of the Tiber.

Slave	Tavern

	Fat Dormouse	IV Seasons	Labyrinth	Quindecim	Tiberside Inn	Clarissus	Delius	Fanius	Nigelus	Pruus	Beef patty	Dough disk	Fish cena	Fowl	Meat package
Branelus															
Cluelus															
Euselus															
Gormlus															
Hopelus															
Beef patty															
Dough disk															
Fish cena															
Fowl															
Meat package															
Clarissus															
Delius															
Fanius															
Nigelus															
Pruus															

Owner	New dish

Bargain Board

The bulletin board in my kitchen has five vouchers offering discounts from various stores hoping to persuade me through their doors. From the clues, can you work out the title on the voucher and the percentage savings it is offering?

Clues

1. The Value Ticket from the drug store, which is not number 5, offers 10% higher savings than the offer to its left on the board.

2. The Super Saver from the sports store in the mall, which is directly below the 25% discount, offers a larger percentage than is being offered on coupon 1, but a lower one than is on the Mega Coupon.

3. The Bumper Voucher from the supermarket has an even number on the board.

4. The Diamond Token from the local coffee shop is diagonally adjacent to the slip offering the 20% discount.

Titles: Bumper Voucher; Diamond Token; Mega Coupon; Super Saver; Value Ticket
Savings: 20%; 25%; 30%; 35%; 40%

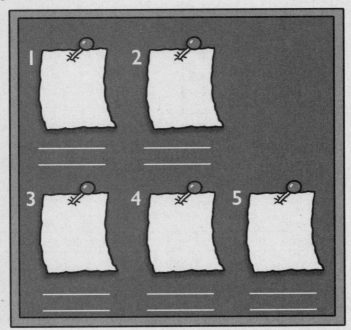

Starting tip: Begin by working out who is offering the 20% savings.

Mrs. Robinson

Keighshire State Council employs three ladies by the name of Mrs. Robinson. From the clues, can you work out in which departments they work, their job titles within that department, and the number of years they have held that position?

Clues

1. Mrs. Jocelyn Robinson, who is a Department Manager, has been with the Council for longer than the Mrs. Robinson from H.R.

2. Keighshire State Council's Finance Director has been in her position for more than three years.

3. Mrs. Katrina Robinson has just passed her four-year anniversary working for the Council.

	Finance	Parks	H.R.	Director	Manager	Secretary	3 years	4 years	5 years
Jocelyn									
Katrina									
Lucille									
3 years									
4 years									
5 years									
Director									
Manager									
Secretary									

Name	Department	Job title	Years

Homeward Bound

At the end of the working day, Keighshire State Council's Mrs. Robinsons head home in different directions and by different modes of transportation. From the clues, can you work out by what means they each make their way home, in which location that is, and how long it takes them to get there?

Clues

1. Mrs. Lucille Robinson's journey home is ten minutes shorter than that of the Mrs. Robinson who catches the bus.

2. Mrs. Katrina Robinson's journey home is longer than the commute to Lower Crispin.

3. One Mrs. Robinson lives in Netherlipp and is lucky enough to be able to walk home.

4. The Mrs. Robinson who catches the train takes 50 minutes to get home, although most of it is spent waiting on the platform.

	Bus	Train	Walk	Lower Crispin	Stonekeigh	Netherlipp	30 mins	40 mins	50 mins
Jocelyn									
Katrina									
Lucille									
30 mins									
40 mins									
50 mins									
Lower Crispin									
Stonekeigh									
Netherlipp									

Name	Mode	Location	Time

Battleships

Do you remember the old game of battleships? These puzzles are based on that idea. Your task is to find the vessels in the diagram. Some parts of boats or sea squares have already been filled in, and a number next to a row or column refers to the number of occupied squares in that row or column. The boats may be positioned horizontally or vertically, but no two boats or parts of boats are in adjacent squares—horizontally, vertically, or diagonally.

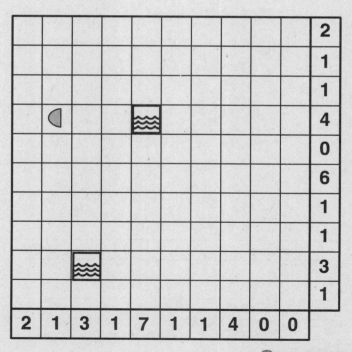

Aircraft carrier:

Battleship:

Cruiser:

Destroyer:

String Stuff

As the days warm up and the daylight stretches into the evenings, the streets of Netherlipp ring to the sounds of street performers entertaining shoppers and revelers. From the clues, can you say which performer is playing which song on which stringed instrument where?

Clues

1. Bertram Bowman is a fiddle player par excellence.

2. Keith Kord is currently giving passersby his version of the old classic *Streets of Netherlipp*.

3. Stella Strummet, who is serenading early evening shoppers in the Mall, isn't the banjo player whose version of *Wallingfen Lineman* is turning a few heads (and a couple of stomachs).

4. The guitarist is entertaining people getting off buses at the bus station.

5. Penny Picker isn't the performer making a noise in the Town Square, which wasn't the location in which you could hear a version of *24 Hours from Keighshire*.

Performer	Song

	I Belong to Stonekeigh	Streets of Netherlipp	24 Hours from Keighshire	Wallingfen Lineman	Banjo	Fiddle	Guitar	Mandolin	Bus station	Main Street	Mall	Town Square
Bertram Bowman												
Keith Kord												
Penny Picker												
Stella Strummet												
Bus station												
Main Street												
Mall												
Town Square												
Banjo												
Fiddle												
Guitar												
Mandolin												

Instrument	Location

Strong Stuff

Four residents of Moonshine Lane in Stonekeigh have been brewing and maturing their own wine since last fall. They've crushed, fermented, clarified, and matured but, although the taste is not unpleasant, their "vinos" are lacking a little kick. So, when no one was looking, they each added a splash or two (or twelve) of something a little stronger to help things along. From the clues, can you work out the type of wine each brewer made, what he or she used to pep it up, and the word used by their friends to describe the result?

Clues

1. The brewer who gave their brew a bit of a kick with the contents of a bottle of vodka, creating a concoction that was judged as "brutal," is the same sex as the one who used a bottle of gin to help the rhubarb wine along.

2. Pamela Plonque, who hadn't made the elderflower wine, was quietly pleased with her friends' verdict of "ruthless."

3. The best the tasters of the fortified gooseberry wine could manage, once they'd regained the power of speech, was a spluttered "That's barbaric!"

4. Hortense Hooch sipped her brew, and thought, "What's needed here is a generous splash of brandy."

5. Gorgon Grogue's brew wasn't the one described as "uncompromising."

Brewer	Wine

	Beetroot	Elderflower	Gooseberry	Rhubarb	Brandy	Gin	Schnapps	Vodka	Barbaric	Brutal	Ruthless	Uncompromising
Gordon Grogue												
Hortense Hooch												
Larry Likka												
Pamela Plonque												
Barbaric												
Brutal												
Ruthless												
Uncompromising												
Brandy												
Gin												
Schnapps												
Vodka												

She was only the moonshiner's daughter, but he loved her still

Addition	Description

Range of Interests

Some celebrities are pretty stupid, but some aren't, and in this problem we're looking at five of the latter type. In the last few years, each of them has published an erudite book on a subject totally unconnected with his or her career. From the clues, can you work out each person's field of celebrity, the subject of their book, and the year in which it was published?

Clues

1. Rosie Swan's book came out in 2013, two years after the volume written by the Neo-Vorticist painter—who isn't Ken Lee or Lucy Merritt—came out.

2. The jazz band leader, whose book was on historic Chinese coinage, has a surname one letter shorter than that of the celebrity whose book came out in 2012; the 2010 publication was a biography of the notorious pirate Captain Kidd.

3. Neither the novelist, whose normal output is in the field of historical fantasy, nor Emma Foley wrote the book called *Ghosts of London,* which—fairly obviously—deals with hauntings in England's capital city.

4. Lucy Merritt is not the famous TV chef, and has never written a book about—or even taken any interest in—any aspect of Easter Island.

5. Alan Blake is a soccer player, playing as striker for the Merseyport Rangers and, occasionally, for England.

6. Ken Lee's book deals with the history and topography of Yeovil, Somerset, where he was born and brought up.

Name	Occupation

	Soccer player	Jazz band leader	Novelist	Painter	TV chef	Captain Kidd	Chinese coinage	Easter Island	London ghosts	Yeovil	2010	2011	2012	2013	2014
Alan Blake															
Emma Foley															
Ken Lee															
Lucy Merritt															
Rosie Swan															
2010															
2011															
2012															
2013															
2014															
Captain Kidd															
Chinese coinage															
Easter Island															
London ghosts															
Yeovil															

Subject	Publication date

Battleships

Do you remember the old game of battleships? These puzzles are based on that idea. Your task is to find the vessels in the diagram. Some parts of boats or sea squares have already been filled in, and a number next to a row or column refers to the number of occupied squares in that row or column. The boats may be positioned horizontally or vertically, but no two boats or parts of boats are in adjacent squares—horizontally, vertically, or diagonally.

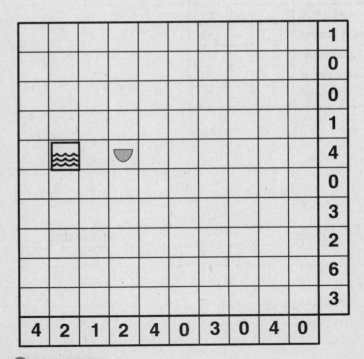

Aircraft carrier:

Battleship:

Cruiser:

Destroyer:

USA TODAY

Logi-5

Each line, across and down, is to have each of the letters A, B, C, D, and E, appearing once. Also, every shape—shown by the thick lines—must also have each of the letters in it. Can you fill in the grid?

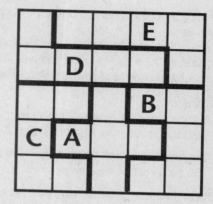

Killer Sudoku

The normal rules of Sudoku apply. In addition, the digits in each inner shape (marked by dots) must add up to the number in the top corner of that box.

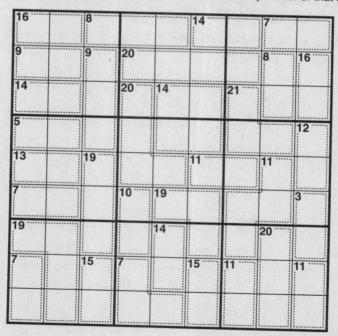

Five Macs

PennyCorp's Civil Engineering Division is busy building a dam in the African republic of Askanda and, so far, the only problem they've had is that six of the engineers are all nicknamed Mac. One of them was Theodore "Big Mac" MacDonald, the chief engineer, so the other five had to find new nicknames. From the clues, can you work out the full name of each ex-"Mac," where he's from, and his new nickname?

Clues

1. The man from Glasgow, now known as "Sparks" because of his career in electrical engineering, isn't McSorley or Macleod.

2. Ulysses Macleod isn't the man from New York City, and isn't the six-foot-four, 250-pound engineer whose new nickname is "Tiny."

3. "Skip" has been given that nickname because he was once Captain McCardle, commander of one of PennyCorp's oil-rig service vessels.

4. The engineer named Mackamotzi is not the one named Ian.

5. The Aberdonian named Maclean isn't Eddie, whose new nickname is "Cat"—he sometimes tells people that it's because he can sleep anywhere and sometimes because he is light and agile on his feet, but actually it's short for "catastrophe," about which, enough said.

6. Arnold, despite his non-Scots first name, was born and bred in Edinburgh.

First name	Surname

	Mackamotzi	Maclean	Macleod	McCardle	McSorley	Aberdeen	Dundee	Edinburgh	Glasgow	New York City	Cat	Lucky	Skip	Sparks	Tiny
Arnold															
Eddie															
Ian															
Oscar															
Ulysses															
Cat															
Lucky															
Skip															
Sparks															
Tiny															
Aberdeen															
Dundee															
Edinburgh															
Glasgow															
New York City															

CIVIL ENGINEERING

After you with the spanner, old chap

No, you have it first, my good man

Home	New nickname

Crispin in Bloom

Marston Bagshot—the city bigshot who has retired to Crispin Manor in Upper Crispin and is now ruling the roost in that village—wants to enter and win the Keighshire in Bloom competition. To that end, he is now ruling with a rod of iron, and tonight, his henchmen have brought five villagers before him and his committee to answer charges of "actions likely to harm Crispin." From the clues, can you say in what order the villagers were dragged before the committee, of what they were charged, and the punishment handed out?

Clues

1. Lawrence Lax was the second wrongdoer to be frog-marched in front of the committee.

2. Simon Slappe-Dasche was brought before the committee on the heinous charge of reckless planting, immediately before Roberta Remisce and immediately after the miscreant sentenced to a month of trash collection.

3. The third person dragged before the committee was charged with the odious crime of careless hedging; the last person to face the committee stood head bowed as they were sentenced to forty-five yards of fence-painting.

4. Bagshot's recent trip to see *The Mikado* resonated as he "let the punishment fit the crime" and sentenced the person charged with under-weeding to twenty-five hours of hard weeding of the curbs around Upper Crispin.

5. Sylvia Slack was sentenced to edge the town square by hand, but not for the despicable act of miserly mulching.

Order	Villager

	Lawrence Lax	Roberta Remisce	Sheryl Shoddy	Simon Slappe-Dasche	Sylvia Slack	Careless hedging	Miserly mulching	Negligent mowing	Reckless planting	Under-weeding	Fence painting	Square edging	Curb weeding	Trash collection	Easement watering
First															
Second															
Third															
Fourth															
Fifth															
Fence painting															
Square edging															
Curb weeding															
Trash collection															
Easement watering															
Careless hedging															
Miserly mulching															
Negligent mowing															
Reckless planting															
Under-weeding															

Charge	Punishment

Second-Hand Siblings

There are five newborn babies in the maternity ward, and their young brothers and sisters are visiting for the first time. From the clues, can you discover the first name and surname of each new baby, the name of its brother or sister, and the toy that each sibling has been persuaded, reluctantly, to bring and donate to the new arrival?

Clues

1. Little Charlotte Newcome has come to see her baby brother for the first time and, when no one's looking, tell him who's boss right from the start; Mark is excited to be seeing his new brother Daniel (at least, that's what he told his parents).

2. Alexandra's visitor is not Harry and her present is not a rattle; the visitor to baby Lily has brought a wooden train, but it's just on loan.

3. George has not been given and Joshua has not brought a teddy bear.

4. Chloe has brought her rag doll to the hospital—and if she's got anything to do with it, will take it back home too; the name of her new baby sibling is one letter shorter than that of Mrs. Bourne's new arrival.

5. The Goodchild baby's present is a musical toy.

6. The until-now only child of the Little family has come to inspect their new brother Simon—"he'll be OK as long as he doesn't get any bigger," was their reaction.

Baby's name	Surname

	Bourne	Goodchild	Little	Newcome	Young	Charlotte	Chloe	Harry	Joshua	Mark	Musical toy	Rag doll	Rattle	Teddy	Wooden train
Alexandra															
Daniel															
George															
Lily															
Simon															
Musical toy															
Rag doll															
Rattle															
Teddy															
Wooden train															
Charlotte															
Chloe															
Harry															
Joshua															
Mark															

MATERNITY UNIT

PUSH-
pant,
pant,
PUSH

DELIVERY
ROOM

Young sibling	Present

Scent to Your Room

A new selection of room fresheners has been released, and Mary Tile, a tester for the Choose It section of the *Netherlipp Sunday Courier*, is currently carrying out an experiment at her home using five different brands to see which lasts longest. From the clues, can you discover which brand of air freshener is in which room, the fragrance of each, and how long each has lasted so far?

Clues

1. The air freshener in the dining room is not made by either Aromist or Atmosfear; the Aromist fragrance has not refreshed a room for thirty-eight days and is not Dusty Lane, which has provided its essence of grit for thirty-two days.

2. Baker's Parlor—the delicate scent of Managing Director Montague Baker's front room—has not lasted for thirty-six or forty days and is not made by Atmosfear; it is not in use in the kitchen, where the air freshener has lasted for thirty-four days.

3. Coffee House Blues is not made by Waftair, whose fragrance has lasted the longest.

4. Strawbale—probably not the first choice for hay fever sufferers—is refreshing the bedroom.

5. The Freshayr product is in use in the hall.

6. Zephyr makes the Odor Killer fragrance which doesn't actually kill odors but smells just like those air fresheners that do.

Room	Maker

	Aromist	Atmosfear	Freshayr	Waftair	Zephyr	Baker's Parlor	Coffee House Blues	Dusty Lane	Odor Killer	Strawbale	32 days	34 days	36 days	38 days	40 days
Bedroom															
Dining room															
Hall															
Kitchen															
Sitting room															
32 days															
34 days															
36 days															
38 days															
40 days															
Baker's Parlor															
Coffee House Blues															
Dusty Lane															
Odor Killer															
Strawbale															

Fragrance	Number of days

Action and Reaction

Fay Nassle is employed by *What?* magazine as a secret shopper. Her job is to visit stores and check out both their facilities and the helpfulness of the staff. Most of the time, she satisfies herself asking for odd sizes, trying on everything in the store, or attempting to return items to inappropriate stores, but this week she's been tasked with doing something a little more dramatic in five of Netherlipp's department stores. From the clues, can you say on which day she visited each store, what she did, and how the staff responded?

Clues

1. Fay visited Harry Spencers in the Mall the day after her antics left one store assistant screaming at the top of their lungs and running around the store in hysterics (Old Mr. Withers will never live it down!), and the day before she fainted onto a divan in the bed department and was covered with a blanket by an assistant who thought it best to pretend she was part of the display.

2. Fay's intentionally ham-fisted attempt at stealing a vacuum cleaner happened the day after she made a nuisance of herself in Mark Rods on Main Street, and the day before her antics were completely ignored.

3. Fay's foray into Debbie Nicks in the Station Approach was the day after one store assistant panicked and dialed 911 asking for the police, the fire brigade, and the coast guard, and the day before she staggered around the soft furnishing department pretending to be drunk.

4. Fay dropped her shopping bags, which she had carefully filled with marbles, rice, and sawdust, later in the week than she popped into Harvey's in the Town Square, which was some time after Fay stuffed a pillow up her blouse and pretended to go into labor in the personal electronics department.

Day	Store

	Debbie Nicks	Mark Rods	Harry Spencers	Harvey's	Selfenhams	Appear drunk	Drop bags	Faint	In labor	Stealing	Call 911	Cover	Ignore	Laugh	Scream
Monday															
Tuesday															
Wednesday															
Thursday															
Friday															
Call 911															
Cover															
Ignore															
Laugh															
Scream															
Appear drunk															
Drop bags															
Faint															
In labor															
Stealing															

Action	Reaction

USA TODAY   201

Diggers

It's a sunny Saturday morning in Storbury, and five locals have armed themselves with shovels, spades, and picks and are hacking away at the ground somewhere. From the clues, can you work out each digger's full name, the location at which they are installing a hole in the ground, and why they are excavating?

Clues

1. Ian, who's a picture framer during the week but gets his spade out most weekends, is not Delve, nor Wells.

2. The person named Wells isn't digging his or her garden and isn't the digger clearing a weedy, muddy pond at the Blackfriars development.

3. Neither the amateur archaeologist, who is working on what is hopefully the site of a medieval abbey gatehouse, nor the person doing a DIY drain repair, are working at the riverside open space called The Croft, which isn't where digger Delve is digging.

4. Una, who has an apartment with no garden, is digging on a community project that is not at the area known as The Croft.

5. Edna Pitt works for the multinational Penny Corporation, as does Alan, who is digging on Friars Meadow.

6. The digger digging on Plough Lane is digger Burrows; the drain repairer, Quarry, is not working on Molford Road.

First name	Surname

	Burrows	Delve	Pitt	Quarry	Wells	Blackfriars	Friars Meadow	Molford Road	Plough Lane	The Croft	Archaeology	Clearing pond	Community project	Digging garden	Repairing drain
Alan															
Edna															
Ian															
Oliver															
Una															
Archaeology															
Clearing pond															
Community project															
Digging garden															
Repairing drain															
Blackfriars															
Friars Meadow															
Molford Road															
Plough Lane															
The Croft															

Location	Reason

Noah Trouble

It had rained for many days, and parts of Churchminster were more lake than land. But Noah Arkwright knew what to do. His mission, he was sure, was to save two of every kind of living creature from the rising waters in the town, so he mounted his garden shed on a rowboat and set off collecting the bemused animals. From the clues, can you discover the order in which he paddled down each of the town's flooded streets, the depth of the water he encountered, and the types of animals he collected?

Clues

1. On the first street, which was not Bridge Street, he took on board two ducks.

2. The water was deepest on the third street he floated down.

3. The pair of goats was collected on the street he visited immediately after Southbank Road, and immediately before the one where the water was four feet deep.

4. The water was shallowest on Wharf Road, which he paddled down immediately after having picked up the two rabbits.

5. The cats joined the menagerie on the street where the water was five feet deep.

6. The guinea pigs came from Weir Street, where the water was less than five feet deep.

Order	Street

	Bridge Street	Mill Road	Southbank Road	Weir Street	Wharf Road	3 feet	4 feet	5 feet	6 feet	7 feet	Cats	Ducks	Goats	Guinea pigs	Rabbits
First															
Second															
Third															
Fourth															
Fifth															
Cats															
Ducks															
Goats															
Guinea pigs															
Rabbits															
3 feet															
4 feet															
5 feet															
6 feet															
7 feet															

Perhaps bringing the woodworm was a bad idea.

ARK

Depth	Animals

Dawdling Duos

Schooldays are, proverbially, the best times of your life, so these five pairs of friends usually loiter on their way to school, not wishing to waste these good times in class. They delay the inevitable with various time-wasting activities on the short walk to the school gates. From the clues, can you discover who the dawdling duos were today, what they were doing, and how many minutes late for school each pair was?

Clues

1. Henry and Sam were three minutes later arriving at school than the pair who swapped playing cards on the way.

2. Billy's watch was a little fast, so he and his friend, who was not Joe, were only four minutes late.

3. Matthew and his friend were playing hide-and-seek, but that didn't make them five minutes late.

4. The Power Rangers pairing were a minute later arriving to class than Rory and his companion, who were an even number of minutes late.

5. Shaun was one of the pair reported six minutes late through the school gates.

6. James wasted time by playing football.

Child	Friend

	Gareth	James	Joe	Sam	Shaun	Buying candy	Football	Hide-and-seek	Playing Power Rangers	Swapping cards	4 mins late	5 mins late	6 mins late	7 mins late	10 mins late
Billy															
Henry															
Matthew															
Rory															
Tom															
4 mins late															
5 mins late															
6 mins late															
7 mins late															
10 mins late															
Buying candy															
Football															
Hide-and-seek															
Playing Power Rangers															
Swapping cards															

Activity	Time late (minutes)

Meet and Greet

Cherilyn Challey, a tour representative based on the Mediterranean island of Ibjorcos, was due to meet five incoming flights one busy summer Saturday. From the clues, can you name the airport the plane arriving at each of the listed times set out from and the airline operating it, and work out the number of people aboard whom Cherilyn was scheduled to meet, greet, and send on their way to their resorts and hotels?

Clues

1. The Plainair flight from Gatside had an afternoon arrival time.

2. Cherilyn had more passengers to meet off the Cloudbase flight than were on the plane from Glaston, which arrived in Ibjorcos earlier in the day.

3. There were more people to be met off the Jetaway flight than on the one arriving at 10:15, which was not its immediate predecessor.

4. Seventeen tourists booked with Cherilyn's firm were aboard the plane from Humbergow airport.

5. The largest group of clients for Cherilyn flew in on a plane that arrived sometime before the one from Stanwick.

6. The 1:35 plane was carrying fourteen people Cherilyn needed to meet, greet, and dispatch on their way.

7. The plane from Heathsted, which was not operated by Skyways, touched down at an earlier time than the FlyOff flight, which had more of Cherilyn's company's customers aboard.

Arrival time	From

	Gatside	Glaston	Heathsted	Humbergow	Stanwick	Cloudbase	FlyOff	Jetaway	Plainair	Skyways	6	14	16	17	28
10:15 a.m.															
11:00 a.m.															
1:35 p.m.															
2:55 p.m.															
3:45 p.m.															
6															
14															
16															
17															
28															
Cloudbase															
FlyOff															
Jetaway															
Plainair															
Skyways															

Flight Delays

We apologise for the severe delays. Normal delays will resume as soon as possible

Carrier	Number

First Jobs

Five self-employed tradesmen in the town of Workwell had undertaken to deal "first thing" with repairs or decoration jobs for clients in outlying villages, who learned that "first thing" is a rather elastic term. From the clues, can you work out the names and trades of the men, to what village each traveled, and at what time he reached his client?

Clues

1. No man's trade and name have the same initial letter; the plasterer's name is alphabetically next after that of the plumber.

2. The joiner turned up more than fifteen minutes earlier than Mr. Smiley, but later than the man who traveled to the picturesque Little Hynge.

3. Neither the roofer nor the man who went to Dun Planking was first or last to arrive.

4. The painter, who was not the man who arrived at his first job at a quarter to ten, arrived fifteen minutes before Mr. Jolly, while Mr. Joynson, who is not a plasterer, appeared next before the man who went to Higher Poynting.

5. Mr. Rafter proved a better timekeeper, or at least arrived earlier, than the chap who turned up, totally unabashed, at Lower Stipple.

6. The Much Flushing job began receiving attention fifteen minutes after Mr. Potts, who was not the first to turn up, got down to work elsewhere.

Village	Name

	Mr. Jolly	Mr. Joynson	Mr. Potts	Mr. Rafter	Mr. Smiley	Joiner	Painter	Plasterer	Plumber	Roofer	9:45 a.m.	10:15 a.m.	10:30 a.m.	10:45 a.m.	11:00 a.m.
Dun Planking															
Higher Poynting															
Little Hynge															
Lower Stipple															
Much Flushing															
9:45 a.m.															
10:15 a.m.															
10:30 a.m.															
10:45 a.m.															
11:00 a.m.															
Joiner															
Painter															
Plasterer															
Plumber															
Roofer															

Trade	Time

Logi-5

Each line, across and down, is to have each of the letters A, B, C, D, and E, appearing once. Also, every shape—shown by the thick lines—must also have each of the letters in it. Can you fill in the grid?

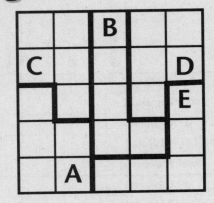

Killer Sudoku

The normal rules of Sudoku apply. In addition, the digits in each inner shape (marked by dots) must add up to the number in the top corner of that box.

16	13	20	9		19		19	
	12		12		23	22		
19		12						
8			9	15	8			15
	14				25	6		
13		11		8				
13	3		10			24	11	
	8						8	

Battleships

Do you remember the old game of battleships? These puzzles are based on that idea. Your task is to find the vessels in the diagram. Some parts of boats or sea squares have already been filled in, and a number next to a row or column refers to the number of occupied squares in that row or column. The boats may be positioned horizontally or vertically, but no two boats or parts of boats are in adjacent squares—horizontally, vertically, or diagonally.

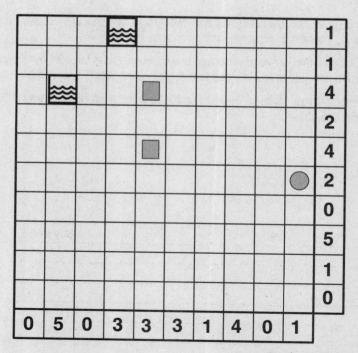

Aircraft carrier:

Battleship:

Cruiser:

Destroyer:

Spycatcher

During World War II, FBI agent Marvin Lee was one of the USA's most successful spy catchers. Over five years, he was responsible for breaking up five major spy rings. From the clues, can you work out the name of the spy ring dealt with in each year, where in the US it was based, and the code name of Lee's FBI operation that broke it up?

Clues

1. In December 1941 (immediately after the attack on Pearl Harbor), Agent Lee headed up Operation Puma, which didn't end up with the arrest of seven members of the Windmill spy ring, set up, bizarrely, by the Hungarians but reporting to their German allies.

2. The Wintersky network, which operated in Miami, Florida, to provide information on coastal shipping in the Atlantic, was closed down by Lee's team the year after he headed up Operation Coyote.

3. Operation Tiger took place the year after Lee arrested the members of the Cabaret group, and the year before the operation against the spy ring in Dayton, Ohio.

4. In mid-1943, Lee and his agents were working in New York against a spy ring passing information on transatlantic shipping.

5. Stormcloud, the Japanese espionage and sabotage group targeted by Operation Fox, did not operate in a city that includes the word "New" in its name.

6. Operation Grizzly broke up the spy ring based in the great US Navy port of San Diego, California.

Year	Spy ring

	Cabaret	Oaktree	Stormcloud	Windmill	Wintersky	Dayton	Miami	New Orleans	New York	San Diego	Coyote	Fox	Grizzly	Puma	Tiger
1941															
1942															
1943															
1944															
1945															
Coyote															
Fox															
Grizzly															
Puma															
Tiger															
Dayton															
Miami															
New Orleans															
New York															
San Diego															

U.S. city	FBI operation

Poster Palace

The CineMaster is a store in Eddsbury that sells movie memorabilia of all kinds and displayed on the wall behind the cash register are four posters from classic movies. They're for sale at a remarkably cheap price—because they're not the English versions. From the clues, can you fill in the details on each—the star's name, the movie title, and its language?

Clues

1. Poster D, which isn't for the Chuck McRay action movie, is in German.

2. The poster for the thriller starring Dean Morley is displayed between the Spanish-language one and the one for *White Dragon*.

3. The poster for Jayne Busby's historic drama *Gunpowder* is next to the one for *Home Ground,* which is not the one printed in Hindustani advertising the Susan Starr comedy.

4. The movie featured on poster B is called *Snowbird*.

Stars: Chuck McRay; Dean Morley; Jayne Busby; Susan Starr
Movies: *Gunpowder*; *Home Ground*; *Snowbird*; *White Dragon*
Languages: French; German; Hindustani; Spanish

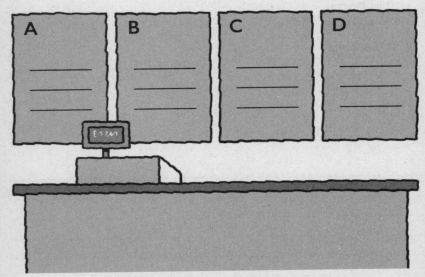

Starting tip: Work out the movie on poster A.

Battleships

Do you remember the old game of battleships? These puzzles are based on that idea. Your task is to find the vessels in the diagram. Some parts of boats or sea squares have already been filled in, and a number next to a row or column refers to the number of occupied squares in that row or column. The boats may be positioned horizontally or vertically, but no two boats or parts of boats are in adjacent squares—horizontally, vertically, or diagonally.

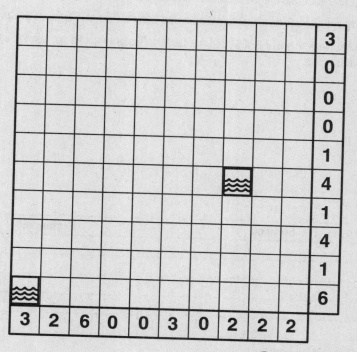

Aircraft carrier:

Battleship:

Cruiser:

Destroyer:

Mysterious Flatland

The Tennessee town of Flatland has a number of Chinese restaurants from which its hungry residents can choose, and last Friday, five local couples each decided to treat themselves to a proper sit-down meal in one of them. From the clues, can you work out which establishment each couple visited, the type of Chinese cuisine served there, and the price of the meal?

Clues

1. Charlie Chan's restaurant on Brewster Street—which isn't really run by Charlie Chan (the boss is called Colin Chan)—serves what could be described as "Anglo-Chinese" food.

2. The Szechuan-style meal cost $56, including wine and oyster crackers.

3. Lewis and Bren Gunn (she's Brenda, really) ate at the Cantonese restaurant, where they spent $8 more than the cost of the meal at the Jade Dragon.

4. The Pekingese-style meal was not the one that cost $48—which, of course, didn't include gratuities.

5. Matt and Pat Ernal ate the most expensive of the five meals.

6. Rusty and Olive Brown chose to dine at the Red Pavilion on Stamford Boulevard.

7. The couple who spent just $40 at the Lantern Restaurant was not Lennox and Beverley Hills.

Surname	Restaurant

	Charlie Chan's	Jade Dragon	Lantern	Red Pavilion	Wong Ping's	Anglo-Chinese	Cantonese	Pekingese	Shanghai	Szechuan	$40	$48	$56	$64	$72
Brown															
Ernal															
Gunn															
Hills															
Katt															
$40															
$48															
$56															
$64															
$72															
Anglo-Chinese															
Cantonese															
Pekingese															
Shanghai															
Szechuan															

Cuisine	Price

Fathom It Out

Sergeant Franklin Fathom works for Utah State Police. In each of the last five years, he has successfully tackled a difficult murder inquiry and eventually brought the villain to justice. From the clues, can you work out the location in which each year's crime took place, name the guilty party, and identify the main evidence on which Fathom's case was based?

Clues

1. Karl Crooke was convicted as a result of Fathom's psychological assessment of his makeup, which eventually led to his obtaining a confession; this was a later case than the one that took Fathom to Crowhampton.

2. The soil sample sufficed to bring the Littlechurch killer to justice.

3. Sergeant Fathom did not work in Misselton during the 2013 investigation, during which the guilty man did not prove to be Anthony Black.

4. The 2012 murder took place in Hambury.

5. The 2009 killing was committed by Leslie Baddey.

6. The vital witness in the 2011 inquiry was finally located as a result of Franklin Fathom's persistence.

7. Gerry Savage was the Pridewell murderer, who was charged the year before the investigation whose solution hinged on fingerprint evidence.

Year	Location

	Crowhampton	Littlechurch	Hambury	Misselton	Pridewell	Anthony Black	Gerry Savage	Karl Crooke	Leslie Baddey	Marlon Hood	Confession	DNA sample	Fingerprints	Soil sample	Vital witness
2009															
2010															
2011															
2012															
2013															
Confession															
DNA sample															
Fingerprints															
Soil sample															
Vital witness															
Anthony Black															
Gerry Savage															
Karl Crooke															
Leslie Baddey															
Marlon Hood															

Villain	Evidence

Les Autres Reliques

Browsing through an internet auction site, I came across a number of items that were claimed to be the former property of members of the seventeenth-century French soldiers known as The Other Musketeers (or Les Autres Mousquetaires, en Francais). From the clues, can you work out which item allegedly belonged to each man, the person selling it, and the city in which he lives?

Clues

1. The item described as the one-time property of Uramis isn't the one offered for sale—for a fortune in euros—by Marc Vaurien from St. Malo.

2. The spurs are being sold by a man in Toulon; the man who supposedly wore the belt buckle had either the first or last name in the alphabetical list.

3. Raoul Dingue wants 10,000 euros for the crucifix described as "wooden, with metal decorations, possibly silver;" the powder horn, designed for use with a flintlock pocket pistol, isn't for sale in Nice, which isn't where Louis Poisseux is based.

4. Jules Sangsue is selling something he claims used to belong to Maximos.

5. One of the items for sale is a leather dice box which is supposed to have once belonged to the notorious gambling Musketeer Damos; the item that was once the property of Silvis, which isn't the powder horn, isn't being offered by Marc Vaurien.

6. The relic of Archamos is being sold by a man in Grenoble; the item offered by Jean Bourricot is not described as having belonged to either Archamos or Uramis.

Musketeer	Item

	Belt buckle	Crucifix	Dice box	Powder horn	Spurs	Jean Bourricot	Jules Sangsue	Louis Poisseux	Marc Vaurien	Raoul Dingue	Dijon	Grenoble	Nice	St. Malo	Toulon
Archamos															
Damos															
Maximos															
Silvis															
Uramis															
Dijon															
Grenoble															
Nice															
St. Malo															
Toulon															
Jean Bourricot															
Jules Sangsue															
Louis Poisseux															
Marc Vaurien															
Raoul Dingue															

Seller	City

Dear Sir

Five regular contributors to the Letters to the Editor page of their chosen Keighshire newspaper each had one of their efforts published on a different day last week. From the clues, can you say whose letter was printed on which day in which paper, and work out the aspect of modern society about which each writer complained?

Clues

1. Colonel Crusty's epistle to the *Wallingfen Recorder*, which did not have anything to do with television, was printed the day before one of the letters that did.

2. The topic of young men's fashion was raised later in the week than the appearance of one reader's letter to the *Netherlipp Courier*.

3. The Monday letter complained at great length, and a lot greater length before it was edited, about trash disposal.

4. It was the regular reader of the *Churchminster Sentinel*, who was not Mr. Cross, who had a letter published in Thursday's edition.

5. Miss Sharp was the sender of the letter printed on Tuesday.

6. In her letter, Mrs. Short criticized a number—a particularly large number—of government policies of which she disapproved; this letter was featured later in the week than the one to the *Crispin Tribune*, which was not written by a woman.

Day	Writer

	Mr. Cross	Colonel Crusty	Major Quarrell	Miss Sharp	Mrs. Short	Churchminster Sentinel	Crispin Tribune	Netherlipp Courier	Stonekeigh Advertiser	Wallingfen Recorder	Garbage	Gov. policies	Cyclists	TV programs	Men's fashion
Monday															
Tuesday															
Wednesday															
Thursday															
Friday															
Garbage															
Gov. policies															
Cyclists															
TV programs															
Men's fashion															
Churchminster Sentinel															
Crispin Tribune															
Netherlipp Courier															
Stonekeigh Advertiser															
Wallingfen Recorder															

Paper	Topic

Classic B and Ps

Brewster and Percival started making cars in a small garage just outside Storbury in 1912. Nowadays, they belong to a Japanese company and simply assemble components made overseas into family sedans, but in the foyer of their factory, they still exhibit four of their classic vehicles. From the clues, can you fill in the model name, type, and year of manufacture of each one? (We've drawn them all the same so as not to give it away.)

Clues

1. The B and P Blenheim (for some reason, all their model names began with a B, perhaps Mr. Brewster was the stronger character) was made eleven years after the sports car.

2. Vehicle 1 is a Grand Prix car—the only one B and P ever built—that finished third in the Irish Grand Prix in the year of its manufacture.

3. The 1949 touring car, which is not vehicle 3 in the drawing, was manufactured some years after the Bulldog.

4. The B and P Beaufort limousine is eleven years older than vehicle 2.

Models: Baltimore; Beaufort; Blenheim; Bulldog
Types: Grand Prix car; limousine; sports car; touring car
Dates: 1927; 1938; 1949; 1960

Starting tip: Decide which type of car dates from 1960.

Chase the Ace

A card shark has set up his portable table in the underpass leading to Netherlipp Station, and a few people have gathered around. "I'm going to lay out the spades," said the card shark, fanning out the cards for all to see. "Place a dollar on the Ace and win a $50 bill. What could be easier?" He spread out the cards face down, as shown. From the clues, can you work out where the cards are—can you find the Ace of Spades and win the cash?

Clues

1. No two adjacent cards on the table are of adjacent value in the suit.

2. The card on the immediate left is a face card (Jack, Queen, or King); the 10 is the second card from the right; the furthest right card isn't the 6.

3. The 8 is four cards left of the Jack, and three cards right of the 2; the Queen is immediately left of a card with an odd number.

4. The 7 has the 9 on one side, and the 4 on the other; the 3 is further to the right than the 5.

Starting tip: Start by positioning the Jack.

Person of the Year

Despite the year only being half done, there has been a spate of "People of the Year" competitions for different occupations in Netherlipp recently, five of which are featured in this problem. From the clues, can you work out the full names and ages of the winners for each occupation?

Clues

1. Kath is the next older after the window cleaner, whose windows were much admired. but is younger than the winner with the surname Bland.

2. The stallholder (commended for their top-quality sales patter, and a very decorative stall awning), who is nearer in age to the person surnamed Rooney than to Anne, though older than both, has a surname with the same number of letters as that of the thirty-seven-year-old, but a shorter first name.

3. The bar attendant (no one mixes a margarita with quite as much panache or, indeed, splash) is younger than the winner named Mills and younger still than Reg.

4. The mailman (there's no package he can't force through a mailbox) is male and older than Gordon and has the surname alphabetically next after his.

5. The winner called Parker is younger than Jim but older than the lunch lady—no child leaves without finishing their cabbage.

Occupation	First name

	Anne	Gordon	Jim	Kath	Reg	Bland	Doherty	Mills	Parker	Rooney	36	37	49	52	64
Bar attendant															
Lunch lady															
Mailman															
Stallholder															
Window cleaner															
36															
37															
49															
52															
64															
Bland															
Doherty															
Mills															
Parker															
Rooney															

Surname	Age

Barbies

By coincidence, the four research students who run the small bar at the Manor House Postgraduate Residence Hall at Netherlipp University have BB as their initials and are known, perhaps unsurprisingly, as the Barbies. The bar is open only from Friday evening to Sunday lunchtime, and each of the Barbies take one shift. From the clues, can you work out the full name of each Barbie, the field in which they carry out their research, and the time they run the bar?

Clues

1. Bettina runs the bar the day after it's under the control of the researcher from the Chemohistory Department.

2. Bruce is on duty on Saturday but isn't the medicoliterature researcher; Battersby is busy on Saturdays and doesn't work in the bar that day.

3. Brian, who spends his weekdays researching in the biogeology labs, works in the bar the day before Birkenshaw takes a shift.

4. Buchanan is an astropolitics researcher and has been developing a theory of Cometary Gerrymandering.

5. Miss Browning works an evening shift.

First name	Surname

	Battersby	Birkenshaw	Browning	Buchanan	Astropolitics	Biogeology	Chemohistory	Medicoliterature	Fri. evening	Sat. lunch	Sat. evening	Sun. lunch
Bettina												
Brian												
Bridget												
Bruce												
Fri. evening												
Sat. lunch												
Sat. evening												
Sun. lunch												
Astropolitics												
Biogeology												
Chemohistory												
Medicoliterature												

Research field	Bar time

Queue

The roads across Keystone County are usually reasonably free-flowing, but on public holidays, especially public holidays that have been forecast to be sunny and warm, certain spots can become glorified parking areas. We drop in on four families who have turned off their engines and are amusing themselves with a game while the traffic jam unjams. From the clues, can you name the family at each location, the game they are playing, and the coastal location that is their intended destination?

Clues

1. "I spy with my little eye something beginning with C," said eight-year-old Jessica Kew. "Is it car . . . again?" asked her Dad with as little cynicism as he could muster. "Yes," she replied delightedly; the Kews weren't the family whose trip to Sandy Cove had been halted at the confusing freeway tunnel arrangement known as Macaroni Junction.

2. The family sitting in their car at the notorious Crispin Bottleneck are playing the famous-person guessing game of Botticelli, hampered only by the fact that no one knows the rules.

3. The Lyne family set out early, hoping for a day at Shingle Head.

4. The family currently playing consequences instead of making progress towards their intended destination of Rock Banks is not the Oldupps.

5. It's not the Jamme family who is gridlocked in the well-known traffic choke point of Moorland Cutting.

Location	Family

	Jamme	Kew	Lyne	Oldupp	Botticelli	Charades	Consequences	I-Spy	Pebble Bay	Rock Banks	Sandy Cove	Shingle Head
Crispin Bottleneck												
Macaroni Junction												
Moorland Cutting												
Stonekeigh Bypass												
Pebble Bay												
Rock Banks												
Sandy Cove												
Shingle Head												
Botticelli												
Charades												
Consequences												
I-Spy												

Joe was winning the game of hide and seek — until the traffic cleared.

Game	Destination

Logi-5

Each line, across and down, is to have each of the letters A, B, C, D, and E, appearing once. Also, every shape—shown by the thick lines—must also have each of the letters in it. Can you fill in the grid?

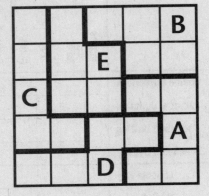

Killer Sudoku

The normal rules of Sudoku apply. In addition, the digits in each inner shape (marked by dots) must add up to the number in the top corner of that box.

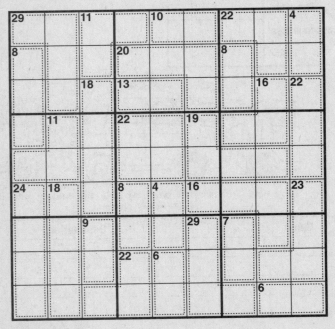

USA TODAY

Domino Search

A standard set of dominoes has been laid out, using numbers instead of dots for clarity. Using a sharp pencil and a keen brain, can you draw in the lines to show where each domino has been placed? You may find the check grid useful—crossing off each domino as you find it.

3	2	2	6	6	6	4	6
3	5	1	2	5	5	2	5
1	1	2	3	6	2	0	6
4	0	2	3	4	5	4	0
4	1	6	6	4	0	1	5
4	1	2	1	1	3	5	0
5	4	3	0	3	0	0	3

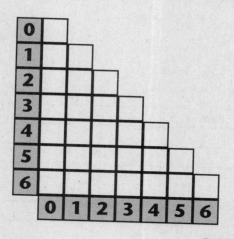

The Bodyguard

Tommy Farmer was a soldier for twenty years, but retired in 2010 and became a professional bodyguard; since then, he's had to do nothing more violent than stand next to his clients wearing sunglasses and looking tough. Next month, he's been hired for five one-day assignments at various events. From the clues, can you work out the name and description of his client on each date, and what event Tommy will be attending with them?

Clues

1. On the 11th, Tommy will be protecting the novelist whose most recent book has attracted hostility and death-threats from a section of the political spectrum.

2. On the 9th, Tommy will be acting as bodyguard to a client who will be a witness at a court hearing; neither this client nor the one who has booked Tommy for the 14th are the outspoken journalist.

3. The pop singer who Tommy is to accompany on a visit to a friend in the hospital in an attempt to stir up speculation and publicity is neither his client for the 24th nor Donald Ellis.

4. Tommy will be looking after Stuart Temple ten days after he escorts another client to a celebrity wedding.

5. Tommy's day with the media tycoon will be later in the month than the charitable organization's prize-giving that he will be attending with Gary Horton.

6. Ray Sellars is a racing driver who has been threatened because he drives for a team financed by an extremely unpopular energy company.

Date	Client

	Carolyn Dunne	Donald Ellis	Gary Horton	Ray Sellars	Stuart Temple	Journalist	Media tycoon	Novelist	Pop singer	Racing driver	Court appearance	Hospital visit	Literary lunch	Prize-giving	Wedding
9th															
11th															
14th															
19th															
24th															
Court appearance															
Hospital visit															
Literary lunch															
Prize-giving															
Wedding															
Journalist															
Media tycoon															
Novelist															
Pop singer															
Racing driver															

Description	Event

Number Series

Writer Ernie Bundell has become a prolific author of books for young children, having hit upon the goldmine of a series of books all based on the same sort of story and formula, and the perfect length for the exhausted parent to read to their little darlings at bedtime. Each title begins with a number, followed by a synonym for "diminutive," then a type of lovable creature and ending with a phrase summarizing the story line. From the clues, can you work out the full title of each of his last five books?

Clues

1. There are two more *Kittens* than there are *Lambs Feeling Sad*.

2. The four creatures in one title are not described as *Tiny*.

3. The diminutive stature of *Five* animals in one title are described with the word *Itsy-Bitsy*.

4. The creatures who *Come to Play* in one book are described as *Wee* in its title; they number one more than the ones who *Ran Away*.

5. One book describes the events as *Three* animals *Have a Party*.

6. The best-selling of Ernie's output, so far, features a number of *Little Mice*.

7. The book featuring *Two Puppies* is Ernie's longest effort so far, spanning twenty pages including illustrations.

Number	Diminutive

	Itsy-Bitsy	Little	Tiny	Wee	Young	Ducklings	Kittens	Lambs	Mice	Puppies	...and Their Friends	...Come to Play	...Feeling Sad	...Have a Party	...Run Away
Two															
Three															
Four															
Five															
Six															
...and Their Friends															
...Come to Play															
...Feeling Sad															
...Have a Party															
...Run Away															
Ducklings															
Kittens															
Lambs															
Mice															
Puppies															

Creatures	Conclusion

Grove Wood

The Grove, in Colnecaster, is a short cul-de-sac in the old part of the town that is occupied by four antique stores, and last week, my friends Don and Sharon bought a wooden object from each of them. From the clues, can you fill in the name of each store, the nature of Don and Sharon's purchase there, and from what wood it was made?

Clues

1. The rosewood dice box, once used by Regency gambler Beau Tifull, came from a store with a higher number than Cobwebs's premises.

2. The mahogany object was bought at a store further right than Darby and Jones.

3. Don and Sharon bought the eighteenth-century wooden rocking horse from Number 3, The Grove.

4. Relics, where the jewel box was purchased, is immediately next to the even-numbered store that supplied the nineteenth-century bamboo antique.

Stores: Cobwebs; Darby and Jones; Father Time; Relics
Antiques: bedside table; dice box; jewel box; rocking horse
Woods: bamboo; mahogany; pear wood; rosewood

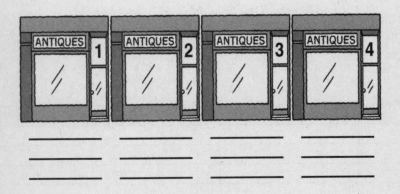

Starting tip: Determine the type of wood bought from store 1.

Coolers

The swim-up bar at the Hotel Splendido offers a wide range of soft drinks to quench the thirst of those who have spent a little too long in the sun, and the most popular section is the serve-yourself "cooler" selection. Each pitcher contains a different combination of two juices, and most vacationers like to mix more than one of these pairings to make their own super-mixture. From the clues, can you say what two juices are mixed in each pitcher?

Clues

1. Patrons who make a mixture from jugs A, B, and E will end up with a drink containing only banana, coconut, orange, and pineapple.

2. Mixing jugs A and D will give you a banana, pineapple, mango, and orange concoction.

3. Jug C doesn't contain coconut.

4. Each jug that contains liquidized banana is to the immediate right of one that contains orange juice.

Juices: banana; coconut; mango; orange; pineapple

Starting tip: Begin by deciding which two jugs have mango juice.

Mentioned in Dispatches

At the central distribution warehouse of the Netsparks.com internet electrical goods store, the items are stacked on vast shelving systems, accessed by forklift trucks when orders arrive. Five trucks are currently trundling around the warehouse accessing items to be dispatched to eagerly waiting customers. From the clues, can you work out the nature of the appliance they each are collecting, and the row, bay, and level number of each location?

Clues

1. The appliance on level 3 of row 3 is in a bay numbered less than ten, while the item in bay 15 is used for washing something.

2. The dishwasher is to be found in an even-numbered bay, but not at level 1, while all the fridges are stored on level 2.

3. The oven is in row 1, but not in bay 12; the television is in bay 6.

4. One of the forklift trucks is collecting something from level 5 of bay 4.

5. The item that was in bay 3 of row 2 only moments ago is now being processed through the dispatch department.

6. The appliance being collected from level 4 of one of the racks is not in row 4.

Appliance	Row

	Row 1	Row 2	Row 3	Row 4	Row 5	Bay 3	Bay 4	Bay 6	Bay 12	Bay 15	Level 1	Level 2	Level 3	Level 4	Level 5
Oven															
Dishwasher															
Fridge															
Television															
Washing machine															
Level 1															
Level 2															
Level 3															
Level 4															
Level 5															
Bay 3															
Bay 4															
Bay 6															
Bay 12															
Bay 15															

OPTICAL ILLUSIONS

Bay	Level

Night Duty

Brightbourne is a great place to spend a seaside vacation (or so it is asserted by the Tourist Information Office) but it does have some law enforcement challenges during the summer season. That's why five pairs of police officers are on duty tonight in civilian clothes at certain local hostelries, watching for trouble and ready to pounce. From the clues, can you name each pair of officers, where they are, and how they're dressed?

Clues

1. Luke Mason and his partner aren't dressed as Goths, nor is he the officer dressed in biker leather who is working with the similarly-clad Diane Ellis.

2. Brian Cook and Kay Lovell are working together, but they're not the two plain-clothes officers (well, perhaps their outfits aren't as plain as all that) who are working in what used to be the Seaman's Rest but is now known as Number 99.

3. Peter Quinn is the senior officer on duty at the Spider's Web; Jim Kelly's senior partner at Area 51 is female.

4. Grace Hall and her partner are dressed as cyclists in tight, brightly colored Lycra tops and shorts—nothing plain-clothed about them!

5. The two coppers disguised as students—who are neither Luke Mason and his partner nor Vicky Wills and hers—aren't the ones watching (or looking?) for trouble at the Lotus Eater, formerly known as the Nelson's Head.

6. One pair of officers is working at the Plum and Peacock, wearing the distinctive pink uniforms of bar staff.

Senior officer	Junior officer

	Alec Brown	Diane Ellis	Jim Kelly	Kay Lovell	Vicky Wills	Area 51	Lotus Eater	Number 99	Plum and Peacock	Spider's Web	Bar staff	Bikers	Cyclists	Goths	Students
Brian Cook															
Grace Hall															
Luke Mason															
Peter Quinn															
Tina Stone															
Bar staff															
Bikers															
Cyclists															
Goths															
Students															
Area 51															
Lotus Eater															
Number 99															
Plum and Peacock															
Spider's Web															

Pub	Disguise

Critter's Creatures

Christine Critter owns and runs Critter's Creatures in Stonekeigh, and supplies pets and all the paraphernalia that go along with them to the animal lovers of the town. Along one side of her store, she has a display of modern gerbil cages, each with a sitting tenant. You may well think that all the cages are the same, having been bought in bulk from Netherlipp Plastic, but you'd be wrong, as each have an upper layer described in a different way. From the clues, can you name each plastic habitude's resident and the name given to the upper story?

Clues

1. Benedict is in residence in a house directly below and on the shelf below the dwelling that boasts, at least according to Christine, loft storage; his immediate right-hand neighbor is a girl gerbil.

2. Beatrice's abode is directly above and on the shelf above the lodgings whose upper floor has been named a garret; her immediate left-hand neighbor is a boy gerbil.

3. The gerbil whose accommodation comes with a penthouse has a boy gerbil for its left-hand neighbor and a girl gerbil for its right-hand neighbor.

4. Cleopatra's habitation is directly below and on the shelf below the property of another girl gerbil; Cleopatra is not the right-hand neighbor of Antony, who doesn't occupy gerbil apartment number 1, which has an upper floor gallery.

5. Kate's domicile on the top shelf has a playroom on its upper level.

6. The home with the attic bedroom is numbered one lower than the set of rooms occupied by Hamlet; Juliet's property has an odd number higher than 1.

7. The quarters whose upper level has been described as an observatory is on the left-hand end of one of the shelves.

Gerbils: Antony; Beatrice; Benedict; Cleopatra; Hamlet; Juliet; Kate; Romeo (male gerbils have male names, female ones have female names—Christine has checked)
Upper floors: attic bedroom; gallery; garret; loft storage; observatory; penthouse; playroom; studio space

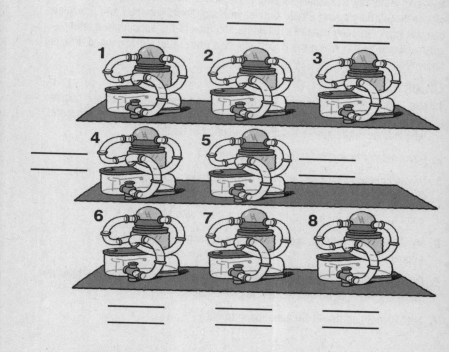

Starting tip: Begin by deciding which gerbil lives in home number 1.

Dysart Five

Dysart, Dysart, Dysart, Dysart, and Dysart is a firm of lawyers specializing in family law, and yesterday, five ladies seeking to begin divorce proceedings came to their offices on Storbury's King Street to meet with a different Dysart. From the clues, can you work out each woman's full name, the time of the appointment, and the old-fashioned way in which the Dysart she saw (they're an old-fashioned firm) is known?

Clues

1. Mrs. Jones' appointment was with Mr. Godfrey, the senior partner who shares his name with the man who founded the firm in 1874—and also with his son, who is known throughout the firm as "young Mr. Godfrey."

2. Olivia did not have the 10:00 a.m. appointment.

3. Ursula Lambert's husband Howard owns Storbury's luxury Regency Hotel—though she hopes to be able to force him to sell it!

4. Irene had the 11:00 a.m. appointment, but not with Mr. Monty.

5. Mr. Ronald met with his client at 10:30 a.m., sometime before Alice's appointment; Alice is not the soon-to-be-ex Mrs. Naylor.

6. Ellen met with Mr. Tobias, the youngest of the partners, thirty minutes after Mrs. Ward arrived right on time for her appointment.

7. Mrs. Clarke had the 11:30 a.m. appointment.

First name	Surname

	Clarke	Jones	Lambert	Naylor	Ward	10:00 a.m.	10:30 a.m.	11:00 a.m.	11:30 a.m.	12:00 noon	Mr. Godfrey	Mr. Monty	Mr. Ronald	Mr. Tobias	Young Mr. Godfrey
Alice															
Ellen															
Irene															
Olivia															
Ursula															
Mr. Godfrey										
Mr. Monty										
Mr. Ronald										
Mr. Tobias										
Young Mr. Godfrey										
10:00 a.m.					
10:30 a.m.					
11:00 a.m.					
11:30 a.m.					
12:00 noon					

Appointment	Dysart

Vacation Homes

The picture below shows the seaward end of Beach View Road in Sandhaven, and the six buildings shown are vacation homes—but they weren't originally, and even now we wouldn't recommend you rent any of them. From the clues, can you fill in each building's name, what it was originally, and why it's not ideal as a vacation home? (For the sake of clarity, the picture shows a straight road running east to west, and we are looking due west. Shacks 5, 3, and 1 are in a line east to west, as are shacks 6, 4, and 2.)

Clues

1. What is now Crow's Nest Cottage, but was built in 1854 as a cart shed for use by fishermen, is on the same side of Beach View Road as—but further east than—the vacation home with rotting floorboards on the first floor.

2. The former beer store—that's like a bar but less respectable—that is claimed to be haunted by the ghost of a sailor who died there back in 1809 is not known as Neptune's Nook.

3. Building 4 is the one with no heating of any kind—unless you take your own, of course!

4. The rat-infested Benbow Villa, which is not the building that began life as a beached, derelict sailing trawler, is numbered one higher than the vacation home that has a nasty reputation as the scene of five mysterious deaths since 1948.

5. The building that was originally a shanty built by unknown persons for unknown purposes is somewhere west of Fisherman's Cottage and somewhere east of Safe Harbor.

6. The former net storage, where nineteenth-century fishermen used to store their nets—oh, you knew that?—is building 5 on the plan; it doesn't have a leaking roof.

7. Building 3 is called Nelson House, though the great English Admiral had no connection with Sandhaven.

Names: Benbow Villa; Crow's Nest Cottage; Fisherman's Cottage; Nelson House; Neptune's Nook; Safe Harbor
Original uses: beer store; cart shed; net storage; shanty; stable; trawler
Drawbacks: death scene; haunted; leaking roof; no heating; rats; rotting floor

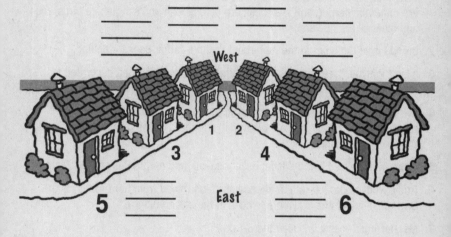

West

East

1 2

3 4

5 6

Starting tip: Work out the drawback of shack 5.

Water Nymphs

It's a bright, warm Saturday morning in Eastshire, and at the little town of Catley Bridge, on the River Wann, five young ladies have taken to the water in boats of various kinds. From the clues, can you work out each woman's full name, and the name and type of boat she's using?

Clues

1. Thanks to one of those coincidences on which we thrive, none of the girls have a surname drawn from the same category of items as the name of her boat—that is, if there was an Ann Lion and a boat called the *Tiger*, that wouldn't be her boat. (For the sake of clarity: claymore and cutlass are swords; flint and diamond are minerals; herring and swordfish are fish; pigeon and seagull are birds; rose and bluebell are flowers.)

2. Brenda is at the helm of the motorboat that her father uses for fishing.

3. It isn't Pauline Rose who's using the brightly painted rowboat, decorated in Mediterranean style with eyes on each side of the bow.

4. The *Bluebell* is a twin-hulled catamaran (there is, of course, no other type!) propelled normally by sail, although the young lady at the wheel today is using the auxiliary engine.

5. Laura is not Miss Flint, the local beauty queen, and her boat is not the *Diamond*.

6. Trudy, whose boat (or, rather, the one she's borrowed from her brother) is the *Swordfish*, is not Ms. Claymore, who is in the sailing dinghy.

7. Ms. Herring's vessel is called the *Seagull*.

First name	Surname

	Claymore	Flint	Herring	Pigeon	Rose	Bluebell	Cutlass	Diamond	Seagull	Swordfish	Catamaran	Inflatable	Motorboat	Rowboat	Sailing dinghy
Brenda															
Edna															
Laura															
Pauline															
Trudy															
Catamaran															
Inflatable															
Motorboat															
Rowboat															
Sailing dinghy															
Bluebell															
Cutlass															
Diamond															
Seagull															
Swordfish															

Boat	Type

In the Aria

The famous and prolific nineteenth-century composer Rigatoni wrote a multitude of symphonies and concertos, but only five operas. From the clues, can you work out in which year they each were composed, its title, the title of the most famous aria from each, and the character that sings it?

Clues

1. *Uno Cornetto* is not an aria from the 1841 opera *Cosi Fan Belt*, nor is it sung by the ditch digger Grandebusti.

2. *Rigomortis* was composed two years after the opera famous for the aria *Nissan Dormobile*, and two years before the one featuring the aria sung by blind pin-maker Fiatuno.

3. The character called Figarol, who always appears drunk, appears in the 1835 opera, which is not *Don Johnsoni*.

4. *I Monna Mobile* is an aria from the 1839 work, although most people recognize it as the music from the TV ads for diapers.

5. *Topo Gigio* is the most famous aria from *Carmenda*, and has been borrowed (and adapted in a way that shouldn't be repeated in polite company) by the fans of Netherlipp United.

6. The Grand Duke's finance minister Lancia Ferrari sings the beautiful *Pizza di Actione* in one of the operas.

Year	Opera

	Carmenda	Cosi Fan Belt	Don Johnsoni	La Travesti	Rigomortis	I Monna Mobile	Nissan Dormobile	Pizza di Actione	Topo Gigio	Uno Cornetto	Alf Aromeo	Fiatuno	Figarol	Grandebusti	Lancia Ferrari
1835															
1837															
1839															
1841															
1843															
Alf Aromeo															
Fiatuno															
Figarol															
Grandebusti															
Lancia Ferrari															
I Monna Mobile															
Nissan Dormobile															
Pizza di Actione															
Topo Gigio															
Uno Cornetto															

I've won a tenor on the scratchcards

Aria	Character

Sign In

Each row and column is to contain the digits 1-5. The given signs tell you if a digit in a cell is plus 1 (+) or minus 1 (-) the digit next to it. Signs between consecutive digits always work from left to right or top to bottom. Examples: 3 + 4 or 2 ALL occurences of consecutive digits have been marked by a sign.

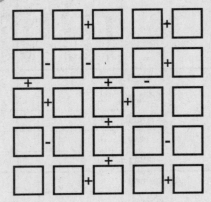

Sudoku

Complete this grid so that each column, each row, and each marked 3 X 3 square contains each of the numbers 1 to 9.

		7			4			
				2		3	7	
		1		5			4	
		2						5
7	4		3			2	1	
6				1				
5	6				9	7		3
		4		7				
		9	6	3				

Battleships

Do you remember the old game of battleships? These puzzles are based on that idea. Your task is to find the vessels in the diagram. Some parts of boats or sea squares have already been filled in, and a number next to a row or column refers to the number of occupied squares in that row or column. The boats may be positioned horizontally or vertically, but no two boats or parts of boats are in adjacent squares—horizontally, vertically, or diagonally.

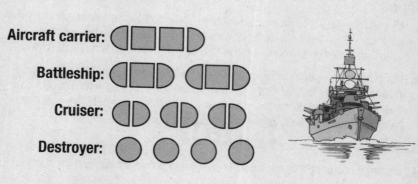

Aircraft carrier:

Battleship:

Cruiser:

Destroyer:

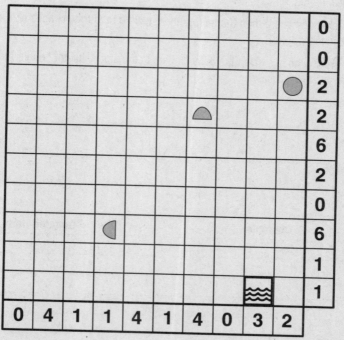

Sweet Charity

Stonekeigh's Hospice owns a small charity store on High Street where it makes a little money to help with running costs and purchases for the hospice. This morning, there are five customers visiting the store, each having brought in a donated item and each buying something to take home. From the clues, can you work out the identity of the items in each case and the price being paid for the purchased item?

Clues

1. Mrs. Barginn has brought in some blouses she's decided no longer suit her—the color isn't right, the collar isn't her style anymore and, just by the way, they seem not to fit her anymore—and is spending $1 less than Mrs. Pryce-Lowe.

2. The person who has brought in the toys is spending more than the person who has donated the coat, while the person who no longer has use for the CDs, since they split up with their partner who took the CD player, has paid twice as much for a lampshade as Mrs. Pryce-Lowe has spent.

3. Mr. Steele hasn't donated the CDs.

4. Mr. Sayle has bought himself a tie—yellow and purple stripes, just the thing for his new image.

5. The jacket cost more than the tie (but then, having read the previous clue, you'd have guessed that!).

6. The person who has given the baby clothes to the store has not bought the jacket or the $2 jigsaw.

Customer	Donated item

	Baby clothes	Blouses	Coat	CDs	Toys	Jacket	Jigsaw	Lampshade	Set of plates	Tie	$1	$2	$3	$4	$5
Mrs. Barginn															
Mrs. Pryce-Lowe															
Mr. Sayle															
Miss Snipp															
Mr. Steele															
$1															
$2															
$3															
$4															
$5															
Jacket															
Jigsaw															
Lampshade															
Set of plates															
Tie															

Purchased item	Cost

Courier Favor

The Farnwyde Industrial estate on the outskirts of Stonekeigh is home to a number of small businesses that include on their order books a number of overseas clients. Usually, these orders are needed quickly, so the firms use international couriers to collect packages from their premises and whisk them across the world. From the clues, can you work out the contents of the package collected by each courier firm, its weight, and its final destination?

Clues

1. The package being collected by Rapidispatch from Libresco Services contains important documents, while Speedway Couriers has collected a package that needs to go to Paris.

2. The package being consigned by Lectex Components via Interswift does not contain computer software and weighs less than the one being picked up from Transco Development by Speedway.

3. The books do not weigh exactly one pound and are not being sent to Frankfurt; the lightest package, bearing an address in Milan, does not contain books or computer software.

4. The package of fashion samples is one pound heavier than the package being sent to New York.

5. The package being picked up by Packageprompt from the reception desk of Multichem Systems weighs one and a half pounds.

6. The spare parts (digressors and hydraulic-maximaters for a Series 2 Mechamixer, if you're interested) form the heaviest consignment.

Courier	Contents

	Books	Computer software	Documents	Fashion samples	Spare parts	0.5 lb	1 lb	1.5 lb	2 lb	2.5 lb	Frankfurt	Madrid	Milan	New York	Paris
Fastline															
Interswift															
Packageprompt															
Rapidispatch															
Speedway															
Frankfurt															
Madrid															
Milan															
New York															
Paris															
0.5 lb															
1 lb															
1.5 lb															
2 lb															
2.5 lb															

PONY EXPRESS

PONY STANDARD DELIVERY

Weight	Destination

Muddelle's Muddle

Malcolm Muddelle, emeritus professor of Theoretical Hypotheses at the University of Netherlipp, frequently works on projects at home, wandering aimlessly through the house as he ponders. His long-suffering wife Marie frequently returns home from work to find the house strewn with bits of uneaten takeout meals her husband had ordered for lunch, and other objects abandoned in the strangest places. From the clues, can you say for each day last week—while the professor was working on his new theory of Indeterminable Specificity—what takeout Marie found and which other object she discovered where?

Clues

1. Marie discovered a half-eaten Chinese spring roll the day after she discovered something odd next to the bacon in the fridge and the day before she discovered a carton of milk in an unexpected place.

2. It wasn't on Thursday that Marie found a dirty coffee mug in the washing machine; on Wednesday, Professor Muddelle had a kebab for lunch—or, more accurately, half of it before putting it down and forgetting where it was.

3. On Monday, Marie discovered a strange object in the laundry basket; it wasn't the book, which wasn't discovered the day before Malcolm ate two or three mouthfuls of fish and fries before becoming distracted; the day he ate fish and fries was not the day that he left something peculiar in the pantry.

4. Marie found an old pair of rugby socks in an odd place later in the week than she found cold Indian curry in the house, which wasn't her husband's intended lunch the day after he left his laptop somewhere.

5. It wasn't to scattered remains of a pizza that Marie returned home on Friday.

Day	Takeout

	Chinese	Fish and fries	Indian curry	Kebab	Pizza	Book	Dirty mug	Laptop	Milk carton	Old socks	Linen closet	Fridge	Laundry basket	Pantry	Washing machine
Monday															
Tuesday															
Wednesday															
Thursday															
Friday															
Linen closet															
Fridge															
Laundry basket															
Pantry															
Washing machine															
Book															
Dirty mug															
Laptop															
Milk carton															
Old socks															

Object	Location

Great Non-Escape

In 2009, five employees of the multinational Penny Corporation defrauded the company of more than ten million dollars, then fled the country, thinking they had got away—but they were wrong. Over the next five years, all were tracked down in their exotic (mostly) new homes by officers from Interpol's Quite Serious Crimes Indeed Unit. From the clues, can you work out when and where each of the five embezzlers was arrested, and the name of the arresting officer?

Clues

1. The fraudster arrested in 2010, who wasn't the gang member captured in Southend (as I said, not all were exotic) was taken into custody by Inspector Heddlu; Don Caster was arrested in 2011, but not by Inspector Vigilis.

2. Ken Ilworth wasn't arrested in 2012; the 2013 arrest took place in Bangkok.

3. Inspector Vigilis tracked down his quarry before Mary Kirk was arrested.

4. Joan Town was taken into custody by Inspector Mouchard before the fraudster in Quito was arrested.

5. It was Inspector Bell, who was at Scotland Yard before he joined Interpol, who made the arrest in Maputo in Mozambique.

6. Peter Head was arrested in Nassau, in the Bahamas.

Criminal	Year

	2010	2011	2012	2013	2014	Bangkok	Maputo	Nassau	Quito	Southend	Inspector Bell	Inspector Heddlu	Inspector Jager	Inspector Mouchard	Inspector Vigilis
Don Caster															
Joan Town															
Ken Ilworth															
Mary Kirk															
Peter Head															
Inspector Bell															
Inspector Heddlu															
Inspector Jager															
Inspector Mouchard															
Inspector Vigilis															
Bangkok															
Maputo															
Nassau															
Quito															
Southend															

City	Detective

Address Unknown

Amongst their many great (and some unpleasant) innovations, one of the areas in which the Romans failed was to invent a precise system of street numbering. Instead of saying "Take this to XXIII Nero Street," they were reduced to using much more imprecise descriptions. So when our five friends, the Roman household slaves, were told to deliver an important message, finding the correct location proved to be a severe test of their limited powers of deduction. From the clues, can you find the location to which each slave was sent and the time he took to find it?

Clues

1. Cluelus was sent to deliver a message to an oak door; it wasn't Hopelus who was sent to an address in the cobblers' quarter.

2. Branelus, whose destination was near the olive grove, didn't take exactly two hours to find the house (although he did spend a few minutes sampling the olives).

3. The slave looking for the house behind the old wall beside the Tiber found it one hour faster than Euselus found the location he was looking for.

4. The address at the third milestone would have been OK if the direction of the three miles had been specified. As it was, it took one slave four hours of trudging to find the right place.

5. The search for the house with no garden took thirty minutes longer than the one that took place on the Caelian Hill.

6. Gormlus took an hour longer to find his address than the slave who was looking for the big villa.

There is a story from the US Postal Service about a letter addressed in this way. It was apparently decoded into a first name, surname, town, and state, and safely delivered. Can you match their decoding skills?

Slave	First part

	Behind the wall	House with no garden	Near the pear tree	The big villa	The oak door	At third milestone	Beside Tiber	In cobblers' quarter	On Caelian Hill	Near olive grove	1½ hours	2 hours	2½ hours	3½ hours	4 hours
Branelus															
Cluelus															
Euselus															
Gormlus															
Hopelus															
1½ hours															
2 hours															
2½ hours															
3½ hours															
4 hours															
At third milestone															
Beside Tiber															
In cobblers' quarter															
On Caelian Hill															
Near olive grove															

HILL
JOHN
MASS

Second part	Time

Imaginary Memoirs

Publishing house Starr and Carson publish a series of real-life memoirs of men who have lived exciting and violent lives, but they're not too fussy about the "real-life" part. From the clues, can you work out the names of the hack writers responsible for each of the latest five books in the series, the nom de plume they used, and the title and theme of the book?

Clues

1. George Gordon, whose book pretends to be the memoir of a champion cage fighter, is not the writer who has, using the pen name Guy Darrell, written *No Way Back*.

2. Austin Caxton's book—or, at least, the book with that name on the cover—is an account of his alleged life as a London gang boss and rival of the Kray brothers, but its title isn't *Bad Medicine*; Austin Saxton is really male, but the user of the pseudonym Marc le Roux is female.

3. Geoff Lester is actually Michael Warden, whose main output is articles on military history and famous battles for hobby magazines.

4. Edith Granger has penned (or perhaps that should be keyboarded) *Dark City*, which isn't the autobiography of a Mafia hitman based in 1990s New Jersey.

5. *Hellbender*, supposedly the story of a Spitfire pilot from one of the American volunteer "Eagle squadrons" who fought in the Battle of Britain, is not the book Belinda Waters wrote between turning out romantic short stories for a popular magazine.

Real name	Pen name

	Austin Caxton	Frank Vance	Geoff Lester	Guy Darrell	Marc le Roux	Bad Medicine	Dark City	Hellbender	No Way Back	The Seesaw	Cage fighter	Cold War spy	London gang boss	Mafia hitman	Spitfire pilot
Belinda Waters															
Edith Granger															
George Gordon															
John Dawkins															
Michael Warden															
Cage fighter															
Cold War spy															
London gang boss															
Mafia hitman															
Spitfire pilot															
Bad Medicine															
Dark City															
Hellbender															
No Way Back															
The Seesaw															

Title	Theme

West End Girls

Laura West started work in a high-end fashion store in New York just this morning, and on her first day was thrilled to serve five celebrities whom she recognized. From the clues, can you work out why each customer is famous, what she bought, and how much it cost her?

Clues

1. The baseball player's wife who bought silk underwear by the Italian designer Skimpi spent less than Donna Essex.

2. "$360, the swimsuit was!" Laura told her sister Katy. "Supposed to be an exclusive Sicilian design, but it didn't look any different from the one I got for $25!"

3. "It's no wonder that Verity Wild's become a top model," Laura said. "She's so thin, she was almost knocked over by a draft."

4. Selina Rolf spent eighty dollars more than the purchaser of the jacket by the Spanish designer Don Qui.

5. Alison Bolt bought a cotton sundress.

6. "Leah Maxim spent $400," Laura reported to Katy.

7. "That actress—you know, that skinny blonde one that's always on TV—spent $320!" Laura told her sister.

8. "The TV presenter had a look at the clogs by designer Klumper," said Katy. "But it was someone else who had the bad taste to actually buy the horrible things."

Name	Description

	Actress	Baseball player's wife	Model	Pop singer	TV presenter	Dress	Jacket	Shoes	Swimsuit	Underclothes	$280	$320	$360	$400	$440
Alison Bolt															
Donna Essex															
Leah Maxim,															
Selina Rolf															
Verity Wild															
$280															
$320															
$360															
$400															
$440															
Dress															
Jacket															
Shoes															
Swimsuit															
Underclothes															

Do you have this in a smaller price?

Item bought	Amount spent

Identifying the Unidentified

The Randolph Hotel in Thetford, Massachusetts, is hosting a weekend convention for people interested in Unidentified Flying Objects, which will include Saturday afternoon workshops conducted by five experts of different kinds. From the clues, can you work out each speaker's full name, what qualifies them to talk about UFOs, and in which room they'll be presenting their workshops?

Clues

1. Toby, who is a movie actor and played an alien pilot in the movie *Flying Saucer Invasion*, will be displaying his expertise in a conference room numbered three higher than that where Mr. Munro's workshop will take place.

2. Mr. La Rue's assigned room is numbered one above Ross's, which isn't room 2.

3. Conference Room 1 has been assigned to Brad, who is not the journalist who writes the *UFO Notes* column for the *American Enquirer* magazine.

4. Floyd Conrad won't be presenting his workshop in Conference Room 2.

5. Room 3 is being used by the man who has, apparently, had regular contact with aliens from the distant planet Raisa and has been taken for a trip in one of their "esirpretne," or starships.

6. Mr. Wasson is the science fiction writer responsible for the successful *UFO Hunter* series.

First name	Surname

	Brady	Conrad	La Rue	Munro	Wasson	Movie actor	Journalist	Science fiction writer	UFO contactee	UFO researcher	1	2	3	4	7
Brad															
Floyd															
Jonah															
Ross															
Toby															
1															
2															
3															
4															
7															
Movie actor					
Journalist					
Science fiction writer					
UFO contactee					
UFO researcher					

The four-legged ones must be in charge. Wherever they go the two-legged ones run along behind.

Qualification	Room

Battleships

Do you remember the old game of battleships? These puzzles are based on that idea. Your task is to find the vessels in the diagram. Some parts of boats or sea squares have already been filled in, and a number next to a row or column refers to the number of occupied squares in that row or column. The boats may be positioned horizontally or vertically, but no two boats or parts of boats are in adjacent squares—horizontally, vertically, or diagonally.

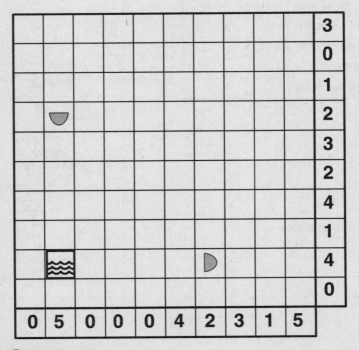

Aircraft carrier:

Battleship:

Cruiser:

Destroyer:

Sign In

Each row and column is to contain the digits 1-5. The given signs tell you if a digit in a cell is plus 1 (+) or minus 1 (-) the digit next to it. Signs between consecutive digits always work from left to right or top to bottom.

Examples: $\boxed{3}$ + $\boxed{4}$ or $\boxed{2}$
 $\genfrac{}{}{0pt}{}{-}{\boxed{1}}$

ALL occurences of consecutive digits have been marked by a sign.

Sudoku

Complete this grid so that each column, each row, and each marked 3 X 3 square contains each of the numbers 1 to 9.

Vacation Reading

Jakki Redburn is a keen reader with a wide range of interests, and intends to spend her week vacation in Boston reading in the hotel sunroom (her interests don't include geography), so she's taking six books with her, as shown below. From the clues, can you fill in the title of each volume, its author, and what sort of book it is?

Clues

1. Tricia Lane's *Shadows of Blood* is lower in Jakki's pile of books than the volume of crime fiction, and both of them are lower than the Carol Kaine.

2. The authors of the true crime book and *Grand Tour* are of different sexes; the latter tome is higher in the pile than the former, and both are higher than Steven Bauer's book.

3. Book 4 in the pile is about US wildlife.

4. The book by Victoria Ray is lower in the pile than *The Road* but higher than the science fiction volume.

5. The James Portman book is a history, detailing the life and death of King Richard III.

6. The book on the top of the stack is *Warriors*, which may sound like fantasy fiction but isn't; the book on the bottom is the work of a male author.

7. *Private Lives*—not the Noel Coward one!—is two places above *Treasure*.

Titles: *Grand Tour*; *Private Lives*; *Shadows of Blood*; *The Road*; *Treasure*; *Warriors*
Authors: Bernard Joyner; Carol Kaine; James Portman; Steven Bauer; Tricia Lane; Victoria Ray
Genres: crime fiction; fantasy fiction; history; science fiction; true crime; wildlife

1 _____

2 _____

3 _____

4 _____

5 _____

6 _____

Starting tip: Work out the genre of the book on the top of the pile.

Paragon in Europe

The Paragon, the vigilante/criminal created by Charles Litoris for *Detective Adventure* magazine in the 1920s, enjoyed adventures across most of the world, but this problem is concerned just with Europe. From the clues, can you work out in which city each of the listed stories (the titles of which all begin *The Paragon and the . . .*) is set, the crime involved, and the name of the villain or villainess?

Clues

1. In Budapest, the Paragon, whose real name was Peter Galahad, was up against a very dangerous man indeed.

2. The blonde and beautiful Helen Marcus claimed to be a wealthy tourist, but actually she was a burglar who tried to frame Peter Galahad for a crime she had committed.

3. The story that pits the Paragon against a ruthless smuggling gang in Danzig (known today as Gdansk) is not *The Paragon and the Ghostly Galleon* and doesn't involve criminal mastermind Dr. Stella Piper.

4. Chick Lumsky, the New York gangster the Paragon dealt with in Oporto, had nothing to do with the kidnappings in *The Paragon and the Red Roadhouse*.

5. Neither *The Paragon and the Poisoned Patriot*, in which Peter Galahad hunts down the unfrocked clergyman Zebedee Wyatt, nor *The Paragon and the Diamond Dragon*, set in Antwerp, are concerned with either smuggling or murder.

Title	City

	Antwerp	Budapest	Corunna	Danzig	Oporto	Burglary	Fraud	Kidnapping	Murder	Smuggling	Chick Lumsky	Enzo Dragoti	Helen Marcus	Stella Piper	Zebedee Wyatt
The Paragon and the …															
…*Angry Archer*															
…*Diamond Dragon*															
…*Ghostly Galleon*															
…*Poisoned Patriot*															
…*Red Roadhouse*															
Chick Lumsky															
Enzo Dragoti															
Helen Marcus															
Stella Piper															
Zebedee Wyatt															
Burglary															
Fraud															
Kidnapping															
Murder															
Smuggling															

Crime	Villain

Music and Words

Composer Sandy Banks Spyder and lyricist Ken Grane wrote several successful musicals together before deciding to go their own ways. Last year, Sandy announced five new projects, none of which has yet come to fruition and for each of which he has collaborated with a different wordsmith. From the clues, can you work out in which month each new show was announced, the name of its lyricist, its title, and its theme?

Clues

1. The musical about werewolves, tentatively titled *Werewolves*, was the next announced after the collaboration with lyricist and comedian Piers Send.

2. In June, Sandy told the press that he had agreed to work on a new show with American singer-songwriter Berry Likely.

3. *Celebration* was announced later in the year than *Next Day*.

4. *The Fountain*, with lyrics by former pop singer Jack Hammer, had no connection at all with pool; it was announced next before the show based on events during the Great Depression.

5. In April, Sandy announced a project based on the story of Dr. Hawley Harvey Crippen, representing the medico as a tragic romantic hero, and went on to say that a leading African-American singer had agreed to take the role.

6. Oscar-winning lyricist Roy De France was named as Sandy's partner on the musical based on the disastrous Battle of Narvik in 1940; this announcement was made earlier than the one about *Early to Bed*, which was issued either immediately before or immediately after the one about the collaboration with Aussie songwriter Mack Iavelli.

Month	Lyricist

	Berry Likely	Jack Hammer	Mack Iavelli	Piers Send	Roy De France	Celebration	Early to Bed	Next Day	The Fountain	Werewolves	Battle of Narvik	Dr. Crippen	Great Depression	Pool	Werewolves
January															
April															
June															
September															
December															
Battle of Narvik															
Dr. Crippen															
Great Depression															
Pool															
Werewolves															
Celebration															
Early to Bed															
Next Day															
The Fountain															
Werewolves															

Title	Theme

Old-Time Horrors

Last night, Albion-TV presented a documentary called *Old-Time Horrors*, about some classic horror movies from the early years of sound movie theater, featuring interviews (recorded ones, from the archives, of course—all the gentlemen died before 1990) with members of the production teams. From the clues, can you identify each man, his cinematic role, and the title and date of his most famous movie?

Clues

1. *The Crawling Horror* was released in 1929, just two years after the first sound movie, *The Jazz Singer*.

2. One of the taped interviews was with the producer of the original version of *The Faceless Killer* (since remade three times, most recently in 2012), which came out the year before the movie on which Wilbur Francke worked.

3. Benedict De Forest worked on *House of the Hell Maiden* (they don't write titles like that anymore), which was released the year before the movie on which one of the five interviewees was responsible for the groundbreaking stop-motion animation.

4. Freeman McMichael was a costume designer and was once nominated for an Oscar—though not for the horror movie he talked about.

5. One of the five men had been the chief makeup artist on the movie that came out in 1932.

6. Kurt Vorster worked on the 1933 movie, but not as a scriptwriter; he had no connection with the Hollywood classic *Food for the Ghoul Woman*.

Names	Role

	Costume designer	Makeup artist	Producer	Scriptwriter	Stop-motion animator	Day of the Death Bat	Food for the Ghoul Woman	House of the Hell Maiden	The Crawling Horror	The Faceless Killer	1929	1930	1931	1932	1933
Benedict De Forest															
Freeman McMichael															
Kurt Vorster															
Randall Bancroft															
Wilbur Francke															
1929															
1930															
1931															
1932															
1933															
Day of the Death Bat															
Food for the Ghoul Woman															
House of the Hell Maiden															
The Crawling Horror															
The Faceless Killer															

Title	Date

Trail Drive

In the year 1872, the owners of four small ranches located near the town of Eagle Ridge, Texas, decided to combine their herds for a trail drive to Kansas. From the clues given, can you fill in on the map below the brand used by each ranch, the number of cows it contributed to the drive, and the name of the ranch's owner?

Clues

1. The Box M ranch provided more cattle to the trail herd than the spread immediately to its west.

2. Ranch D sent 650 longhorn cows to Kansas with the combined herd.

3. Jack Nelson's ranch was next west from the one that sent 850 cattle with the herd.

4. Dan Addison, owner of the Rocking A, who acted as trail boss, sent one hundred more longhorns on the drive than the Lazy K, which was either next east or next west from his spread; the owner of the Lazy K wasn't Mack McLean.

5. Slim Leamas's ranch contributed more cattle to the drive than the Flying H.

Ranches: Box M; Flying H; Lazy K; Rocking A
Heads of cattle: 650; 750; 850; 950
Ranch owners: Dan Addison; Jack Nelson; Mack McLean; Slim Leamas

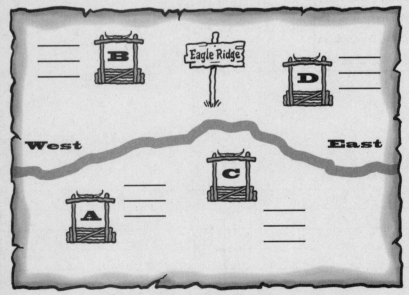

Starting tip: Work out who owns ranch D.

Circuit Training

Spandeco Transitors, Ltd., has released a new computer circuit board, the Flux Deconcentrator, which for anyone in the know is a major leap forward in one-dimensional digression approval analysis, and for the rest of us is an electronic item that takes flux and deconcentrates it. From the clues and the diagram, can you name each of its component parts?

Clues

1. The Loss Collector has one more direct connection to another component than the Antisender.

2. Component 3 is the Preregulator and is directly connected to both the Expeller and the Disaccumulator.

3. The Upsweller, one of the three components on the bottom level of the board, has one fewer direct connection than does the Expeller.

4. The Redischarger, which is an even-numbered component, is not directly connected to the Upsweller; the Undirector doesn't have the largest number of direct connections.

Components: Antisender; Disaccumulator; Expeller; Loss Collector; Preregulator; Redischarger; Undirector; Upsweller

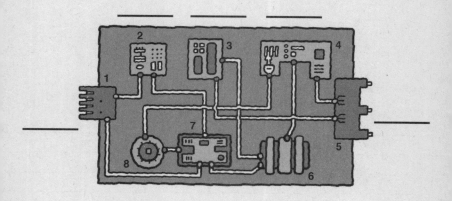

Starting tip: Begin by positioning the Expeller.

Bloop Bloop

Movie Bloopers is a website that lists bloopers (or errors) in movies, and among the latest entries are five related to the new thriller *Tumbler*. From the clues, can you work out the name of the character featured in each blooper, what's happening, where it's happening, and what the error is?

Clues

1. Dr. Adam Baxter's blooper occurs in the scene where Agent Kelly of the CIA is shot; Pete Ramsey, who is the hero Sean Marshall's sidekick, appears in the blooper at police headquarters; the scene where one female character meets Sean shows her with a changing hairstyle—up in some shots, down in others.

2. Russian spy Lara Mazova, who is not present when the bomb is defused, shares one shot with a movie camera that shouldn't be visible.

3. The German thug Teller isn't the character who has a scene with a replenishing glass of beer—half-empty in some shots, full in others.

4. The person being pursued by Sean in the Chinatown sequence is male—and a particularly large and ugly specimen at that, though the actor who plays him has a nice smile.

5. It's in the airport lounge that one of the characters has a vanishing jacket, worn in the close-ups but not in the long shots.

6. The scene in which one character has breakfast with Sean doesn't take place in the coffee shop.

Character	Action

	Breakfast with Sean	Chase scene	Defusing bomb	Kelly shot	Meeting with Sean	Airport lounge	Coffee shop	Chinatown	Joe's Diner	Police HQ	Camera in shot	Changing hairstyle	Color-changing shirt	Replenishing beer	Vanishing jacket
Dr. Adam Baxter															
Gail Hadley																
Lara Mazova																
Pete Ramsey																
Teller																
Camera in shot																
Changing hairstyle																
Color-changing shirt																
Replenishing beer																
Vanishing jacket																
Airport lounge																
Coffee shop																
Chinatown																
Joe's Diner																
Police HQ																

Location	Blooper

To All in Tents

Guy Roap runs a small campsite in the depths of rural Eastshire, and one of the small fields is set aside for those who book early and want to avoid the marshy ground if or, more likely when, it rains. The plan below shows the site last Saturday; from the clues, can you work out the name of the family occupying each tent, their hometown, and how many nights they were booked to stay?

Clues

1. The family from Bellford had pitched their tent next left, from our point of view, to that of the people booked for 12 nights.

2. As we look at the picture, the McClure family's tent was further left than both the one belonging to the family from Domecaster and the one booked for a 9-night stay.

3. The family in tent 3 had booked a shorter stay than the Fawcetts but a longer one than the people from Ridgewood.

4. The Doughty family's tent was on a higher-numbered pitch than that occupied by the people from Framebury, and was booked for a stay three nights longer.

5. The Wilkins family had booked a stay three nights longer than the people in tent 4.

Families: Doughty; Fawcett; McClure; Wilkins
Hometowns: Bellford; Domecaster; Framebury; Ridgewood
Nights booked: 6 nights; 9 nights; 12 nights; 14 nights

Starting tip: Find the hometown of the family who has booked for 12 nights.

USA TODAY

Domino Search

A standard set of dominoes has been laid out, using numbers instead of dots for clarity. Using a sharp pencil and a keen brain, can you draw in the lines to show where each domino has been placed? You may find the check grid useful— crossing off each domino as you find it.

6	0	2	4	4	0	2	4
5	5	1	4	3	6	5	4
6	1	1	0	0	6	3	5
2	6	2	2	1	5	4	5
3	5	6	4	5	0	2	0
6	1	2	0	2	1	6	4
3	1	3	3	3	3	0	1

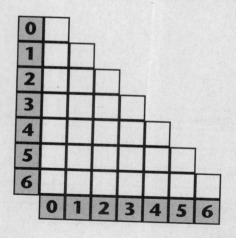

Careering Along

Five members of the Coral Beach Golf and Country Club were sitting in the bar one wet Sunday afternoon while the greenkeepers tried desperately to make the course playable, and were reminiscing about their start in business. Each had been taken on as a callow youth fresh from school by a small local firm in a different line of business, each bearing the name of its two principal partners, and had risen to the level of partner. From the clues, can you work out the full title and description of the firm each man joined?

Clues

1. Both the firm Walter worked for and the insurance brokers had names in which the initial letter of the second partner's name came earlier in the alphabet than that of the first partner.

2. Harold worked for the firm where one of the partners was Mr. Devonish; they were not in the business of giving investment advice.

3. Mr. Rumford was one of John's original employers, and it was he who John eventually eased aside to become Managing Director.

4. One firm's business name was Duncan and Jackson; their employee was not Arthur.

5. Mr. Stokes was a qualified lawyer; his business partner was not Mr. Archer.

6. Mr. Tomkins was a partner in the real estate agents' business, but Mr. Bates was not.

Employee	First partner

	Archer and...	Bellamy and...	Duncan and...	Rumford and...	Tomkins and...	Bates	Devonish	Jackson	Russell	Stokes	Accountants	Real estate agents	Insurance brokers	Investment advisers	Lawyers
Arthur															
Harold															
John															
Norman															
Walter															
Accountants															
Real estate agents															
Insurance brokers															
Investment advisers															
Lawyers															
Bates															
Devonish															
Jackson															
Russell															
Stokes															

Second partner	Business

Surfing

Internet shopping late at night is never a good idea, and tonight these five "surfers" have fallen for the exuberant marketing found on many a website and have parted with their hard-earned cash. From the clues, can you say what each person has just bought, the marketing phrase on the page that caught their eye, and the price they have paid?

Clues

1. Boris Brass was tempted enough to buy the wine prop—a small stand to hold a wine bottle upright and stop it from toppling over.

2. The sock presser—for those for whom ironing socks is a must—is on sale for $6.99; it didn't tempt Delia Dosh, who bought one last month!

3. One sale page read "The fabulous knee pillow—No more uncomfortable knees— Only a few left!"

4. The kettle lock—a device to stop your cat from switching on the kettle—is more expensive than the item advertised with the phrase "Don't miss out!"

5. One customer was tempted by the "Last chance to buy—only $5.99" blurb.

6. Bruce Bucks spent $1 more than the customer who was persuaded to buy the so-called "Limited offer"—limited, that is, to those who buy it.

Shopper	Item

	Kettle lock	Knee pillow	Sock presser	Wine prop	Don't miss out	Last chance	Limited offer	Only a few left	$4.99	$5.99	$6.99	$7.99
Boris Brass												
Bridget Bread												
Bruce Bucks												
Delia Dosh												
$4.99												
$5.99												
$6.99												
$7.99												
Don't miss out												
Last chance												
Limited offer												
Only a few left												

Splash	Price

You Essay

Last week, Anita Lushon, the organizer of the creative writing evening class at Netherlipp College, set her pupils the task of writing a 1000-word piece with, as she put it, "you" in the title. She was hoping for essays including some personal insight into her class, but either out of misunderstanding or an attempt to prove how creative they can be, her class members veered a little off course. From the clues, can you say which pupil produced which of these short stories, its setting, and the event it chronicled?

Clues

1. Perhaps not surprisingly, *Bless Shoes* involves a blizzard; *After U* was set on a university campus in the 1960s but wasn't penned by Sophie Scribel.

2. Jeremy Jotter's 1000 words was entitled *Thank Hugh*.

3. Norman Noat's short, riveting story was set in the foyer of a famous art gallery.

4. The thousand-word story that told of a riot in a casino in Monte Carlo was not entitled *Good for Ewe*.

5. Deirdre's creative effort didn't involve a fire, and the fire wasn't the event that sparked up the story in an eighteenth-century market.

Class member	Title

	After U	Bless Shoes	Good for Ewe	Thank Hugh	Art gallery	Casino	Market	University	Blizzard	Concert	Fire	Riot
Deirdre Dashov												
Jeremy Jotter												
Norman Noat												
Sophie Scribel												
Blizzard												
Concert												
Fire												
Riot												
Art gallery												
Casino												
Market												
University												

Location	Event

Ars Pro Gloria Artis

The art competition run by the Keighshire Daubers Art Society is a regular summer fixture, and the five artists featured here are delighted to have made it into the top ten as decided by the judging panel. That there were only ten entries in total apparently disheartened them not one bit. From the clues, can you say in what medium each artist has produced their work, its main (and indeed only) color, and the position it achieved in the competition?

Clues

1. Delia Dye's canvas, simply a solid red color entitled *Ketchup Slick,* is not the piece painted with acrylic paint that placed sixth in the contest.

2. The canvas that comprised a solid green color and was called *Lawn in Soft Focus* placed ninth.

3. Horace Hue's entry finished one place behind the solid white canvas called *Outlook of a Bear (Polar)*, and one place ahead of the oil painting.

4. William Wash's work in pastels didn't place seventh.

5. Sheryl Shade's entry to the competition finished higher than the solid black canvas entitled *Panther at Night*, which itself had a better placing than the entry in crayon.

6. The solid pink watercolor canvas makes no sense until you read the title, *Flamingo—A Close-Up*, and not much even then.

Artist	Medium

	Acrylic paint	Crayon	Oil paint	Pastel	Watercolors	Black	Green	Pink	Red	White	6th	7th	8th	9th	10th
Delia Dye															
Horace Hue															
Sheryl Shade															
Theresa Tint															
William Wash															
6th															
7th															
8th															
9th															
10th															
Black															
Green															
Pink															
Red															
White															

Color	Position

Crazy Games

Crazy golf (aka miniature golf) has been with us for over a hundred years, so five businesses along the coast have decided that, following that reasonably successful trial period, it's time to branch out. From the clues, can you work out the name of the business in each coastal location, the crazy sport they have invented, and the "signature" obstacle they have included to crazy-up their game?

Clues

1. Crazy billiards, which isn't played at either of the two diners, includes a large King Kong model with flailing arms and swirling biplanes.

2. Patrons at the Pirate's Parrot bar can enjoy a game of crazy bocce on AstroTurf in the parking lot; Sandy Cove is not the location of the crazy chessboard and pieces.

3. The game at the ice cream parlor involves negotiating a waterwheel, which spins ever faster as the game progresses.

4. The Beach Diner at Shingle Head isn't the place that has a large model of a lighthouse, which isn't the obstacle in the game of crazy darts.

5. Visitors to Pebble Bay, which isn't the location of the Promenade Diner, can collect mallets and balls and crash helmets and play a game of crazy croquet.

6. The owners of the establishment at Coral Dunes have manufactured a huge dragon with waving tail and nostrils that light up as an obstacle in the crazy ball game.

Location	Business

	Beach diner	Ice cream parlor	Pirate's Parrot bar	Promenade diner	Sunken Wreck bar	Crazy billiards	Crazy bocce	Crazy chess	Crazy croquet	Crazy darts	Dragon	King Kong	Lighthouse	Waterwheel	Windmill
Coral Dunes															
Pebble Bay															
Rock Banks															
Sandy Cove															
Shingle Head															
Dragon															
King Kong															
Lighthouse															
Waterwheel															
Windmill															
Crazy billiards															
Crazy bocce															
Crazy chess															
Crazy croquet															
Crazy darts															

How crazy golf began

Crazy sport	Obstacle

Disaster TV

Some form of calamity—personal or collective—is the stock-in-trade of the soap opera writer, and this week's Netherlipp TV offerings have included five prime examples. From the clues, can you discover the crisis affecting each character, the soap in which they appear, and the evening on which the episode was broadcast?

Clues

1. Annie Moane is a character in *Brook Street*, which is broadcast the evening before the ongoing story of *Jubilee Square*.

2. Dan Hartid found out that his business was failing the evening before the broadcast of the latest episode of *Home Affairs*, which does not feature Damon Gloom, who doesn't appear on the screen on Tuesday evenings.

3. Thursday's soap featured a no-hope character with a drinking problem whose surname is longer than that of the person whose marriage was breaking up.

4. The upsetting tale of a secret love affair becoming not so secret anymore in the never-ending story of *Farmside* was broadcast sometime after Tuesday.

5. The character Taylor Woe wasn't the one who was losing their job.

6. *Eastdale* is broadcast by Netherlipp TV on Wednesdays at 7:05 p.m.

Evening	Soap

	Brook Street	Eastdale	Farmside	Home Affairs	Jubilee Square	Damon Gloom	Dan Hartid	Ed Hunglow	Annie Moane	Taylor Woe	Affair discovered	Business failing	Drinking problem	Lost job	Marriage failing
Monday															
Tuesday															
Wednesday															
Thursday															
Friday															
Affair discovered															
Business failing															
Drinking problem															
Lost job															
Marriage failing															
Damon Gloom															
Dan Hartid															
Ed Hunglow															
Annie Moane															
Taylor Woe															

Character	Crisis

Women's Writes

The Housewives Writing Circle is an organization for, as you might expect, housewives with aspirations to write. They recently ran a competition on their website for short stories, expecting the entries to be mainly romances or childhood memories—but they were wrong. From the clues, can you work out the details of the five prize winners—their names and the titles and genres of their stories?

Clues

1. Selina Stokes, a mother of two from the town of Shalestoke, entitled her story *Shadow of Doubt*.

2. The science fiction story by New Hampshire housewife Peggy O'Dwyer won her the prize immediately above that awarded to the story called *City Lights*.

3. *Green Shoes*, which won second prize, is not the fantasy story featuring elves, dragons, and a mysterious warrior-maiden with a magic sword.

4. The war story, *A Bargain,* deals with the battle of El Alamein in 1942.

5. The third-placed crime story was not the work of Helena Flower.

6. Laura Bell's story won first prize.

7. The story by Emily Blades from California won an even-numbered prize.

Prize	Writer

USA TODAY

	Emily Blades	Helena Flower	Laura Bell	Peggy O'Dwyer	Selina Stokes	A Bargain	City Lights	Green Shoes	Shadow of Doubt	Sun Rise	Crime	Fantasy	Science fiction	Vampire	War
First															
Second															
Third															
Fourth															
Fifth															
Crime															
Fantasy															
Science fiction															
Vampire															
War															
A Bargain															
City Lights															
Green Shoes															
Shadow of Doubt															
Sun Rise															

Dear Publisher,
I am in receipt of
your rejection letter.
Sadly it is not up to
the standard I require

Title	Genre

On Your Medal

With the completion of the events in the annual All-Countryside Games, the medal ceremony can begin. The eight engraved gold medals to be awarded are arranged on a presentation frame from where guest of honor Marston Bagshot will pluck them to dangle around the necks of this year's winners. From the clues, can you say for which event each of the numbered medals is to be awarded and to whom?

Clues

1. The medal for Top Plowman, awarded to the competitor who made the best cheese and pickle-based lunch and which is in position 8, will not be awarded to Peter Pessant; Peter, who hasn't won the gold medal for Archery (a quiz competition based on the events of a fictional farming community in Ambridge) will receive a medal from the same horizontal row as the one to be given to the winner of Boxing after they proved their packing technique to be top of the pile.

2. Medal number 1 will be hung around the neck of a female winner, as will that for the winner of the 100m Butterfly, a colorful-insect netting competition.

3. Cow Wrestling, in which the bravest and strongest try their luck at wrestling one of Farmer Groam's best milkers, has been won in a surprise result by Rosebud the cow; her medal, which isn't number 6, is directly below that of the one to be awarded to Horace Hick.

4. Theresa Tyke's medal is diagonally below the one to be awarded to the winner of Rowing, who proved to be the best, loudest, and most obstreperous arguer.

5. Stan Swain's name has been engraved on medal number 2.

6. The medal that Yasmin Yoakel will take home is shown immediately to the left of the gold medal for the 4x4 Relay, in which competitors have to replace an electrical relay in a 4x4 truck, which has been won by a woman.

Events: Archery; Boxing; Cow Wrestling; 4x4 Relay; 100m Butterfly; Rowing; Top Plowman; Welly Throw
Winners: Horace Hick; Peter Pessant; Ricky Rube; Rosebud; Stan Swain; Sylvia Serff; Theresa Tyke; Yasmin Yoakel

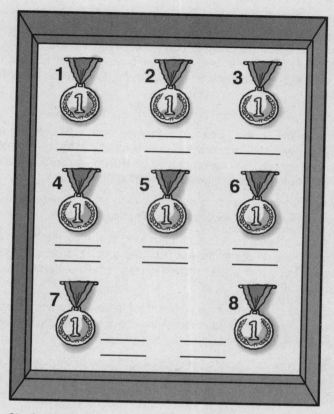

Starting tip: Begin by determining which medal is for Cow Wrestling.

Cocktails and Crimes

For once, those ladies of a certain age who meet occasionally for lunch weren't lunching together. Last Friday, they met at New York's Dominion Hotel for just long enough to sip a cocktail and reminisce briefly about their criminal pasts—or, at least, occasions when they had been accused of crimes. From the clues, can you work out what each woman drank, where she "committed" a crime, and what that crime was?

Clues

1. Neither Sally Van Der Waal, who admitted she had once, quite justifiably, been accused of being drunk and disorderly, nor her friend who had been convicted—again, quite justifiably—of espionage, was the woman who drank a Moscow Mule while talking about an offense committed in Cairo.

2. Judith McVitie told her friends of an amusing experience in Shanghai back in the 1970s—an experience that wasn't all that amusing at the time.

3. Diana Flambard, who drank an Earthquake cocktail, was not the woman who fell afoul of the police in Oporto; nor was Diana the woman charged at Warsaw's airport with trying to smuggle forbidden literature into Poland, back in the bad old days.

4. Patricia Paolucci was neither the drinker of the Bellini nor the woman who had once been charged with assault, though the charge was later dropped because of the influence of an old friend.

5. The woman once accused of burglary but acquitted on an obscure point of local law (plus the fact that she had only been recovering her own property from a friend's home) drank a Zombie.

Name	Cocktail

	Bellini	Earthquake	Gimlet	Moscow Mule	Zombie	Cairo	Leipzig	Oporto	Shanghai	Warsaw	Assault	Burglary	Drunk and disorderly	Espionage	Smuggling
Colette Barwick															
Diana Flambard															
Judith McVitie															
Patricia Paolucci															
Sally Van Der Waal															
Assault															
Burglary															
Drunk and disorderly															
Espionage															
Smuggling															
Cairo															
Leipzig															
Oporto															
Shanghai															
Warsaw															

City	Crime

Lesson Notes

Making Music, Ltd., is an agency based in Upper Crispin that offers music lessons across Baltimore to anyone with the urge to learn, the instrument to play, and the $50-a-lesson fee. The agency employs a number of teachers who visit homes and schools, trying to turn tinklers and tooters into maestros. Today, five of these teachers are each visiting different schools teaching different instruments. From the clues, can you discover when and where each teacher has his or her next lesson, and the instrument each teaches?

Clues

1. Mrs. Gifford is not the teacher giving the trumpet lesson at 11 o'clock; her next lesson is later than the one due to take place at King John School.

2. Mr. Adley is not teaching at King John School today.

3. Miss Morgan's next lesson is after midday, but not at St. Edward's School.

4. The piano teacher is due at Round Hill School more than 70 minutes before Mr. Manning starts his next lesson at Northfield School.

5. The clarinet lesson is not due to take place at Bishop Sutton School.

6. Mr. Griffiths teaches violin.

Time	Teacher

	Mr. Adley	Mrs. Gifford	Mr. Griffiths	Mr. Manning	Miss Morgan	Bishop Sutton	King John	Northfield	Round Hill	St. Edward's	Cello	Clarinet	Piano	Trumpet	Violin
10:00 a.m.															
11:00 a.m.															
11:20 a.m.															
12:30 p.m.															
12:50 p.m.															
Cello															
Clarinet															
Piano															
Trumpet															
Violin															
Bishop Sutton															
King John															
Northfield															
Round Hill															
St. Edward's															

MAKING MUSIC
MUSIC LESSONS

BACK IN 5 MINUETS

School	Instrument

First Things First

Five male executives for Hay, Wyre, and Company have busy working weeks minutely organized by their personal assistants. But when left off the leash on the weekend, their social lives tend to fall apart, leaving the first thing on each PA's list of things to do on Monday morning as "Send apologies for the weekend." From the clues, can you work out the name of the organized lady who steers each executive through the week, what he forgot last weekend, and what the PA sent as an immediate apology before greater reparations could be organized later?

Clues

1. "I'm afraid I forgot my wedding anniversary," said one executive. "I imagined you would, so I've already sent three dozen red roses," replied his PA.

2. Mr. Termoyle forgot to turn up for a charity golf day on Saturday.

3. "Miss Frydeigh," began one executive, "it was my mother's birthday on Saturday. Send her something to apologize for me, would you?"

4. "I think a bottle of malt whiskey will do to start with," said Miss Mundy, after her boss explained what he had forgotten to do; he isn't Mr. Mayhemme, who wasn't the executive who forgot to go to his mother-in-law's house for Sunday lunch.

5. Without Miss Chewsday, Mr. Kayos's working life would be . . . well, you know; she didn't send the large box of chocolates.

6. Neither Mr. Avock nor Mr. DeSarray forgot to turn up for a meal. Mr. DeSarray's PA sent a large bouquet of cheerful sunflowers; Mr. Avock's PA, who isn't Miss Wensdee, also chose a floral apology.

Executive	PA

	Miss Chewsday	Miss Frydeigh	Miss Mundy	Miss Thirsdie	Miss Wensdee	Anniversary	Birthday	Golf game	Saturday dinner	Sunday lunch	Chocolates	Chrysanthemums	Malt whiskey	Red roses	Sunflowers
Mr. Avock															
Mr. DeSarray															
Mr. Kayos															
Mr. Mayhemme															
Mr. Termoyle															
Chocolates															
Chrysanthemums															
Malt whiskey															
Red roses															
Sunflowers															
Anniversary															
Birthday															
Golf game															
Saturday dinner															
Sunday lunch															

Forgot	Sent

Gone to Market

Vic Toryan has a small antiques store in Storbury and is always looking out for items at swap meets to mark up and stock his shelves. At the swap meet in Storbury's People's Park last weekend, he found six containers for knock-down prices that he thought he'd be able to knock back up again. From the clues, can you fill in the name of each of the stall-holders Vic bought from, and both the country of origin and the description of the container?

Clues

1. Vic found the pewter jug at Errol's stall, which was numbered next lower than the stall with the item of Italian origin, and immediately thought of the proprietor of the Rusty Bucket, who likes to have these sorts of things on the shelf behind his bar.

2. The large earthenware pitcher, which Vic thought he could pass on to The Old Mill Hotel as a period decoration, was not at stall 8.

3. The item of Belgian origin was at Sandy's stall, numbered one higher than the one where Vic found the porcelain vase, which Vic thought would do best in the window of his store.

4. Vic found the Dutch item at stall 6; the silver hip flask that Vic planned to pass straight on to Bidemme and Gavil Auctioneers for their special silver collectors' sale next week, wasn't at stall 7 or stall 8.

5. Barney's stall wasn't stall 2 or stall 11, and the French item wasn't at Jane's stall.

6. Vic found the gold etui, which wasn't made in Britain, amongst the clutter at stall 2, and it was so cheap he knew that even if he couldn't find a buyer, he could make a profit on the scrap value; Steve and his wife were at stall 4.

7. The brass pillbox, which Vic knew would be taken off his hands by Major Wanstead-Bucks (retired) for his famed "collection of not very useful things," had been crafted in the German city of Munich, probably as an apprentice's training piece.

Stall-holders: Barney; Errol; Jane; Kirk; Sandy; Steve
Items: brass pillbox; earthenware pitcher; gold etui; pewter jug; porcelain vase; silver hip flask
Countries of origin: Belgian; British; Dutch; French; German; Italian

Starting tip: Work out what item Vic bought from Sandy.

Rescue Party

Officers from the Keighshire Animal Rescue services were busy in Stonekeigh yesterday, responding to five emergency calls made by members of the public. From the clues, can you work out where each officer went, the animal concerned, and the problem each successfully tackled?

Clues

1. Lenny Lama was called to Burlington Road, but not to deal with the goat; the Burlington Road incident was also not the location of the duck trapped in the outhouse, which was

2. also not the Hopkins Farm problem.

3. Clare Coogar wasn't called to Alexandra Street or to the animal caught in the snare, which was not the fox.

4. The incident involving the dog was on Lindsay Street.

5. One animal had jumped into the old canal on Wharf Street but couldn't climb back up the vertical sides.

6. Paul Possem rescued the animal that was stuck on a roof, having climbed the fire escape but reluctant to make the return journey.

7. Caroline Cammelle dealt with the cat.

Officer	Location

	Alexandra Street	Burlington Road	Hopkins Farm	Lindsay Street	Wharf Street	Cat	Dog	Duck	Fox	Goat	Caught in snare	Jumped in canal	Knocked over	Stuck on roof	Trapped in outhouse
Bob Bear															
Caroline Cammelle															
Clare Coogar															
Lenny Lama															
Paul Possem															
Caught in snare															
Jumped in canal															
Knocked over															
Stuck on roof															
Trapped in outhouse															
Cat															
Dog															
Duck															
Fox															
Goat															

Animal	Problem

Love and Death

Although Shee-La the Golden is often described as "the peerless sword-maiden of Fantasyland," she has actually enjoyed an extensive and varied love life, but most of her relationships have ended badly, very badly. From the clues, can you work out the details of her latest five lovers—his name and occupation, the city where he was based, and how he died?

Clues

1. Van the Axeman turned out be a nasty piece of work who, far from reciprocating Shee-La's love, had been hired to kill her—but his attempt failed, and he fell victim to her deadly sword.

2. Garin of the Hills was not the pirate captain—let's face it, you can't easily get a ship up a hill!

3. The man from Eurali who gave his life to save Shee-La when they were ambushed by Zupushtu tribesmen was neither Donal the Red (who wasn't the man murdered with the poison of the chlenic fish) nor the pit-fighter (a sort of gladiator-in-a-hole), who, like the man who died at Shee-La's side in battle against the forces of the Dark Empire, is not from the Fantasyland metropolis of Kroprom.

4. Mordok the Shark came from the island-city of Kuhhrl, and the mercenary warrior came from Ogravar; despite his occupation, the latter did not die in battle.

5. The City Guard officer, whose name is either first or last in the list, died in a tragic accident while riding to meet Shee-La at a clifftop rendezvous.

Name	Occupation

	City Guard officer	Mercenary	Outlaw leader	Pirate captain	Pit-fighter	Eurali	Kroprom	Kuhhrl	Ogravar	Phoeba	Accident	In battle	Murdered	Saving Shee-La	Trying to kill Shee-La
Aeric Ormson															
Donal the Red															
Garin of the Hills															
Mordok the Shark															
Van the Axeman															
Accident															
In battle															
Murdered															
Saving Shee-La															
Trying to kill Shee-La															
Eurali															
Kroprom															
Kuhhrl															
Ogravar															
Phoeba															

City	Cause

Bertram's Hotel

Bertram Percival is the general manager of the Homecroft Hotel in Manhattan, which caters mainly to overseas guests flying in and out of La Guardia Airport. Last Monday morning, he found himself having to deal with complaints from five guests—luckily, English-speaking ones, as Bertram's foreign language skills are minimal. From the clues, can you work out each guest's hometown, room, and complaint? (In traditional fashion, the first digit of each room number is the floor of the hotel on which it stands.)

Clues

1. Susan Terry's complaint concerned the faulty shower, which would provide only ice-cold water; her room had a higher number than that of the guest from Calgary, Canada.

2. The guest occupying room 26 was a jewelry salesman from Sydney, Australia.

3. The complaint about the wrong newspaper—fairly trivial, you might think, even if was the tabloid *Daily Lantern* instead of the prestigious *Manhattan Financial Recorder*—came from the guest born and bred in New York City.

4. It was the guest in Room 35 who complained about not being able to sleep—not because of insomnia, but owing to the noise from the nearby elevator shaft.

5. Frank Glen occupied room 42, up on the fourth floor.

6. Andy Brock, who comes from Kingston, Jamaica, did not have a room on the floor immediately above Jack King's; it wasn't Jack who complained about the poor quality of the food served at breakfast.

Name	Hometown

	Calgary	Dunedin	Kingston	New York	Sydney	Room 05	Room 26	Room 35	Room 42	Room 51	Couldn't sleep	Faulty shower	Passport stolen	Poor food	Wrong paper
Andy Brock															
Frank Glen															
Jack King															
Pamela Quayle															
Susan Terry															
Couldn't sleep															
Faulty shower															
Passport stolen															
Poor food															
Wrong paper															
Room 05															
Room 26															
Room 35															
Room 42															
Room 51															

Those are the five stars, sir

413

Room	Complaint

College Hall Saturday

Every Saturday morning, five different organizations meet in various rooms of the College Hall in Flatland, Idaho. From the clues, can you work out which of the numerous rooms in the Hall is used for each Saturday morning meeting, the time the meeting starts, the name of the group meeting, and the name of the person in charge?

Clues

1. The Crafters' Club (handicrafts such as candle making, greeting-card making, jewelry making—you know the sort of thing) meets half an hour later than the group that uses the Draw-Wing Room, named for a family of local benefactors.

2. Flatland's U3A group (that stands for University of the Third Age) is headed by retired teacher Jean Poole.

3. The Sayle Room, named for former Flatland mayor Marmaduke Sayle (1784-1848), is a comparatively small chamber used for meetings of the local Writers' Circle.

4. The Tower Room (which isn't named for anybody named Tower—it just happens to be in the tower of the Town Hall) is used for the 9:15 a.m. meeting, which is not that of the U3A.

5. May Flower's group meets at 9:30 a.m. on Saturday mornings; Ruby Wryng's group meets at an earlier time than Dawn Brakes's.

6. The Flab-Fighters meet at 9:45 a.m., but not in the Garde Room—which is named, of course, for local Civil War hero and magnate Colonel Zachary Garde.

7. Rose Garden is chairperson of the group that meets in the room named for 1950s Senator Bill Yard, which was coincidentally formerly used for playing a tabletop ball game.

Room	Time

	9:00 a.m.	9:15 a.m.	9:30 a.m.	9:45 a.m.	10:00 a.m.	Crafters' Club	Dancercise	Flab-Fighters	U3A	Writers' Circle	Dawn Brakes	Jean Poole	May Flower	Rose Garden	Ruby Wryng
Bill Yard Room															
Draw-Wing Room															
Garde Room															
Sayle Room															
Tower Room															
Dawn Brakes															
Jean Poole															
May Flower															
Rose Garden															
Ruby Wryng															
Crafters' Club															
Dancercise															
Flab-Fighters															
U3A															
Writers' Circle															

Group	Leaders

Crème de la Crème

The picture below appeared in the last issue of *Hippolitan*, school magazine of Queenshill High School for Girls, a very ritzy educational establishment; it shows four of the pupils who appeared in this year's school play, and it accompanied an article about their achievements and aspirations. From the clues given, can you work out each girl's full name, her dramatic role, the sport at which she excels, and her stated ambition?

Clues

1. The girl who played Donalbain (this is a girls' school, remember; Miss Brodie, the teacher who produced the play whose title I'm planning not to mention had to cast females in all the roles) is figure 2 in the picture.

2. Helen is further right in the picture than Miss Cooper, but somewhere left of the volleyball star and team captain, who played the title role in that notorious Scottish play.

3. The tennis star, who some see as a future Wimbledon champion (but whose stated ambition is to become a physicist and build her own fission reactor!), has a surname beginning with a letter in the second half of the alphabet; she is standing to the left of the young lady who Miss Brodie cast as Third Witch, whose surname initial is in the first half of the alphabet.

4. The girl whose simple ambition is to, one day (as soon as possible), be President is standing immediately right of the captain of Queenshill's championship-winning hockey team.

5. Angela's ambition is to be an army officer—preferably a general.

6. Sonia Polk's father is a famous businessman and philanthropist.

7. Miss Sutton is standing somewhere left of Judith.

8. The girl on the extreme left is an oarswoman recognized as one of the outstanding rowers of her generation.

First names: Angela; Helen; Judith; Sonia
Surnames: Cooper; Freeman; Polk; Sutton
Play roles: Donalbain; Lady Macduff; Macbeth; Third Witch
Sports: hockey; volleyball; rowing; tennis
Ambitions: army officer; President; physicist; lawyer

_____ _____ _____ _____
_____ _____ _____ _____
_____ _____ _____ _____
_____ _____ _____ _____
_____ _____ _____ _____

Starting tip: Work out the role taken in the play by girl number 1.

Wanted Men

In January 1878, the notorious outlaw Joe Massey and his gang held up the Cattleman's Bank in Painted Rock, Texas, and fled with $12,000—but they didn't go far. None of them left Texas, and within nine months all were dead or in custody, tracked down by lawmen of various varieties. From the clues, can you work out each man's name, when and where he was caught, and what type of lawman caught him?

Clues

1. Waco Shaw, who was arrested in Eagle Creek, was on the run longer than Pat O'Kelly, who died in a gunfight with the infamous bounty hunter Mustang Dillard, but not in June.

2. The outlaw who was tracked down by agent Mick Campbell of the Pinkerton Detective Agency was caught before the gang member who was made prisoner by US Marshal Roy Lynch.

3. The outlaw captured by Sheriff Luke Adams of High Points County in February 1878 was arrested on the main street in the county seat, which wasn't White Rock.

4. Dan Griffin was arrested on April 1st, 1878, which was his thirtieth birthday.

5. It was in June that one of the gang members was tracked down to Fort Keppel.

6. One outlaw was wounded and then arrested by Texas Ranger Teddy Sturtevant in the Rosebud Saloon in the little town of Belltower, two months before gang leader Joe Massey was captured.

Outlaw	Month

	February	April	June	August	October	Belltower	Eagle Creek	Fort Keppel	San Pietro	White Rock	Bounty hunter	County Sheriff	Pinkerton agent	Texas Ranger	US Marshal
Buck Crane															
Dan Griffin															
Joe Massey															
Pat O'Kelly															
Waco Shaw															
Bounty hunter															
County Sheriff															
Pinkerton agent															
Texas Ranger															
US Marshal															
Belltower															
Eagle Creek															
Fort Keppel															
San Pietro															
White Rock															

Town	Lawman

Answers

Martial Arts, p. 1

Tuesday's class starts at 7:00 p.m. (clue 1) and Sunday's belt is green (clue 2), so the 6:00 p.m. class, at which he wears a yellow belt (clue 4) must be on Thursday. It's not Karate, at which Marshall is a white belt (clue 2), or Aikido, which begins at 5:00 p.m. (clue 3), so he must be a yellow belt at Thursday's 6:00 pm Taekwondo session. The white karate belt isn't worn on Sunday (clue 2), so it must be donned on Tuesday at 7:00 p.m., leaving Sunday's session as the 5:00 p.m. Aikido class for which Marshall wears a green belt.

Sunday, 5:00 p.m., Aikido, green.
Tuesday, 7:00 p.m., Karate, white.
Thursday, 6:00 p.m., Taekwondo, yellow.

Stand and Deliver, p. 2

E. Schioppe's parcel was in the trash can (clue 1), so the Interswift parcel in the barbecue which wasn't for E. Byer (clue 4) must have been for E. Perchess, leaving E. Byer's parcel as the Tuesday delivery left under the car (clue 3). E. Perchess's delivery wasn't on Wednesday (clue 2), so it must have been on Monday that Interswift left her package in the barbecue and, from clue 2, Fastline must have left E. Byer's parcel under the car on Tuesday. By elimination, Speedway must have left E. Schioppe's parcel in her trash can on Wednesday.

Monday, E. Perchess, Interswift, in barbecue.
Tuesday, E. Byer, Fastline, under car.
Wednesday, E. Schioppe, Speedway, in trash can.

Battleships, p. 3

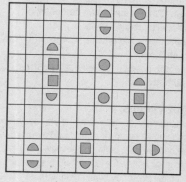

Winter Games, p. 4

Bobby Blatherton reported on the win by Walter Wytout (clue 5), and Solomon Sleat competed on the school playground (clue 2), so the man whose victory on the baseball field was reported by Barry Babble must have been Dominic Driffed. Fiona Flayk won the snowman demolish (clue 6), so the person who won the no-sled sledding as reported by Rex Rabbit (clue 2), who wasn't Solomon Sleat (clue 2), must have been Beatrice Blizzard. We have now matched four winners with either their event or location, so the playground slide in the supermarket parking lot must have been won by ace slider Walter Wytout and reported by Bobby Blatherton. Dominic Driffed didn't win the icicle javelin (clue 4), so he must have won the snowball fight on the baseball field witnessed by Barry Babble, leaving Solomon Sleat's school playground event as the icicle javelin. It wasn't reported on by Clive Chattaway, so it must have been seen by Perry Prattle, leaving Clive Chattaway watching Fiona Flayk's discomfiting demolition of a snowman with a blowtorch. This wasn't on Main Street (clue 6), so it must have been on the tennis courts, leaving Rex Rabbit reporting on the no-sled sledding on Main Street won by Beatrice Blizzard in her garbage can.

Barry Babble, snowball fight, baseball field, Dominic Driffed.

Bobby Blatherton, playground slide, parking lot, Walter Wytout.

Clive Chattaway, snowman demolish, tennis courts, Fiona Flayk.

Perry Prattle, icicle javelin, playground, Solomon Sleat.

Rex Rabbit, no-sled sledding, Main Street, Beatrice Blizzard.

Knight Visions, p. 6

Philomena was the heroine in the Thursday dream (clue 4), so, from clue 1, Sir Poltroon's dream cannot have been on Tuesday, Thursday, or Friday. Sir Sorely had the Monday dream (clue 6), so, by elimination, it must have been on Wednesday night that Sir Poltroon had his. So, from clue 1, Joanne was rescued from the band of thieves in the Friday dream. We have now matched two nights with knights, and another two with damsels, so Sir Coward, who dreamed of rescuing Elaine (clue 5), must have done so on Tuesday. Sir Timid's opponent was the wizard (clue 3), so he cannot have dreamed of rescuing Joanne on Friday, and must have had the Thursday dream, leaving the Friday dreamer as Sir Spyneless. Rosanna was not in Sir Poltroon's Wednesday dream (clue 2), so she must have been rescued by Sir Sorely in his Monday dream, leaving Melanie as the damsel Sir Poltroon dreamed of. So, Melanie's oppressor was not the ogre (clue 2), nor was he the evil knight (clue 6), so it must have been the dragon. Nor was the evil knight Sir Sorely's Monday night antagonist (clue 6), so he must have appeared with Elaine in Sir Coward's Tuesday dream, which leaves Rosanna's oppressor in Sir Sorely's dream as the ogre.

Monday, Sir Sorely à Frayde, Rosanna, ogre.

Tuesday, Sir Coward de Custarde, Elaine, evil knight.

Wednesday, Sir Poltroon à Ghaste, Melanie, dragon.

Thursday, Sir Timid de Shayke, Philomena, wizard.

Friday, Sir Spyneless de Feete, Joanne, band of thieves.

Mouse Sale, p. 8

The animal in pairing 1 isn't Jerry (clue 1), Philida (clue 2), Harvey (clue 3), or Dora (clue 4), and so it must be Mickey. So, from clue 4, the Klikkit mouse must be part of pair 3. It's not paired with Philida (clue 2) or Dora (clue 4), and Harvey is paired with a mouse from Logiput (clue 3), so the Klikkit mouse in place 3 must be paired with Jerry Mouse and, from clue 1, Mickey Mouse in place 1 must come with a free Microtek mouse. Now, from clue 2, Philida can't be in either combination 2 or 4 and must be mouse 5, and the Poynter mouse must be in combination 4. Now, by elimination, the combination of Harvey Mouse and the Logiput mouse must be number 2, Mouse 4 must be Dora, and Mouse 5 must be from the Kerser company.

1, Mickey, Microtek.

2, Harvey, Logiput.

3, Jerry, Klikkit.

4, Dora, Poynter.

5, Philida, Kerser.

Sporting Ladies, p. 9

Figure 1's sport can't be roller skating (clue 1) nor is it golf (clue 5). Since Maude Young, aged 76 (clue 4), can't be figure 2, who is 73 (clue 2), clue 4 also rules out figure 1 as the fencer, so she must play table tennis. She can't be 70 or 79 (clues 3 and 5), so she must be the 76-year-old, Maude Young. Clue 4 now tells us that figure 2's sport must be fencing and, from clue 3, her name must be Emily Ross. Beryl Owen can't be figure 4 (clue 1), so she must be figure 3 and, from clue 1, figure 4 must be the roller skater, leaving Beryl Owen's sport as golf. By elimination, Joan White must be the roller-skating figure 4. Finally, clue 5 tells us Beryl Owen is 79, leaving Joan White's age as 70.

1, Maude Young, 76, table tennis.

2, Emily Rose, 73, fencing.
3, Beryl Owen, 79, golf.
4, Joan White, 70, roller skating.

Injured at the Gym, p. 10

Annie's surname is Flore (clue 6) and Ms. Rings hurt her elbow (clue 6), so Irene, who hurt her finger but isn't Ms. Barr or Ms. Beame (clue 3), must be Irene Hawse and injured herself on the exercise bike (clue 2). The shoulder injury occurred on the shoulder press (clue 2), so the knee injury, which didn't happen with the medicine ball or the pec deck (clue 4), must have occurred on the leg press, to Edna (clue 1). She isn't Ms. Beame (clue 4), so she must be Edna Barr. Ms. Rings isn't Ursula (clue 6), so she must be Olive Rings and, by elimination, Ursula must be Ursula Beame. From her injury, Olive Rings wasn't hurt on the shoulder lift (clue 2) and she wasn't hurt on the pec deck (clue 5), so she must have been using the medicine ball. Ursula Beame wasn't on the pec deck (clue 5), so she must have been on the shoulder lift and must have hurt her shoulder, and Annie Flore must have been on the pec deck and injured her nose (which isn't difficult, if you don't keep your head up).
Annie Flore, nose, pec deck.
Edna Barr, knee, leg press.
Irene Hawse, finger, bike.
Olive Rings, elbow, medicine ball.
Ursula Beame, shoulder, shoulder lift.

Looks Familiar, p. 12

Helen's familiar is named Tip (clue 4) and Drogo is a squirrel (clue 6), so Katy's familiar, a rabbit with a one-word name (clue 5), must be Smaug. Fran O'Lochlainn (clue 3) hasn't called her familiar Poor John, which is the name of Mrs. Potter's animal (clue 1), or Cuddy Wifter (clue 3), so she must have named it Drogo. From clue 7, Cuddy Wifter doesn't belong to Millie, so it must be Beryl's familiar, leaving Millie as Millie Potter, owner of Poor John. So, Poor John isn't the bat, which belongs to Mrs. Faust (clue 2). Nor is Mrs.

Faust Beryl (clue 2), so she must be Helen Faust. Smaug's owner Katy isn't Mrs. Merlyn (clue 8), so it must be Katy Daniels, and, by elimination, Mrs. Merlyn must be Beryl Merlyn. Finally, Millie's familiar isn't a hedgehog (clue 1), so it must be a platypus and the hedgehog must be Beryl Merlyn's animal.
Beryl Merlyn, Cuddy Wifter, hedgehog.
Fran O'Lochlainn, Drogo, squirrel.
Helen Faust, Tip, bat.
Katy Daniels, Smaug, rabbit.
Millie Potter, Poor John, platypus.

Models, p. 14

Hilyard, the cowman (clue 5), can't have been Katie, who modeled for *The Dreamer* (clue 6), nor was her surname Lester (clue 6). Danvers was Edgar (clue 2) and Price modeled for *The Medium* (clue 4), so Katie must have been Digby. So, she wasn't the lady's maid (clue 7), and so, since there were only two female models, she must have been the housemaid. So, the model for *The Visitor* must have been the footman (clue 1) and Vera must have been the lady's maid. Hilyard wasn't Alfred (clue 5), so he must have been Simon Hilyard the cowman. He didn't model for *The Pilgrim* (clue 3) and his surname rules out *The Medium*, so he must have posed for *The Artist*. Price wasn't the gardener (clue 4), so it must have been the lady's maid, Vera Price. By elimination, Alfred must have been Alfred Lester. Clue 6 rules him out as the footman, who must therefore have been Edgar Danvers, leaving Alfred Lester as the gardener and model for *The Pilgrim*.
The Artist, **Simon Hilyard, cowman.**
The Dreamer, **Katie Digby, housemaid.**
The Medium, **Vera Price, lady's maid.**
The Pilgrim, **Alfred Lester, gardener.**
The Visitor, **Edgar Danvers, footman.**

Sable Ovines, p. 16

Caroline is Caroline Noble (clue 1) and Franklin is a poet (clue 3), so the burglar Bonar-Fydes (clue 4), who isn't Fiona (clue 2) or Matthew (clue 4) must be Joseph Bonar-Fydes. So, his father isn't the landowner (clue 3), the Archbishop, who is Fiona's father (clue 2), the judge, father of the model (clue 5), or the General (clue 6), and must be a Senator. Pridefull's father is a landowner (clue 3), so Pridefull isn't Franklin (clue 3) and must be Matthew Pridefull. Fiona isn't Wellborn, who is male (clue 6), so she must be Fiona Loftey, leaving Franklin as Franklin Wellborn. The artist is not Matthew (clue 3) or Caroline (clue 1), so it must be Fiona Loftey. Matthew Pridefull, son of the landowner, isn't the model (clue 5), so he must be a social worker, leaving Caroline Noble as the judge's model offspring, and Franklin's father as General Wellborn.

Caroline Noble, judge, model.
Fiona Loftey, Archbishop, artist.
Franklin Wellborn, general, poet.
Joseph Bonar-Fydes, senator, burglar.
Matthew Pridefull, landowner, social worker.

Safe and Sound, p. 18

The gold coins are immediately below Jimmy the Jemmy's wads of cash (clue 2), so they can't be in any of boxes 1, 2, 3, 8, or 12. Box 8 contains gold (clue 7), so the gold coins can't be below it in box 11. Box 6 contains gemstones (clue 7) and box 7 doesn't contain gold (clue 8), so the gold coins must be in box 4 and Jimmy the Jemmy must rent box 1. Box 7 is rented by Don the Drill (clue 8), so the gold in box 8 (clue 7) can't be gold watches (clue 5) and must be gold bars. Now, from clue 5, Jellyman Jake can't have any of boxes 2, 3, 6, 8, or 12, and must have box 11, with the gold watches in box 12. Lugs Larry's odd-numbered box is in the same column as the one containing diamonds (clue 6), so it can't be box 7, since box 4 has the coins and Jimmy the Jemmy's box 1 has cash, so it must be box 3, and box 6 must contain the diamonds. The only box left for Numbers Neville's rubies (clue 4) is now box 2 and, also from clue 4, Terry the Torch must rent box 4 with its gold coins. The renter of box 8 can't be Fingers Freddie (clue 3) and isn't

Percy the Picker (clue 7), so it must be Claude the Cracker. Fingers Freddie can't have box 12 (clue 3), so he must have the diamonds in box 6, with Lugs Larry's box 3 being the one containing $80,000 and, by elimination, Percy the Picker renting box 12 full of gold watches. Jellyman Jake's box 11 doesn't contain $50,000 (clue 5) or emeralds (clue 8) and so it must have $100,000. Finally, Jimmy the Jemmy's box 1 must have the $50,000 (clue 2), leaving the emeralds in Don the Drill's box 7.

1, Jimmy the Jemmy, $50,000.
2, Numbers Neville, rubies.
3, Lugs Larry, $80,000.
4, Terry the Torch, gold coins.
6, Fingers Freddie, diamonds.
7, Don the Drill, emeralds.
8, Claude the Cracker, gold bars.
11, Jellyman Jake, $100,000.
12, Percy the Picker, gold watches.

Winter Warmers, p. 20

Someone's daughter lives in Adelaide (clue 4) and Maxine is visiting Sydney (clue 5), so Kelly's bridesmaid, who lives in Australia (clue 1), must be in Perth. This is not Samantha (clue 3). Nor can it be Virginia, who lives in New Zealand (clue 1). Carol's guest is Gloria (clue 2), and Angie's visitor is her sister (clue 5), so the former bridesmaid must be Bronwen. We now know Virginia is not the sister or the bridesmaid, nor is she the old school friend (clue 1). Nor can she be the daughter, who lives in Adelaide (clues 1 and 4), so she must be her visitor's cousin. Therefore, her home city is not Wellington (clue 3), and must be Auckland (clue 1). So, her visitor is not Bernice (clue 5). We know Gloria is staying with Carol, and we have named the cities where Maxine and Kelly are staying, so, by elimination, it must be Stella who is visiting her cousin Virginia in Auckland. Since Maxine is not Angie's sister (clue 5), she must be visiting an old school friend in Sydney, and, by elimination, Angie's sister must be staying with her in Wellington.

She cannot be Gloria, who is staying with Carol, so she must be Bernice, leaving Gloria as the visitor to Adelaide, and Carol as Gloria's daughter. Therefore, by elimination, Maxine's old school friend in Sydney must be Samantha.

Bernice, Angie, sister, Wellington.
Gloria, Carol, daughter, Adelaide.
Kelly, Bronwen, bridesmaid, Perth.
Maxine, Samantha, school friend, Sydney.
Stella, Virginia, cousin, Auckland.

Stake-Out, p. 22

Mike Mallet watched the arrival of the officer (clue 2) and Ricky Wrench witnessed the quarrel (clue 5), so the detective who saw the tall man arrive and hand over cash (clue 6), who wasn't Spike Spanner (clue 1) or Nicky Nail (clue 5), must have been Dick Drill. So, it wasn't at the docks, where Spike Spanner was on stake-out (clue 1) or the office (clue 1), the hotel (clue 4), or the depot, where a fist fight broke out (clue 3) and so it must have been at a house. Nicky Nail's new character was wearing a hat (clue 5) and Ricky Wrench watched the arrival of a diminutive figure (clue 5), so the tall woman must have been seen by Spike Spanner at the docks. She didn't hand over the bag (clue 7), so she must have been kidnapped. Nor did the woman in the hat hand over the bag (clue 7) or take part in a fist fight (clue 3), so she must have been in the quarrel witnessed by Ricky Wrench, leaving Nicky Nail as the detective who watched the man in the hat. So, Nicky Nail's incident wasn't at the hotel (clue 4) or the docks (clue 1), so he must have seen the fight at the depot. By elimination, Mike Mallet must have seen the officer hand over the bag. Finally, the officer didn't arrive outside the office (clue 1), so he must have been at the hotel, leaving Ricky Wrench watching the woman in the hat have a quarrel at the office.

Dick Drill, house, tall man, hand over cash.
Mike Mallet, hotel, officer, hand over bag.
Nicky Nail, depot, man in hat, fist fight.

Ricky Wrench, office, woman in hat, quarrel.
Spike Spanner, docks, tall woman, kidnap.

Adventurous Addifields, p. 24

Joseph was born in 1942 (clue 2) and Edward in either 1867 or 1892 (clue 6). John Addifield was a soldier (clue 5), so the farmer born in 1917, who wasn't Virgil (clue 2), must have been Moroni Addifield, who captured the bank robber (clue 4). So, the man kidnapped by Indians, who was born twenty-five years before the teacher (clue 7), wasn't born in 1892, 1917, or 1942. The man born in 1842 found treasure (clue 3), so the one kidnapped by Indians must have been born in 1867, and the teacher in 1892. The birth date rules out the farmer and the teacher as the kidnap victim, nor was he the printer (clue 7), or the sailor, who was shipwrecked (clue 1), so he must have been John, the soldier. Therefore, the teacher born in 1892 was Edward Addifield (clue 6). By elimination, the man born in 1842 who found treasure must have been Virgil. We now know either the occupation or the adventure for four men, so the sailor who was shipwrecked must have been Joseph. By elimination, Edward, the teacher, must have built a land yacht, and Virgil, who found the treasure, must have been a printer.

Edward, 1892, teacher, built land yacht.
John, 1867, soldier, kidnapped by Indians.
Joseph, 1942, sailor, shipwrecked.
Moroni, 1917, farmer, captured robber.
Virgil, 1842, printer, found treasure.

Stamps of Approval, p. 26

The 1 mirj stamp cost $750,000 (clue 6). Clue 1 rules out the 12 konang stamp as costing $825,000 or $1 million. Since the Lustrian stamp cost $875,000 (clue 3), clue 1 also rules out the 12 konang as costing $625,000, so it must have cost $500,000. From clue 1, the green stamp must have cost $625,000 and the Adari stamp was the $750,000 purchase. The $625,000 stamp isn't Holirran (clue 2), and the Ciwalian stamp is lilac (clue 4), so the Minean stamp must be green. Its face value is not 10 quiral (clue 5), while the 30 galter stamp is orange (clue 7), so the Minean stamp's face value must be 5 buzat. Clue 4 rules out $500,000 as the price of the Ciwalian stamp, so that must have been the cost of the Holirran stamp, and the Ciwalian one must have cost $1 million. The Holirran stamp's face value tells us it isn't sepia (clue 2), so it must be pink. The Adari stamp's face value tells us it isn't orange, so it must be sepia, leaving the orange stamp as Lustrian. By final elimination, the $1 million Ciwalian stamp's face value must be 10 quiral.

$500,000, Holirran, 12 konang, pink.
$625,000, Minean, 5 buzat, green.
$750,000 Adari, 1 mirj, sepia.
$875,000, Lustrian, 30 galter, orange.
$1 million, Ciwalian, 10 quiral, lilac.

Date Nights, p. 28

Marc and Cleo saw the stage musical on the 29th (clue 1). Their meal that night wasn't at the Taj Mahal (clue 2), nor was it at Le Provençal, Maison Marcel, or Gordon's (clue 5), so it must have been at the Riverside, and they therefore went to the Pavilion on the 22nd (clue 3). The visit to the Empire must therefore have been on either the 15th or the 29th, and that to the Regent on the 1st or the 15th (clue 3), so they went to one of these on the 15th. The visit to the Coronet can't have been on the 1st or the 29th (clue 4), so it must have been on the 8th. From the same clue, therefore, the meal at Maison Marcel must have been on the 15th, and the visit to the '60s concert on the 1st. The meal on the 22nd wasn't at the Taj Mahal (clue 2) or Gordon's (clue 5), so it must have been at Le Provençal. Now, from clue 5, the visit to the movie musical can't have been on the 22nd or on the 15th, when Marc and Cleo ate at Maison Marcel, so it must have been on the 8th. Therefore, on the 15th and the 23rd they must have seen the stage thriller and the movie comedy respectively (clue 5), and

so, from the same clue, the meal at Gordon's must have been on the 8th. By elimination, the meal on the 1st was at the Taj Mahal. We can now see that the visit to the Eldorado wasn't on the 1st (clue 2), and we know it wasn't on the 15th, so it must have been on the 29th. So, the visit to the Empire was on the 15th, and that to the Regent on the 1st (clue 3).

1st, Taj Mahal, Regent, '60s concert.
8th, Gordon's, Coronet, movie musical.
15th, Maison Marcel, Empire, stage thriller.
22nd, Le Provençal, Pavilion, movie comedy.
29th, Riverside, Eldorado, stage musical.

Miss Attributed, p. 30

The Capital Bank robbery was in 1900 (clue 5) and Franco Brothers' store was in Paris (clue 2), so the Moscow job of 1894 (clue 6), which wasn't at the Grand Hotel, robbed by the Anarchist Liberators (clue 1) or Hart & Lukas (clue 7), must have been Star House. Billy Boyle was the 1896 robber (clue 4) and clue 1 rules out both 1896 and 1899 for the Grand Hotel theft as the Lisbon job carried out by the Pike Gang, so the Grand Hotel must have been robbed in 1903. We now know that the Hart & Lukas job must have been in 1896 or 1899, so, from clue 7, the Green Skull Gang's job must have been in 1894, at Star House. Franco Brothers weren't robbed by Ivan Lenkov (clue 2), so it must have been the victim of Billy Boyle in 1896 and, by elimination, Ivan Lenkov must have done the 1899 job. The Grand Hotel can't have been in Berlin (clue 3), so it must have been in Rome. Clue 3 rules out Berlin for the Capital Bank job, so the victim there must have been Hart & Lukas, leaving the Capital Bank in Lisbon; by elimination, Hart & Lukas must have been robbed by Ivan Lenkov.

Capital Bank, Lisbon, 1900, Pike Gang.
Franco Brothers, Paris, 1896, Billy Boyle.
Grand Hotel, Rome, 1903, Anarchist Liberators.
Hart & Lukas, Berlin, 1899, Ivan Lenkov.

Star House, Moscow, 1894, Green Skull Gang.

Trubble at Mills, p. 32

Trubble saw the Sales employee on Thursday (clue 2), so, from clue 1, the person seen on Tuesday can't have been from Advertising or Research. Nor was this person from Transport (clue 4), so he must have been the Accounts worker, Barry Dock (clue 6), and, also from clue 6, Trubble must have seen Don Key on Wednesday. Now, from clue 1, the persons from Research and Advertising must have seen Trubble on either Monday and Wednesday or Wednesday and Friday, respectively. We know that Don was seen on Wednesday, so the gender of these two people must be male (clue 1). So, Sue Dann, who saw Trubble on Monday (clue 5), can't be the Research worker, who must be Don Key and the Advertising worker must have been seen on Friday. The Advertising worker was male (clue 1), so he must have been George Cross, leaving Ann Gellick as the Sales person who saw Trubble on Thursday. By elimination, Sue Dann must work in Transportation. George Cross from Advertising was tipsy (clue 1). The person caught playing computer games wasn't Ann Gellick (clue 3) or Barry Dock (clue 6) and, from clue 3, wasn't Sue Dann, who saw Trubble on Monday, so it must have been Don Key. Therefore, from clue 3, Barry Dock must have been rude on the phone. Finally, Ann Gellick from Sales wasn't caught eating at her desk (clue 2), so it must have been reprimanded for bad timekeeping, leaving the at-desk eater as Sue Dann from Transportation, who saw Trubble on Monday.
Monday, Sue Dann, Transportation, eating.
Tuesday, Barry Dock, Accounts, rude on phone.
Wednesday, Don Key, Research, computer games.
Thursday, Ann Gellick, Sales, bad timekeeper.
Friday, George Cross, Advertising, tipsy.

Bernards All, p. 34

Montgomery has an even number and Herman's number is higher (clue1), so neither can be dog 1. Both Shaw and Cribbins have dogs to their left (clue 1), so neither can be dog 1. So, dog 1 must be Matthews and, from clue 2, dog 2 must look after the Encom Pass. From clue 2, the Sur Pass must be the patch of either dog 4 or 5, so Cribbins can't be dog 2, looking after the Encom Pass. Nor does he look after Over Pass (clue 1) or Sur Pass or Tres Pass (clue 2) and must work in Under Pass. So, this isn't the pass tended by dog 5 (clue 1). Nor does dog 5 look after Tres Pass or Over Pass (clue 1), so it must be Sur Pass and, from clue 2, Cribbins must be dog 4. The dog called Shaw is right of both the ones who look after Tres Pass and Over Pass (clue 1). So, since they must now each be either 1 or 3, Shaw must be dog 5. Now from clue 1, Herman must be dog 3, numbered higher than Montgomery, dog 2. Finally, from clue 2, Herman, dog 3, doesn't look after Over Pass, so it must work along Tres Pass, leaving dog 1, Matthews, as the guardian of the Over Pass.
1, Matthews, Over Pass.
2, Montgomery, Encom Pass.
3, Herman, Tres Pass.
4, Cribbins, Under Pass.
5, Shaw, Sur Pass.

Battleships, p. 35

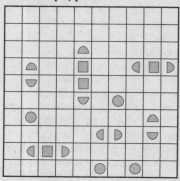

Crew Room, p. 36

The surgeon in position 7 and her neighbor in position 6 are both women (clue 5). Neither of them can be Liz Mond (clue 3), and Ella Beit is in position 3 (clue 7), so officers 6 and 7 must both be either Kate Luce or Zia Welzl. Gus Hill must be in position 3 or 4 (clue 4). So, he must be officer 4, and Zia Welzl is therefore the surgeon in position 7, leaving Kate Luce as officer 6. So, from clue 6, Gus Hill, officer 4, must be the purser, and comms must be officer 2. The sysso is immediately left of Toby Roche (clue 2), which rules out positions 2, 3, 5, and 6; we know the roles of officers 4 and 7, so the sysso must be in position 1 and Toby Roche officer 2. Now, helm Marc Polo (clue 1), must be in position 5. So, by elimination, the sysso must be Liz Mond, and so Ella Beit, officer 3, must be the engineer (clue 3), leaving Kate Luce as the *Firefly*'s master.

1, sysso, Liz Mond.
2, comms, Toby Roche.
3, engineer, Ella Beit.
4, purser, Gus Hill.
5, helm, Marc Polo.
6, master, Kate Luce.
7, surgeon, Zia Welzl.

Clarion Calls, p. 38

The originator of Valentine 1411 cannot be Bonzo (clue 1), Tiger (clue 2), or Cattikins (clue 3), and since the one addressed to Gorjus cannot be 1412 (clue 1), Flossie cannot have devised 1411 (clue 2), so it must be Snazzy who did. He cannot be addressing Apollo (clue 1), Gorjus (clue 2), The It Girl, or Tankman (clue 6), so his Valentine must be Peachy-Pie. Message 1412 is not for The It Girl (clue 6) and cannot be for Apollo (clue 5) or, as we know, Gorjus, so it must be for Tankman. Therefore, Tiger must be the creator of 1413 (clue 2). 1415 cannot be attributed to Flossie (clue 2) or Bonzo (clue 5), so it must be attributed to Cattikins. Since 1413 is not Bonzo's or Flossie's, 1414 cannot be for Gorjus (clue 2) or Apollo (clue 5), so it must be for The It Girl. The message of 1411 cannot

be "Come back darling" or "IOU4 Evva" (clue 4) or "Huggies and kissies" (clue 6), and since it is addressed to Peachy-Pie cannot be "My chocolate soldier," so it must be "UR4Me." Since Snazzy is male (clue 6), "IOU4 Evva" cannot be the text of 1412 (clue 4), nor, from the same clue, can "Come back," so the message in 1412 must be "My chocolate soldier," addressed to Tankman. This is not by the male Bonzo, so it must be by Flossie. Therefore, 1413 must be for Gorjus and 1415 for Apollo, with Bonzo producing 1414. It is now evident that "IOU4 Evva" must be 1413 and "Come back," 1414.

1411, Snazzy, Peachy-Pie, UR4Me.
1412, Flossie, Tankman, My chocolate soldier.
1413, Tiger, Gorjus, IOU4 Evva.
1414, Bonzo, The It Girl, Come back darling.
1415, Cattikins, Apollo, Huggies and kissies.

Lawn Order, p. 40

Mossloss has been delivered to No. 2 (clue 4), so Jeremy Jade, who has ordered Daisyways but doesn't live at number 6 (clue 1), must live at 4 Gardner's Drive. So, Turf Nuts must have delivered their Cloverover to No. 6. We now know the resident or the company for No. 4 and No. 6, so Lucas Lime, a new customer of Sod Supplies (clue 2), must live at 2 Gardner's Drive and Sod Supplies must supply Mossloss. By elimination, Jeremy Jade at No. 4 must have bought Grass Routes's Daisyways and the resident at No. 6 who bought Turf Nuts's Cloverover must be Ellis Emerald.

No. 2, Lucas Lime, Sod Supplies, Mossloss.
No. 4, Jeremy Jade, Grass Routes, Daisyways.
No. 6, Ellis Emerald, Turf Nuts, Cloverover.

Law'n'Order, p. 41

Rowdy Raynes is in jail in Doomstone, so Bruiser Baker, in jail for fighting but not in Smudge City (clue 3), must be in jail in

Leadwood, having been taken there by Sheriff Walter Slurp (clue 2). So, Punk Petersen must be in jail in Smudge City. He wasn't thrown in jail by Sheriff Wally Burp (clue 2), so he must have been jailed by Sheriff Wallis Chirp for cheating at cards (clue 4), leaving Wally Burp as the sheriff of Doomstone who jailed Rowdy Raynes for being drunk.

Doomstone, Wally Burp, Rowdy Raynes, drunk.

Leadwood, Walter Slurp, Bruiser Baker, fighting.

Smudge City, Wallis Chirp, Punk Petersen, cheating.

Pop the Question, p. 42

Wetherby Wise beat Coralie Clutts (clue 1) and Norma Nowell won the CD pen (clue 4), so the competitor who beat Dominic Dimm-Witte to win the calendar, who wasn't Craig Canny (clue 3), must have been Stephanie Smart. The stamps were Wednesday's prize (clue 2), so Stephanie Smart's battle with Dominic Dimm-Witte, which wasn't on Monday (clue 3) or Tuesday (clue 4) must have been on Thursday and, from clue 3, Craig Canny must have won the stamps on Wednesday. By elimination, Wetherby Wise's victory over Coralie Clutts must have won him the photo. Wetherby is male (clue 1), so the loser on Tuesday is also male (clue 5) and must be Chester Chump, leaving Sophie Sapp as the loser to Craig Canny on Wednesday. This leaves Coralie Clutts losing to Wetherby Wise on Monday and Norma Nowell beating Chester Chump on Tuesday to win the CD pen.

Monday, Wetherby Wise, Coralie Clutts, photo.

Tuesday, Norma Nowell, Chester Chump, CD pen.

Wednesday, Craig Canny, Sophie Sapp, stamps for year.

Thursday, Stephanie Smart, Dominic Dimm-Witte, calendar.

Question the Pop, p. 44

The police sergeant is where 12 bottles has gone off (clue 2) and Douglas Doughty is a teacher (clue 3), so Vicky Valiant, who has counted 16 missiles so far (clue 4) but who isn't a firefighter (clue 3) must be the store manager at Cashlow (clue 1). Lucas Lynart is organizing the defense in Pricedeels (clue 2), so teacher Douglas Doughty, who isn't in Savelot (clue 3) must be in Kostov. This isn't where 8 bottles have so far popped and must be where 20 have hit the roof (and walls). Finally, Lucas Lynart isn't the police sergeant (clue 2) and so he must be the firefighter who, by elimination, must have witnessed 8 explosions so far, leaving Belinda Brayve as the police sergeant who has seen 12 bottles go "pop" so far in Savelot.

Cashlow, Vicky Valiant, store manager, 16.

Kostov, Douglas Doughty, teacher, 20.

Pricedeels, Lucas Lynart, firefighter, 8.

Savelot, Belinda Brayve, police sergeant, 12.

Earwigging, p. 46

The conversation with the delivery boy included "many returns" (clue 1), so the one with the parent, which didn't involve "need for candles" or "another year" (clue 3), must have been about "older on Friday." This wasn't the first earwigging of the day (clue 2) and so it could not have been in the conversation with the teacher at breakfast. Nor was that the need for candles (clue 3), so the teacher's conversation must have included "another year", leaving the need for candles overheard by Chris Cockroft (clue 3) as the phone conversation. The "older on Friday" snippet from the parent's conversation wasn't either of the first two overhearings (clue 3), so Hamish Hazel could not have overheard the breakfast chat (clue 2). Martin Masters overheard the midafternoon conversation (clue 4), so it must have been Ben Barton who earwigged at breakfast. Hamish Hazel didn't overhear "older on Friday" (clue 2), so he must have overheard "many returns," leaving Martin Master's midafternoon snippet as "older on Friday." So, from clue 2, Hamish Hazel must have earwigged at lunch and Chris Cockroft must have overheard at mid-morning.

Ben Barton, breakfast, teacher, another year.
Chris Cockroft, mid-morning, on phone, need candles.
Hamish Hazel, lunchtime, delivery boy, many returns.
Martin Masters, midafternoon, parent, older on Friday.

Present Day, p. 48

Ben Barton's family member sent the sherry (clue 4) and the letter resulted in the walking stick present (clue 3), so Martin Masters's text message, which didn't bring the slippers (clue 5), must have produced the marshmallows, so he must have sent the text to Uncle Godfrey (clue 2). Chris Cockroft asked his Aunt Petunia for help (clue 4), so Hamish Hazel, who didn't recruit his grandad (clue 5), must have called his grandmother (clue 1). So, his present wasn't the letter-begotten walking stick and must have been the thermal slippers. By elimination, Chris Cockroft's Aunt Petunia must have been the accomplice who replied to the letter with a walking stick, leaving Ben Barton sending an email to his grandad who sent the sherry.

Ben Barton, grandad, email, sherry.
Christ Cockroft, Aunt Petunia, letter, walking stick.
Hamish Hazel, grandmother, phone, thermal slippers.
Martin Masters, Uncle Godfrey, text, marshmallows.

Long Time in Store, p. 50

Figure A, who joined in 1980 (clue 3), can't be Ruth Candy (clue 1). Nor did Ruth begin working at Gross Brothers in 1991 (clue 1). Mrs. Dime joined in 1989 (clue 4), so Ruth Candy must have joined in 1994. So, from clue 2, Mrs. Chayne must have joined in 1991,

leaving the 1980 starter as Mrs. Seegar. From clue 2, Susie must be Dime. Ruth can't now be figure B (clue 2), and clue 5 rules her out for figure D, so she must be figure C. So, figure B must have joined in 1991 (clue 1) and is therefore Mrs. Chayne, leaving Susie Dime as figure D. Martha isn't Seegar (clue 6), so she must be Martha Chayne and Seegar must be Grace Seegar, the longest-serving of the four.

A, Grace Seegar, 1980.
B, Martha Chayne, 1991.
C, Ruth Candy, 1994.
D, Susie Dime, 1989.

Disaster Area, p. 51

The movie in position 1 isn't *Flood* or *Asteroid* (clue 1), *Landslide* or *Hurricane* (clue 2), or *Blaze* or *Eruption* (clue 3). From clue 2, *Eruption* can't be any of numbers 3, 4, 7, or 8, so, from clue 3, *Earthquake* can't be number 1. So, movie 1 must be *Avalanche*. Similarly, from clues 1 and 2, the movie in position 5 can't be *Flood, Asteroid, Landslide,* or *Hurricane*. Clue 3 rules out *Blaze*, and since, as we have seen, *Eruption* can't be number 7, *Earthquake* can't be number 5, so movie 5 must be *Eruption* and, from clue 3, *Earthquake* must be movie 3. *Hurricane* is left of *Blaze* (clue 3), so it can't be any of movies 2, 4, or 8. From clue 2, it can't be number 6, so it must be movie 7 and *Blaze* must be 8. Neither *Flood* (clue 1) nor *Landslide* (clue 2) can be movie 4, so that must be *Asteroid*. Finally, *Asteroid* and *Avalanche* are both on the upper shelf so, from clue 1, *Flood* must be on the lower shelf in position 6, leaving *Landslide* in position 2.

1, *Avalanche*.
2, *Landslide*.
3, *Earthquake*.
4, *Asteroid*.
5, *Eruption*.
6, *Flood*.
7, *Hurricane*.
8, *Blaze*.

Mall Teaser, p. 52

Brook Lane contains the trees (clue 3), so the area with the open diner and five stores, the first word of which must have five or six letters (clue 2), must be Castle Keep, the central area of the mall (clue 1). The easterly arcade has nine stores and its name is neither the shortest nor the longest (clue 2). It is not Leather Lane, which has seven stores (clue 3), so it must be Dolphin Walk. There are not ten stores in Buckingham Way (clue 5), so there must be six, leaving Brook Lane with ten stores. The distinctive feature in Buckingham Way is neither the carousel (clue 5) nor the sculpture (clue 4), so it must be the fountain, and it is therefore the northerly arcade (clue 6). We know that the first word of the name of the westerly arcade must have seven letters, and is therefore Leather Lane, leaving Brook Lane as the southerly part of the mall. Finally, as the sculpture is not in Dolphin Walk (clue 4), it must contain the carousel, leaving the sculpture as the feature of Leather Lane.

Brook Lane, south, ten stores, trees.
Buckingham Way, north, six stores, fountain.
Castle Keep, center, five stores, open diner.
Dolphin Walk, east, nine stores, carousel.
Leather Lane, west, seven stores, sculpture.

Logi-5, p. 54

D	C	B	A	E
C	D	A	E	B
E	A	D	B	C
A	B	E	C	D
B	E	C	D	A

Killer Sudoku, p. 54

9	3	7	1	2	4	6	8	5
2	8	4	5	6	3	1	7	9
6	1	5	8	9	7	4	2	3
3	2	1	4	8	5	7	9	6
5	9	8	7	1	6	3	4	2
4	7	6	9	3	2	5	1	8
8	5	2	6	7	1	9	3	4
1	4	3	2	5	9	8	6	7
7	6	9	3	4	8	2	5	1

Domino Search, p. 55

0	4	6	2	3	4	3	3
6	5	5	2	2	5	1	1
1	5	0	4	1	5	0	4
5	4	3	1	3	6	5	3
6	6	4	3	1	6	4	2
0	1	4	0	6	6	1	0
0	2	0	2	3	5	2	2

Wayne in Spain, p. 56

Maria's surname is Valladaros (clue 6). Eduardo from Bilbao (clue 4) can't be Ferreira, who lives in Pamplona (clue 5), nor can he be Palmero or Quiroga (clue 2), so he must be Garcia. Joaquin can't be Palmero or Quiroga either (clue 2 again), so he must be Ferreira. Palmero wants Wayne to lead a demonstration (clue 3), so it can't be Jose, who wants him to address students (clue 7), and must be Francesca, leaving Jose as Quiroga. From what we now know, the invitation from Málaga to receive an award (clue 1), must be from Maria Valladaros, So Joaquin Ferreira, who hasn't invited Wayne to address politicians (clue 4), must have asked him to train some activists, and Eduardo Garcia must want Wayne to address the politicians. Finally, from clue 7, Jose Quiroga, who's not from Valencia, must come from Granada, leaving the person in Valencia as Francesco Palmero.

Bilbao, Eduardo Garcia, address politicians.
Granada, Jose Quiroga, address students.
Málaga, Maria Valladaros, receive award.
Pamplona, Joaquin Ferreira, train activists.
Valencia, Francesca Palmero, lead
demonstration.

Knuckle Dusters, p. 58

Toby Swift lost in six rounds (clue 6). He was
not watched by Beau Legges (clue 6). Clue 1
rules out Beau Tighe, who saw the 22-round
fight, and clue 2 rules out both Beau Nydel,
who watched Tom Allen win a longer fight,
and Beau Belles, who saw Esau Creasey
beaten, so Toby must have been watched by
Beau Streate. We know his opponent was not
Tom Allen, nor was he Jem Pendle (clue 6).
Ezra Mason won the 18-round fight (clue 5),
and Jake Smith fought Zach Murphy (clue 4),
so Toby's opponent must have been Adam
Fell. So, from clue 3, the 18-round fight
against Ezra Mason must have been lost by
Ben Keyes. We have matched four Beaux
with a winner, loser, or length of fight, so, by
elimination, the fight between Ezra and Ben
must have been watched by Beau Legges.
This leaves the spectator at the match
between Jake Smith and Zach Murphy as
Beau Tighe. Now, by elimination, Esau Creasey
must have fought Jem Pendle, and Tom Allen
must have beaten Kit Tanner. Finally, from
clue 2, Tom Allen's fight must have lasted 31
rounds, and Jem Pendle's 27.

**Beau Belles, Jem Pendle, Esau Creasey, 27
rounds.**
**Beau Legges, Ezra Mason, Ben Keyes, 18
rounds.**
**Beau Nydel, Tom Allen, Kit Tanner, 31
rounds.**
**Beau Streate, Adam Fell, Toby Swift, 6
rounds.**
**Beau Tighe, Jake Smith, Zach Murphy, 22
rounds.**

Punishing Schedule, p. 60

Captain Boland's pupil wasted water (clue
6) and Ms. Sladek's had to write an essay

(clue 5), so the pupil who, guilty of pre-
programming, had to use a keyboard, who
wasn't in the class of Daneel-41 or Ubik-16
(clues 3 and 2), must be in Mr. Louva's class.
His pupil isn't Suzan Thom (clue 1), Miro
Nothar, who is in Daneel-41's class (clue
2), Helen Ivarson, who was banned from
the surface (clue 4), or Jan Kalli, who was
disobedient (clue 4), so it must be Charli
Bodel. Miro Nothar wasn't caught speaking
Terran (clue 2), so she must have been
playing games in class. So, she didn't have
to clean the airlocks (clue 1) and must have
been sent to the principal. Suzan Thom didn't
clean the airlock either (clue 1), so she must
have had to write an essay. By elimination,
the airlock cleaner must have been the
disobedient Jan Kalli, who must be Ubik-16's
pupil. Therefore, Captain Boland's pupil must
be Helen Ivarson, and Suzan Thom must have
been Ms. Sladek's pupil punished for speaking
Terran by having to handwrite an essay about
Neil Armstrong.

**Charli Bodel, Mr. Louva, pre-programming,
use keyboard.**
**Helen Ivarson, Captain Boland, wasting
water, banned from surface.**
**Jan Kalli, Ubik-16, disobedience, clean
airlock.**
**Miro Nothar, Daneel-41, playing games in
class, sent to principal.**
**Suzan Thom, Ms. Sladek, speaking Terran,
write essay.**

Having a Break, p. 62

Madge, who eats fruitcake, does not take
black or white coffee with it (clue 1), and
the woman who orders a pot of tea eats a
toasted tea cake (clue 2). Since Nancy orders
hot chocolate to drink (clue 5), Madge's drink
must be mineral water. She is an afternoon
customer (clue 1), but there are two others
after her (clue 3), so she must come in at 2
o'clock, and, from clue 3, Ella must be the
3:10 customer, and the gingerbread must be
ordered at 4:15. Now, from clue 6, Lucy must
be the customer who arrives at 11:30, and

Ethel, at 10 o'clock. So, by elimination, Nancy must be the 4:15 customer, and therefore has gingerbread with her cup of hot chocolate. The white coffee drinker, who does not order a scone (clue 7), must eat cookies with it, leaving the scone for the black coffee drinker. This person is not Lucy or Ethel (clue 6), so it must be Ella. The cookies and white coffee are not ordered by Lucy, who comes in at 11:30 (clue 4), so they must be the choice of Ethel, the 10 o'clock customer, leaving Lucy with the pot of tea and the toasted tea cake.

10:00, Ethel, white coffee, cookies.
11:30, Lucy, pot of tea, tea cake.
2:00, Madge, mineral water, fruitcake.
3:10, Ella, black coffee, scone.
4:15, Nancy, hot chocolate, gingerbread.

Ollie Wood's Bowl, p. 64

One Correction will appear on the 8th (clue 2) and Buckled will appear on a Saturday (clue 5), so the band shown in position 5 who will appear on Wednesday the 19th (clue 6), who aren't Take What? (clue 1), The Wasted, 6ix, or Westwife (clue 3) or McWhy (clue 4), must be Boyztwo. So, from clue 1, Take What? must be booked for the 22nd. The band in position 7 isn't Buckled (clue 5), The Wasted, 6ix, or Westwife (clue 3). From clue 3, the band in position 7 can't be the one appearing on the 8th, One Correction, and since Boyztwo is appearing on the 19th, it can't be Take What? on the 22nd, so it must be McWhy. So, from clue 4, the band shown in position 8 must be set to play on the 12th. So, Take What? on the 22nd, which must be on the bottom row (clue 1), must be in position 6. The band that will appear on the 5th isn't shown in position 1, 2, or 3 (clue 5) and we know it isn't places 5, 6, or 8. It's not McWhy in position 7 (clue 3), so it must be the band in position 4 and, from clue 5, Buckled must be shown in place 1. Now, the band in position 3 isn't The Wasted or 6ix or Westwife (clue 3) and so it must be One Correction booked to play on the 8th. Buckled, in position 1, won't be appearing on Saturday the 29th (clue 6), so their Saturday date must

be Saturday the 15th. McWhy in position 7 can't be booked for the 5th or the 26th (clue 3) so it must be slated for the 29th and The Wasted must be set to play on the 26th. By elimination, they must be shown in position 2. Finally, from clue 3, 6ix must be shown in position 4 and will appear on the 5th, and Westwife must be in place 8 and due to play on the 12th.

1, Buckled, Saturday the 15th.
2, The Wasted, Wednesday the 26th.
3, One Correction, Saturday the 8th.
4, 6ix, Wednesday the 5th.
5, Boyztwo, Wednesday the 19th.
6, Take What?, Saturday the 22nd.
7, McWhy, Saturday the 29th.
8, Westwife, Wednesday the 12th.

Flipp Flops, p. 66

Warstar lost $15m (clue 4) and Al Garbidge's movie lost $23m (clue 3), so Sol Rubitch's *Dark Carnival*, which lost an odd number of millions (clue 1), must have lost $19m. The Galactic movie lost $18m (clue 1), so QKQ's *Prime Number* (clue 2) didn't lose $18m or $26m (clue 2), so it must have lost $23m and was therefore produced by Al Garbidge. Therefore, *Interceptor* must have lost $26m (clue 2) and, by elimination, *The Tower* must have been the Galactic movie that lost $18m. It wasn't produced by Jess Torrible (clue 5) or Pat Hettick, who worked for Summit (clue 6), so it must have been an Adam Leuser production. Jess Torrible's movie wasn't made for Dixon (clue 5), so it must have been for Buena Sera, leaving the Dixon movie as *Dark Carnival*, produced by Sol Rubitch. Finally, Jess Torrible's Buena Sera movie wasn't *Warstar* (clue 4), so it must have been *Interceptor*, leaving *Warstar* as the Summit movie produced by Pat Hettick.

Dark Carnival, Dixon, Sol Rubitch, $19,000,000.
Interceptor, Buena Sera, Jess Torrible, $26,000,000.
Prime Number, QKQ, Al Garbidge, $23,000,000.

The Tower, Galactic, Adam Leuser, $18,000,000.
Warstar, Summit, Pat Hettick, $15,000,000.

Attacks Evasion, p. 68

Five men were sent to the bar (clue 3) and Bugsy Brakes sent his two best henchmen (clue 5), so the number of men who almost caught one of our heroes at the station, that couldn't have been one or two (clue 1) or, since it was two more than was sent by Sugsy Stokes (clue 1), four, must have been three. So, from clue 1, Sugsy Stokes must have sent a solitary thug and Mike Mallet must have dodged the two sent by Bugsy Brakes. We now know the gang bosses who sent one and two men and that five thugs went to the bar, so the number of men sent by Lugsy Locks, which was lower than the number sent to the park, must have been the three who visited the station and, by elimination, the gang of four must have just missed the Private Eye in the park. Nicky Nail left the barber shop in a hurry so Mike Mallet, must have dodged two of Bugsy Brakes's men at the diner. By elimination, Nicky Nail must have dodged just one man sent by Sugsy Stokes at the barber shop. Spike Spanner dodged Rugsy Ricks's men, so the dick who evaded the three men from Lugsy Locks at the station, who couldn't have been Dick Drill, must have been Ricky Wrench, leaving Dick Drill as the man who incurred the wrath of Mugsy Maker. Spike Spanner didn't leave O'Malley's bar by the window (clue 3), so he must have dodged four of Rugsy Ricks's men at the park, leaving Dick Drill leaping from the bathroom window of O'Malley's bar to evade five thugs in the pay of Mugsy Maker.

Dick Drill, Mugsy Maker, 5, bar.
Mike Mallet, Bugsy Brakes, 2, diner.
Nicky Nail, Sugsy Stokes, 1, barber shop.
Ricky Wrench, Lugsy Locks, 3, station.
Spike Spanner, Rugsy Ricks, 4, park.

My Grandfather's . . ., p. 70

The mirror in the main bedroom was not left for Roger (clue 1) or Eileen (clue 2). Stella inherited the clock (clue 7) and Owen's item was in the living room (clue 4), so the mirror must have been left to Neil, and therefore dates from 1820 (clue 6). So, from clue 1, Roger must have been left the item manufactured about 1870. We know this was not the mirror or the clock, nor was it the sideboard (clue 3), and the table was made in 1720 (clue 5), so Roger must have been left the chest. We know it was not from the main bedroom or the living room, nor was it from the drawing room (clue 3), and the item in the hallway dated from about 1770 (clue 4), so the chest must have been in Grandad's back bedroom. Owen's living room item cannot have been the table (clue 4), so it must have been the sideboard, leaving the table as Eileen's legacy. Its date rules out its location as the hallway, so it must have been in the drawing room, and, by elimination, the 1770 item from the hallway must have been Stella's clock, which leaves the date of Owen's sideboard as circa 1920.

Eileen, table, 1720, drawing room.
Neil, mirror, 1820, main bedroom.
Owen, sideboard, 1920, living room.
Roger, chest, 1870, back bedroom.
Stella, clock, 1770, hallway.

Quick Getaway, p. 72

The seven-night vacation departs on the 8th but not to Fuquid (clue 4), nor is it to Costa Poco, whose departure date is the day before that of the fourteen-night vacation (clue 3), Nodeira, where the five-night vacation is on offer (clue 5), or Minorcash, which departs on the 6th (clue 2), so it must be the $420 vacation in the Bargin Islands (clue 6). The fourteen-night vacation costs more than that to Fuquid (clue 3), so it is not the $294 package departing on the 5th (clue 2), nor can it be the departure on the 4th (clue 3). As it departs the day after the vacation in Costa Poco (clue 3), the date is not the 7th.

Therefore, the fourteen-night vacation must depart on the 6th to Minorcash, and the one on the 5th must be to Costa Poco, and must cost $294. It is not the fifteen-night, $378 vacation (clue 1), so it must be for ten nights. By elimination, the fifteen-night vacation must be to Fuquid. The five nights in Nodeira cost less than $420, so it must be $336, and the $462 vacation must be the fourteen nights in Minorcash. The fifteen nights in Fuquid does not depart on the 4th (clue 1), so it must be the 7th, leaving the departure on the 4th as the five-night vacation in Nodeira.

4th, Nodeira, 5 nights, $236.
5th, Costa Poco, 10 nights, $294.
6th, Minorcash, 14 nights, $462.
7th, Fuquid, 15 nights, $378.
8th, Bargin Islands, 7 nights, $420.

Ghost Writer, p. 74

The *Beneath the Surface* ghost is a naval officer (clue 5), so, from clue 2, the landmark in that book must be the Royal Opera House, and *Inheritance*'s ghost must be the pirate. *Full Circle*'s ghost isn't the novelist (clue 4) or the poet (clue 7), so it must be the clergyman, who appeared to the cop (clue 1). The landmark in *On the Way Home* is London Bridge Station (clue 6) and the British Museum is the landmark in the book featuring the artist (clue 4), so *The Call*, which features the physician but not Kew Gardens (clue 3), must have its ghost in Highgate Cemetery. Now, the book featuring the British Museum must be *Inheritance*. By elimination, *Full Circle* must feature Kew Gardens. The poet's ghost doesn't contact the physician or the student (clue 7), so it appears to the teacher and, from what we now know, they must feature in *On the Way Home*. Finally, by elimination, the tourist in *Beneath the Surface* must be the student, and the ghost in *The Call* must be the novelist.

Beneath the Surface, **Royal Opera House, naval officer, student.**
Full Circle, **Kew Gardens, clergyman, cop.**
Inheritance, **British Museum, pirate, artist.**

On the Way Home, **London Bridge Station, poet, teacher.**
The Call, **Highgate Cemetery, novelist, physician.**

Pirates, p. 76

Figure 3 is the bosun (clue 5), so Figure 1, "Bristol Bill" (clue 2), who can't be the first mate, who is "Red Jack" (clue 3), or Craddock the gunner (clue 4), must be just a seaman. So Craddock, who isn't "Scar" (clue 4), must be "Bones", leaving figure 3 as "Scar". So, Craddock must be figure 4 (clue 4), leaving the first mate as figure 2. So, Watkins must be the bosun (clue 1). The first mate isn't Jarvis (clue 3), so it is Fisher, leaving Jarvis as "Bristol Bill" the seaman.

1, "Bristol Bill" Jarvis, seaman.
2, "Red Jack" Fisher, first mate.
3, "Scar" Watkins, bosun.
4, "Bones" Craddock, gunner.

Salad Days, p. 77

To order a celery, lettuce, and tomato salad, customers need to press buttons 2, 5, and 6, or 3, 4, and 6 (clue 3), so one of those ingredients must come from chute 6 and none of them can be in chute 1. Nor does chute 1 dispense carrots (clue 2) or cucumbers (clue 1), so it must deliver a portion of onions. Carrots are in the chute numbered two higher than the one with celery (clue 2). We know it's not chute 6, so it must be either chute 4 or 5. If it were chute 4, the celery would be in chute 2 and the only even numbered chute left for the cucumbers would be chute 6, which, as we have seen, can't be the case. So, the carrots must be in chute 5, and celery must be in chute 4. Therefore, the celery, lettuce, and tomato salad must be a combination of 3, 4, and 6, and the cucumbers must be in chute 2. Finally, the lettuce isn't in chute 4 (clue 1) and must be in chute 6, leaving chute 4 as the tomatoes.

1, onion rings; 2, cucumber spears; 3, celery sticks; 4, sliced tomatoes; 5, grated carrots; 6, shredded lettuce.

Sign In, p. 78

2	4	5	1	3
1	2	4	3	5
5	3	2	4	1
4	1	3	5	2
3	5	1	2	4

Sudoku, p. 78

4	2	9	3	8	6	7	1	5
1	6	3	7	5	4	2	9	8
5	8	7	1	9	2	3	6	4
9	7	2	4	3	8	1	5	6
8	3	1	9	6	5	4	2	7
6	5	4	2	1	7	9	8	3
7	4	8	5	2	1	6	3	9
2	9	5	6	4	3	8	7	1
3	1	6	8	7	9	5	4	2

Battleships, p. 79

Mini Maestros, p. 80

Norman has a grandchild aged twelve (clue 6), so the grandfather who is paying for eight-year-old Graham's lessons (clue 4), must be Martin. The would-be harpist is ten (clue 5), and Olive is paying for the euphonium lessons (clue 3), so Graham, whose instrument is not the violin or the cello (clue 4), must be learning the piano. Norman's twelve-year-old grandchild can't be learning the cello (clue 2) and must be the violinist. The ten-year-old harpist isn't Rita's grandchild (clue 5), so it must be Vera's, leaving Rita's grandchild as the cellist. Vera's grandchild isn't Rachel (clue 5 again), or Tim or Lawrence (clue 1) and must therefore be Rebecca. Also from clue 1, Lawrence must be nine, and Tim, eleven. So Norman's grandchild must be Rachel. Olive's grandchild isn't Lawrence (clue 3), so he must be Tim, leaving Rita as the grandmother of Lawrence.

Martin, Graham, 8, piano.
Norman, Rachel, 12, violin.
Olive, Tim, 11, euphonium.
Rita, Lawrence, 9, cello.
Vera, Rebecca, 10, harp.

The Cactus Kid, p. 82

Santa Isabel, visited on May 1 (clue 4) wasn't at the end of an eight-mile or fourteen-mile journey (clue 4). Clue 1 rules out twenty-two miles, clue 2 the twenty-mile journey to the Wagon Wheel saloon, and clue 5 sixteen miles, so the journey to Santa Isabel must have been twenty-four miles. The saloon there wasn't the Bucket of Blood (clue 4), nor the Star of Arizona (clue 3); the Range Rider was in Covenant (clue 1), and clue 6 rules out Santa Isabel for the Fremont House, so the saloon there must have been Texas Annie's. So, from clue 6, the twenty-two-mile journey must have ended with a night in the Fremont House. The Kid can't have been there on May 2 (clue 6). Clue 2 rules out the twenty-mile journey to the Wagon Wheel for May 2, and clue 5 rules out sixteen miles. The eight-mile trip ended on May 4 (clue 3), so it must have been fourteen miles from Santa Isabel to his May 2 stop. On May 3, the Kid wasn't in Fort Barrow (clue 4), Covenant (clues 1 and 3), Apache Butte (clues 3 and 5), or Harmony (clues 2 and 3), so he must have been in Russell's Wells. On May 6, he wasn't in Covenant (clue 1), Harmony (clue 2), or

Apache Butte (clue 5), so he must have been in Fort Barrow. On May 5, the Kid can't have been in Harmony (clue 2), and clue 5 rules out Apache Butte, so he must have been in Covenant. So, from clue 1, the twenty-two-mile journey to the Fremont House must have been on May 6. By elimination, the Wagon Wheel at the end of the twenty-mile trip must have been in Russell's Wells. So, from clue 2, the Kid was in Harmony on May 2, and, by elimination, in Apache Butte on May 4. From clue 5, the sixteen-mile journey was to Covenant. Finally, from clue 3, the Star of Arizona wasn't in Harmony, so it must have been in Apache Butte, leaving the saloon in Harmony as the Bucket of Blood.

May 1, Santa Isabel, Texas Annie's, 24 miles.

May 2, Harmony, Bucket of Blood, 14 miles.

May 3, Russell's Wells, Wagon Wheel, 20 miles.

May 4, Apache Butte, Star of Arizona, 8 miles.

May 5, Covenant, Range Rider, 16 miles.

May 6, Fort Barrow, Fremont House, 22 miles.

Wining On, p. 84

The wines critiqued on the 23rd and the 30th weren't the French white (clue 1), the Australian red (clue 4), or the Spanish red (clue 5), so it must have been the American red and the Italian white. So, Steve Grille, who cooked two weeks before the American red wine was chosen (clue 2) couldn't have been the chef on the 2nd. Nor was the first chef of the month Rita Boyle (clue 1), Dave Baker (clue 3), or Joanne Fry (clue 6), and so it must have been Jeff Cooke. So, from clue 4, the Aussie red must have been tasted on the 9th, and the white wine two weeks later (clue 4) must have been the Italian white chosen by Joanne Fry (clue 6), leaving the American red as the last choice of the month. Now, from clue 6, the Aussie red on the 9th must have been considered "abstract." Since Joanne Fry was the chef on the 23rd, from clue 1, the

French white can't have been featured on the show on the 16th and must have been Jeff Cooke's choice on the 2nd, with Rita Boyle choosing the "abstract" Aussie red on the 9th. Also from clue 1, the wine on the 16th must have been considered "noisy." Steve Grille didn't cook on the 30th (clue 2), so he must have cooked on the 16th and, from clue 2, the Italian white chosen by Joanne Fry on the 23rd must have been thought to be "nervous." By elimination, Steve Grille's "noisy" wine on the 16th must have been the Spanish red, and Dave Baker must have chosen the American red on the 30th. Finally, from clue 5, the American red must have been called "tall," leaving the French white chosen by Jeff Cooke on the 2nd as "distracted."

2nd, Jeff Cooke, French white, distracted.

9th, Rita Boyle, Australian red, abstract.

16th, Steve Grille, Spanish red, noisy.

23rd, Joanne Fry, Italian white, nervous.

30th, Dave Baker, American red, tall.

Officer Material, p. 86

Nancy Oriano plays a K9 Squad officer (clue 2) and Cleo Diaz plays Erica Fell (clue 7), so Lucy McGee of the Robbery Squad—who isn't played by Kate Lockhart, who plays a USAFP officer (clue 6)—or Ella Fremont (clue 3) must be played by Ali Booth. So, Lucy McGee isn't the DPD officer, who's played by an actress with an even number of letters in her surname (clue 1), the NYPD officer, who's in the Homicide Squad (clue 4), or the MSP officer, whose name is Liz Marlowe (clue 5), so they must be in the LAPD. So, Ella Fremont's character isn't in Special Investigations (clue 7) or the Cold Case Squad (clue 3) and must be in the Homicide Squad of the NYPD (cue 4). Now, Liz Marlowe, the MSP officer, must be Nancy Oriano's K9 Squad member and, by elimination, Cleo Diaz's Erica Fell must be in the DPD. She's not in Special Investigations (clue 7), so she must be in the Cold Case Squad, leaving the Special Investigations officer played by Kate Lockhart. Ella Fremont's character isn't Sam Thatcher (clue 3), so she must be Fran Grant, leaving Sam Thatcher as Kate Lockhart's character in the Special Investigations Division of the USAFP.

Ali Booth, Lucy McGee, Robbery, LAPD.
Cleo Diaz, Erica Fell, Cold Case, DPD.
Ella Fremont, Fran Grant, Homicide, NYPD.
Kate Lockhart, Sam Thatcher, Special Investigations, USAFP.
Nancy Oriano, Liz Marlowe, K9, MSP.

Fishing Poll, p. 88

The woman in the fur hat was approached with, "I'm asking about . . ." (clue 2), the person entering the mall was asked, "Do you have . . .?" (clue 3), and both "Excuse me, madam" (clue 2) and "Could I have . . ." (clue 5) were used with women, so the man in the baseball cap, tackled near the mall diner (clue 5), must have been approached with, "Excuse me, sir," and he must have responded with, "I have to catch a bus" (clue 4). By elimination, the other man—the tall one—must have been asked, "Do you have a minute or two?" as he walked through the mall entrance. The person approached on Main Street replied, "No comment!" (clue 2), so the woman with the baby, who brushed off Judy with "Feeding time!", who wasn't approached in the mall center (clue 1), must have been approached in the Town Square. The woman in the fur hat wasn't on Main Street (clue 2), so he must have been in the mall center, leaving the elderly woman as the person stopped on Main Street. She wasn't stopped with, "Excuse me, madam" (clue 2) and must have been approached with, "Could I have a moment of your time?" before responding, "No comment!", leaving the woman with the baby as the target approached with, "Excuse me, madam." Finally, the tall man, approached in the mall entrance with, "Do you have a minute or two?", didn't reply, "I've already given," and so he must have said, "I have a train to catch," leaving the woman in the fur hat in the center of the mall responding to "I'm asking about yogurt," with "I've already given."

Main Street, elderly lady, Could I have . . ., No comment!
Mall entrance, tall man, Do you have . . ., Catch train.
Mall diner, man in cap, Excuse me, sir, Catch bus.
Mall center, woman in fur hat, I'm asking about, Already given.
Town Square, woman with baby, Excuse me, madam, Feeding time!

Aliens, p. 90

Xan Balu from Durdane (clue 1) can't be the alien on a sales trip, who's from Helliconia (clue 3), nor is he (?) shopping (clue 1), and it's Q'inshav Bek who's going to college (clue 4), so Xan Balu must be sightseeing. So, from clue 2, figure 1 can't be from Worlorn, nor can Xan Balu be figure 1 (clue 1). Clue 3 rules out the Helliconian as figure 1, who must therefore be from Poloda. He isn't Q'inshav Bek (clue 4), so he isn't going to college and therefore must be on a shopping trip. The alien from Helliconia isn't Toarn Tumika (clue 3), so it must be Rovedah, leaving Toarn Tumika as figure 1. By elimination, Q'inshav Bek is from Worlorn. Clue 1 tells us Xan Balu is figure 2, so, from clue 3, Rovedah must be figure 4, leaving figure 3 as Q'inshav Bek.

1, Toarn Tumika, Poloda, shopping.
2, Xan Balu, Durdane, sightseeing.
3, Q'inshav Bek, Worlorn, going to college.
4, Rovedah, Helliconia, sales trip.

Casino Royale, p. 91

Percy Punt played roulette (clue 3), so the person who lost $10 playing blackjack (clue 1), who wasn't Stephanie Stake (clue 2), must have been Walter Wager, leaving Stephanie Stake at the poker table with dealer Henry Heinz (clue 2). Percy didn't lose $7.50 (clue 3), so he must have lost $5 and Stephanie Stake must have lost $7.50 at the poker table. So, from clue 2, Yolanda Yankee must have dealt at the blackjack table where Walter Wager lost $10. By elimination, Percy Punt's roulette game must have been run by croupier Thomas Trixie.

Percy Punt, roulette, Thomas Trixie, $5.
Stephanie Stake, poker, Henry Heinz, $7.50.
Walter Wager, blackjack, Yolanda Yankee, $10.

For Your Eyes Only, p. 92

The 10:40 appointment replied, "Not from here" (clue 4), so Saul Blurd, who replied, "E,X,I,T" but who didn't have the 10:00 appointment (clue 1) must have had the 10:20 appointment with Iris Scanne (clue 3). By elimination, the 10:00 patient must have answered, "What chart?" So, this wasn't Luke Strate's patient (clue 3) and must have been Len Sella's patient Justin Haze (clue 2). By elimination, Donna Seyitt must have had the 10:40 appointment with Luke Strate and replied to "Can you read the chart, please?" with "Well, not from here obviously."

10:00, Justin Haze, Len Sella, "What chart?"
10:20, Saul Blurd, Iris Scanne, "E,X,I,T."
10:40, Donna Seyitt, Luke Strate, "Not from here.

Battleships, p. 93

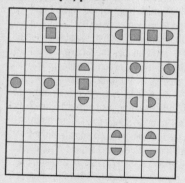

Paint, p. 94

Chris Cockroft encountered wet paint on the landing (clue 1) and Hamish Hazel spent the day partly yellow (clue 2), so the boy who was painted green in the corridor, who wasn't

Ben Barton (clue 5) must have been Martin Masters. Hamish Hazel's yellow hue wasn't acquired in the main entrance (clue 2), so it must have been in the gym. By elimination, it was Ben Barton whose wet paint encounter was in the main entrance. One boy's hands were painted white (clue 3), so the knees, which didn't end up blue (clue 6), must have been painted green and belonged to Martin Masters. By elimination, one boy's hair must have been painted blue. It didn't belong to Chris Cockroft (clue 1), so it must have been Ben Barton's hair that turned blue after a tussle in the main entrance, leaving Chris Cockroft's landing encounter giving him white hands.

Ben Barton, main entrance, hair, blue.
Chris Cockroft, landing, hands, white.
Hamish Hazel, gym, yellow, face.
Martin Masters, corridor, knees, green.

Back in the Swim, p. 96

Martin Masters's breathing device was a length of old hose pipe (clue 2) and the deviser of the Windmill stroke hopes to make do with drinking straws (clue 2), so Chris Cockroft, who invented the Scythe but who doesn't have to stand up every few strokes (clue 1) must be the boy who employs a balloon as an air tank and therefore spent his vacation on the Linnet Islands (clue 4). The Periscope was developed on the island of Crudica (clue 3), so the Eel, which wasn't devised at the Costa del Buoy (clue 5) must have been invented by Hamish Hazel during his vacation on Pilchardia (clue 3) and, by elimination, Hamish must have to stand up every few strokes to take a breath. We now know either the stroke or the vacation spot for three breathing devices, so the Periscope inventor on Crudica must employ the hose pipe and is therefore Martin Masters, leaving Ben Barton as the inventor of the Windmill while vacationing on the Costa del Buoy and hoping a line of straws will help him breathe.

Ben Barton, Windmill, Cost del Buoy, straws.

Chris Cockroft, Scythe, Linnet Islands, balloon.
Hamish Hazel, Eel, Pilchardia, stand up.
Martin Masters, Periscope, Crudica, hose pipe.

Behind the Man, p. 98

The Vulgarian mistress had held sway for four years (clue 3) and Greta for six (clue 6), so clue 1 rules out two years, four years, and eight years for the mistress of the Margrave of Kukuklokz. From clue 4, the Grand-Duke's mistress had been with him ten years, so the Margrave of Kukuklokz must have been linked with Greta for six years. So, from clue 1, Eva had been at the court of Vulgaria for four years. We now know the Grand-Duke's mistress was neither Eva nor Greta. Karen, who was with the ruler of Frankenstein, had not been with him ten years (clue 2) and Heidi was the Regent's mistress (clue 5), so, by elimination, the Grand-Duke's mistress must have been Mitzi. We have now matched three women with countries, so Heidi's Regent, whose country was not Urdigurdi (clue 5), must have been the ruler of Schlossenberg, which leaves the Grand-Duke in charge of Urdigurdi. Karen's protector was not the Prince of Frankenstein (clue 2), so he must have been its Count, leaving Eva's ruler as the Prince of Vulgaria. So, from clue 2, Karen must have been with the Count of Frankenstein for two years, leaving Heidi's period with the Regent of Schlossenberg as eight years.
Count of Frankenstein, Karen, 2 years.
Grand-Duke of Urdigurdi, Mitzi, 10 years.
Margrave of Kukuklokz, Greta, 6 years.
Prince of Vulgaria, Eva, 4 years.
Regent of Schlossenberg, Heidi, 8 years.

The Paragon and . . ., p. 100

The villain of . . . the Jailbird is Joe Bickel (clue 8) and the villain in San Diego is Zack Rovin (clue 5), so, from clue 1, the villain of . . . the Bull's Eye, set in Washington DC, who is also male, must be the jewel thief Roddy Keeler (clue 4). The kidnapping doesn't take place

in Hollywood or San Diego (clue 3) and the crime ring is in New York City (clue 6), so the kidnapping must be in Dallas. So, from clue 3, the Hollywood malefactor is Lola Crocetti. Lola's crime isn't espionage (clue 1), so it must be murder and she therefore appears in . . . the Copycat (clue 2) and, by elimination, the espionage case must be in San Diego. Kitty Jason's not in . . . the Gymnast (clue 7), so that must be the San Diego-set story featuring Zack Rovin, and Kitty Jason must be in . . . the Loup Garou. It isn't set in Dallas (clue 9), so it must be the New York City vice ring story, leaving Dallas as the setting of . . . the Jailbird and Joe Bickel as the kidnapper.
. . . the Bull's Eye, Washington DC, jewel theft, Roddy Keeler.
. . . the Copycat, Hollywood, murder, Lola Crocetti.
. . . the Gymnast, San Diego, espionage, Zack Rovin.
. . . the Jailbird, Dallas, kidnapping, Joe Bickel.
. . . the Loup Garou, New York City, crime ring, Kitty Jason.

The Webster, p. 102

Crispin rented office 5 (clue 2), so, from clue 4, Wilhelm must have rented office 7 and was therefore Homer (clue 1); Goulet, the ex-police sergeant (clue 4), must have rented office 9, and Spurlock must have worked out of office 10. He was therefore the ex-jewel thief (clue 5). By elimination, Valentine Keyes (clue 6) must have used office 8. He was not the ex-attorney, who was Richard (clue 3), or the ex-Pinkerton's man (clue 6), so he must have been a military policeman. Spurlock wasn't Oliver (clue 5), so it must have been Eddie Spurlock. By elimination, Goulet must have been Oliver Goulet, Richard must have been Richard Crispin in office 5, and Homer Wilhelm must have formerly worked for the Pinkerton's Detective Agency.
5, Richard Crispin, attorney.
7, Homer Wilhelm, Pinkerton's.
8, Valentine Keyes, military policeman.

9, Oliver Goulet, police sergeant.
10, Eddie Spurlock, jewel thief.

Quiet Monday, p. 104

Nicky Nail was visited by his client in person (clue 4), the messenger boy was sent by a male (clue 5) and the officer engaged the Private Eye on behalf of the police department (clue 1), so Dick Drill's contact with client Sandra Andersen (clue 6), which wasn't by text (clue 6), must have been via a phone call at 4:15 (clue 3). The detective who was contacted at 5:15 wasn't Mike Mallet (clue 1) or Nicky Nail (clue 4), and Ricky Wrench's snooze was interrupted at 4:45 (clue 5), so it must have been Spike Spanner. Since it was Dick Drill who was contacted at 4:15, the 4:30 client can't have been the San Angelo Police Dept. (clue 1) or Conrad Sanders (clue 4), and Cesar Lopez became a client at 5:00 (clue 2), so it must have been Amanda Jonson. So, this can't have been the time that Mike Mallet was contacted by a male client (clue 1) and so he must have been contacted at 5:00 by Cesar Lopez, leaving Nicky Nail as the private eye contacted at 4:30 by Amanda Jonson in person. Now, from clue 1, Spike Spanner's new client must have been the San Angelo Police Dept., having been contacted at 5:15 by a police officer. By elimination, Conrad Sanders must have contacted Ricky Wrench at 4:45. This first contact wasn't by messenger boy (clue 5), so it must have been by text, leaving Cesar Lopez contacting Mike Mallet at 5:00 by messenger boy.

Dick Drill, 4:15, phone call, Sandra Andersen.
Mike Mallet, 5:00, messenger, Cesar Lopez.
Nicky Nail, 4:30, client visit, Amanda Jonson.
Ricky Wrench, 4:45, text, Conrad Sanders.
Spike Spanner, 5:15, police officer, San Angelo Police Dept.

Welcome Break, p. 106

The Skwurms are in seats C21/22 (clue 4) but haven't ordered the cola, so, from the same clue, the Fijettes, who have seats numbered lower than the cola orderers, can't have seats J16/17. Nor are those seats occupied by the Twichers (clue 1) or the Schuffles (clue 5), so they must belong to the Riggles, who have ordered a shandy (clue 3)—at least for the time being! The draft beer drinker is in row M (clue 5), so the cola drinker, who isn't in row C (clue 4) and can't have the lowest numbered seats (clue 4) must be in seats E8/9 and, from clue 4, the Fijettes must be in seats E5/6. They didn't order draft lager (clue 4) and must have ordered bottled lager, and therefore also whiskey (clue 6), leaving the draft lager as the choice of the Skwurms in row C. Now, from clue 1, the Twichers aren't in seat E8/9, so they must have seats M13/14 and must have ordered the draft beer and port and lemon (clue 1). By elimination, the Schuffles must be in seats E8/9 and have ordered the cola and the vermouth (clue 2). Finally, the Riggles in seats J16/17 didn't order the vodka and tonic, so they must have ordered gin and tonic with the alcohol-free shandy, leaving the Skwurms in row C ordering draft lager and vodka and tonic.

C21/22, Skwurm, draft lager and vodka and tonic.
E5/6, Fijette, bottled lager and whiskey.
E8/9, Schuffle, cola and vermouth.
J16/17, Riggle, shandy and gin and tonic.
M13/14, Twicher, draft beer and port and lemon.

Sporting Writers, p. 108

Jonathan Tanner (clue 7) can't be the author of *Full Tilt*, whose names are the same length (clue 4), and neither can Donald, since he can't have a six-letter surname. Gregory isn't Campion, the yachtsman (clue 3), and Brian's book is *Dead Letter* (clue 2), so the author of *Full Tilt* must be Alan, the showjumper (clue 5), whose surname, from clue 4, must be Wolf. Lynch wrote *Party Piece* (clue 6), and we know that Jonathan Tanner's book isn't *Dead Letter* or *Full Tilt*. Nor is it *Scapegoat* (clue 7), so it must be *In the Bag*, and he is therefore the golfer (clue 8). We have now matched books to three surnames, so Brian, who wrote *Dead Letter* and isn't Goodyear (clue 2), must be Campion, the yachtsman (clue 3). By elimination, *Scapegoat* must be by Goodyear. From clue 1, Donald isn't Lynch, so he must be Goodyear, and Gregory must be Lynch. Donald Goodyear isn't the high jumper (clue 5), so he must be the basketball player, leaving the high jumper as Gregory Lynch, author of *Party Piece*.

Alan Wolf, showjumper, *Full Tilt*.
Brian Campion, yachtsman, *Dead Letter*.
Donald Goodyear, basketball player, *Scapegoat*.
Gregory Lynch, high jumper, *Party Piece*.
Jonathan Tanner, golfer, *In the Bag*.

Logi-5, p. 110

D	B	E	A	C
C	A	B	D	E
E	C	D	B	A
A	D	C	E	B
B	E	A	C	D

Killer Sudoku, p. 110

2	5	9	8	6	7	4	1	3
1	7	3	4	9	2	6	8	5
4	6	8	3	1	5	9	2	7
3	4	7	5	8	9	1	6	2
9	1	2	6	4	3	7	5	8
5	8	6	2	7	1	3	4	9
6	2	4	9	3	8	5	7	1
7	9	5	1	2	4	8	3	6
8	3	1	7	5	6	2	9	4

Domino Search, p. 111

1	3	6	1	2	5	5	4
2	2	0	2	1	4	6	6
4	3	1	1	0	0	0	5
6	6	6	5	4	4	3	6
3	2	0	3	3	2	4	6
4	3	5	3	1	1	0	0
0	5	5	5	2	4	2	1

Can't Wait, p. 112

The spilt wine resulted in a $15 tip (clue 3) and the accident blamed on one diner's feet produced a $20 tip (clue 6), so the tip for the poltergeist excuse, which was $10 more than that left by Brian Bolt's dropped bread rolls (clue 4), can't have been $10, $15, or $25, and so it must have been $30. So, from clue 4, Brian Bolt must have left the $20 tip and his moving feet must have been blamed for the dropped bread rolls. Wilbur Wolf's waving arm was to blame for one incident (clue 2). He didn't leave the $10 tip (clue 2), and Tiffany Tuckin left $25 (clue 3), so Wilbur must have left $15 as a tip after his waving arm caused Algernon to spill the wine over his pants. From clue 1, the earthquake excuse wasn't given to the diner who left the $25 tip, and so they must have left $10, and the overcharging caused by a power surge (clue 1) must have been accompanied by $25 from Tiffany Tuckin. Sylvia Swallow's cutlery wasn't dropped (clue 5), so she must have suffered the spilt soup. So, her accident wasn't excused with an earthquake (clue 1) and she must have left the $30 tip after hearing the poltergeist excuse, leaving Charles Chew as the diner whose cutlery was dropped because of an earthquake and who left a $10 tip.

Brian Bolt, dropped rolls, diner's feet, $20.
Charles Chew, dropped cutlery, earthquake, $10.
Sylvia Swallow, spilt soup, poltergeist, $30.

Tiffany Tuckin, overcharged, power surge, $25.
Wilbur Wolf, spilt wine, diner's arm, $15.

San Guinari Romance, p. 114

Mel Bourne isn't from Kent (clue 1), nor, as her boyfriend is a musician (clue 1), can she be the nurse from Essex, who's in love with the doctor (clue 2). Beverley Hills's home is north of Mel Bourne's (clue 4), so can't be in Kent, Essex, or Suffolk, nor is it in Derbyshire (clue 4), so it must be in Durham. Connie Mara, Diego Mateos' girlfriend, isn't the nurse from Essex who loves the doctor (clue 2), nor is her boyfriend the journalist (clue 2) or the politician, who is Eduardo Huerta (clue 3), so he must be the Army officer. Connie Mara can't be from Kent (clue 5) or Derbyshire, the home of Antonio Rubio's girlfriend (clue 4), so she must be from Suffolk. Eduardo Huerta's girlfriend comes from south of Suffolk (clue 5) and his occupation rules out Essex, so she must be from Kent. The nurse from Essex isn't Sarah Jevo (clue 2), so it must be Pam Plona and, by elimination, Sarah Jevo must come from Kent. Also by elimination, Mel Bourne must be from Derbyshire and Beverley Hills's boyfriend must be the journalist. Pam Plona's boyfriend isn't Manuel Garza (clue 2), so he must be Ricardo Obregon, leaving Manuel Garza as Beverley Hills's boyfriend.

Beverley Hills, Durham, Manuel Garza, journalist.
Connie Mara, Suffolk, Diego Mateos, Army officer.
Mel Bourne, Derbyshire, Antonio Rubio, musician.
Pam Plona, Essex, Ricardo Obregon, doctor.
Sarah Jevo, Kent, Eduardo Huerta, politician.

Writer's Block, p. 116

One man wrote six historical novels (clue 5). The genre of the man who wrote two books wasn't science fiction or whodunits (clue 2), nor horror novels (clue 4), so he must have written war novels and was therefore Hugh

Bookwright (clue 6). So, the man who hired a ghostwriter must have written three or four books (clue 4), but as the six books were historical novels, there must have been five horror books (clue 4) and the ghostwriter employer must have written three books. His genre isn't science fiction (clue 3), so it must be whodunits. By elimination, Perry Scribe's four books (clue 6) must be science fiction. He didn't fake his death (clue 3) and it was Barry Fabler who resorted to plagiarism (clue 1), so Perry Scribe must have become an editor. Jason Hack didn't write whodunits (clue 2), so he hasn't written three books, and, as he wrote fewer than Barry Fabler (clue 1), he can't have written six, so he must have written five horror novels. So, Barry Fabler must have written six historical novels and become a plagiarist (clue 1). By elimination, the whodunits must have been by Mark Besseller, and Jason Hack must have faked his death.

Barry Fabler, historical fiction, 6, plagiarism.
Hugh Bookwright, war novels, 2, became journalist.
Jason Hack, horror novels, 5, faked death.
Mark Besseller, whodunits, 3, hired ghostwriter.
Perry Scribe, science fiction, 4, became editor.

Riding the Rales, p. 118

Ricky Wrench hasn't been working on his case for five days (clue 5), so the man going to see Countess Von Stefl, who has been working on the case for one day fewer (clue 5), can't be the man in seat 4 who has been on the case for four days (clue 2). Nor is the man in seat 4 traveling to see Earl O'Malley (clue 1) or Petula Rigger (clue 7), and the man going to see Sgt. Stanley Hansell has been investigating for six days (clue 2), so the man in seat 4 must be going to see Bugsy Brakes. So, from clue 6, the man in seat 5 with a meeting on Pernod Place (clue 3) must have been working for three days. He isn't going to see Earl O'Malley (clue 1) or Sgt. Stanley Hansell (clue 2), so he must be going to see one of the women. So, from clue 3, the person being met by the Private Eye in seat 3 must also be female. It's not Petula Rigger (clue 7), so it must be Countess Von Stefl, and Petula Rigger must be the person the detective in seat 5 is meeting. We now know the detective meeting Countess Von Stefl hasn't been on the case for six, five, four, or three days, and so he must have been working for two days and is therefore Nicky Nail (clue 2); and, from clue 5, Ricky Wrench must be the detective who has been working for three days and is sitting in seat 5 going to see Petula Rigger on Pernod Place (clue 3). By elimination, the man meeting Earl O'Malley at his bar on Scotch Square must have been investigating for five days. Nicky Nail isn't going to meet the Countess on Tequila Terrace (clue 5) and Mike Mallet is attending the meeting on Bourbon Boulevard (clue 4), so he must be meeting her on Schnapps Street. Now, from clue 1, the detective in seat 4 must be Dick Drill and the one in seat 1 must be going to see Earl O'Malley on Scotch Square, leaving the detective in seat 2 as the one hoping to reinvigorate his stalled six-day investigation with a visit to Sgt. Stanley Hansell. We now know either the detective or the location for four meetings, so the meeting that Mike Mallet is traveling to on Bourbon Boulevard must be with Sgt. Hansell and Mike Mallet is therefore in seat 2. By elimination, the detective in seat 1 must be Spike Spanner and the location of Dick Drill's meeting with Bugsy Brakes must be Tequila Terrace.

1, Spike Spanner, Scotch Square, Earl O'Malley, 5 days.
2, Mike Mallet, Bourbon Boulevard, Sgt. Stanley Hansell, 6 days.
3, Nicky Nail, Schnapps Street, Countess Von Stefl, 2 days.
4, Dick Drill, Tequila Terrace, Bugsy Brakes, 4 days.
5, Ricky Wrench, Pernod Place, Petula Rigger, 3 days.

Bandwagon Books, p. 120

Horace features with the Magic Sword (clue 5). The hero in the *Egyptian Mummy* book by J.K. Rapping is male (clue 1), so isn't Heidi Pibble (clue 2). Nor does she feature with the *Shape-Changer* (clue 2), or the *Imitation Witch*, who's in the book with the hero called Parker (clue 3), so her book must be *Heidi Pibble and the Flying Pig*. Its writer isn't J.K. Ribbing (clue 5), J.K. Rybling, whose hero is surnamed Peters (clue 4), or J.K. Rusting, whose hero is Henry (clue 6), so it must be J.K. Redding. We've identified the "and the" elements of the titles featuring Pibble and Parker, and know that Peters is J.K. Rybling's creation, so J.K. Rapping's hero involved with an *Egyptian Mummy*, who isn't named Pulman (clue 1), must be Pyckle. Henry is J.K. Rusting's hero and his surname contains a K (clue 6) so he must be Parker. J.K. Rapping's hero isn't Harold (clue 1), so it must be Hamish. By elimination, Harold must be in the book with the *Shape-Changer*. His surname isn't Pulman (clue 1), so it must be Peters, and he's therefore J.K. Rybling's hero. This leaves Horace, who features with the *Magic Sword*, as Pulman, and as the hero created by J.K. Ribbing.

Hamish Pyckle and the Egyptian Mummy, **J.K. Rapping.**
Harold Peters and the Shape-Changer, **J.K. Rybling.**
Heidi Pibble and the Flying Pig, **J.K. Redding.**
Henry Parker and the Imitation Witch, **J.K. Rusting.**
Horace Pulman and the Magic Sword, **J.K. Ribbing.**

Model Tea, p. 122

The Ceylon tea is whisked (clue 3), so the pot-swirled tea, that isn't Darjeeling or Nilgiri (clue 1), must be Brian Brewer's Assam tea. The Darjeeling tea didn't finish fourth (clue 1) and we know the special technique for the Assam and the Ceylon, so the double-brewed tea that placed last (clue 4) must have been the Nilgiri.

It wasn't brewed by Betty Boyle, who finished third (clue 6), or Prunella Potter, who employed the high pour (clue 2), so it must have been made by Stewart Steepe. By elimination, Betty Boyle's egg whisk must have been used on the Ceylon tea and Prunella Potter must have high-poured her Darjeeling. So, from clue 1, she didn't come first and must have finished second, leaving Brian Brewer's pot-swirled Assam as the winner of the golden strainer.

Betty Boyle, Ceylon, whisk stir, third.
Brian Brewer, Assam, pot-swirl, first.
Prunella Potter, Darjeeling, high pour, second.
Stewart Steep, Nilgiri, double-brew, fourth.

Student Models, p. 124

The A grade wasn't achieved by Samantha (clue 1), Pamela (clue 2), or Ricardo (clue 4), and so it must have been awarded to Quentin. The C wasn't given to Pamela (clue 2) or Ricardo (clue 3), so it must have been Samantha's grade. Ricardo was asked to feign coyness (clue 4), so the student asked to look surprised, who wasn't Pamela (clue 2) and couldn't have received an A (clue 2) and so wasn't Quentin, must have been Samantha. Her grade rules out Beau Guss (clue 2) and Charlie Tann (clue 1) as her examiner, and Arty Fisher asked for anger (clue 3), so Samantha must have received her C for surprise from Fay Kitt. Charlie Tann didn't ask anyone to pout (clue 1), so he must have asked Ricardo to be coy, leaving Beau Guss requesting the pout. He didn't ask this of Pamela (clue 2) so he must have examined Quentin and awarded an A for some tiptop pouting. By elimination, Pamela must have been asked to display anger by Arty Fisher. Finally, from clue 1, Charlie Tann must have awarded a B+ for some pretty convincing coyness by Ricardo, leaving Arty Fisher awarding a B- for some so-so anger by Pamela.

Pamela, Arty Fisher, anger, B-.
Quentin, Beau Guss, pouting, A.
Ricardo, Charlie Tann, coy, B+.
Samantha, Fay Kitt, surprise, C.

Five Sisters, p. 126

Jean Lebas lives in Monaco (clue 2), and Amanda and her husband live in Dublin (clue 7). Jane's husband Otis Morgan isn't the car salesman from Vancouver (clue 4), nor can he be the man from Auckland, whose first name begins with a consonant (clue 3), so the Morgans must live in North London. Otis isn't the police officer (clue 5) or the dentist, who is married to Margaret (clue 1), and the publisher is Ian Dugdale (clue 6), so Otis Morgan must be a movie producer. Ian Dugdale isn't from Auckland (clue 3), so he must be the Dublin man married to Amanda. The police officer isn't Georgina's husband (clue 5), so he must be married to Susan, leaving Georgina as the wife of the car salesman. So, he isn't Jean Lebas from Monaco (clue 2) and must be either Leo Cox or Nick Dunn. So, from clue 5, Susan's police officer must be either Jean Lebas or Otis Morgan—but we know Otis married Jane, so Susan must have wed Jean Lebas, and, from clue 5, Georgina married Leo Cox. Finally, by elimination, Margaret's husband is Nick Dunn, who he must do his dentistry in Auckland.

Amanda, Ian Dugdale, publisher, Dublin.
Georgina, Leo Cox, car salesman, Vancouver.
Jane, Otis Morgan, movie producer, North London.
Margaret, Nick Dunn, dentist, Auckland.
Susan, Jean Lebas, police officer, Monaco.

Cherry Tree Radio, p. 128

The presenter of the 4pm-7pm show, featuring country music, isn't Roy Ferguson (clue 5), Hazel Roberts, who has the 12 noon-2 p.m. show (clue 2), or Jerry Pye, who plays modern pop (clue 7). Clue 4 rules out Colin Bush for the last show, so the 4 p.m.-7 p.m. show must be hosted by Lucy Murphy. Colin doesn't present the 7:00 a.m.-10:00 a.m. show (clue 4). The 4pm-7pm show doesn't feature 1960s pop, so clue 4 also rules out the 2pm-4pm show for Colin, so he must have the 10:00 a.m.-12 noon slot and, from clue

4, the ex-decorator must run the 7:00 a.m.-10:00 a.m. show. This person's music isn't jazz (clue 1) and the time rules out country. The ex-librarian plays folk (clue 6) and clue 4 rules out 1960s pop, so the 7:00 a.m.-10:00 a.m. music must be the modern pop favored by Jerry Pye. By elimination, Roy Ferguson must host the 2 p.m.-4 p.m. slot. Jerry is a decorator, so, from clue 1, he doesn't offer the jazz. Nor does he play 1960s pop (clue 4), so Colin must play folk and is therefore the ex-librarian. So, from clue 1, jazz isn't Hazel Roberts' 12 noon-2:00 p.m. music, so she must play 1960s pop, leaving the jazz as Roy Ferguson's music. So, from clue 1, Hazel must be the ex-bus driver. Roy wasn't a cashier (clue 3), so he must have been a firefighter, leaving the cashier as Lucy Murphy.

7 a.m.-10 a.m., Jerry Pye, decorator, modern pop.
10 a.m.-12 noon, Colin Bush, librarian, folk.
12 noon-2 p.m., Hazel Roberts, bus driver, 1960s pop.
2 p.m.-4 p.m., Roy Ferguson, firefighter, jazz.
4 p.m.-7 p.m., Lucy Murphy, cashier, country.

Battleships, p. 130

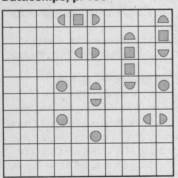

Sign In, p. 131

2	5	1	3	4
5	2	3	4	1
4	3	5	1	2
3	1	4	2	5
1	4	2	5	3

Sudoku, p. 131

2	8	4	5	6	1	3	9	7
1	7	6	2	9	3	5	4	8
5	9	3	7	8	4	1	2	6
3	2	7	6	4	8	9	5	1
4	6	9	1	7	5	8	3	2
8	1	5	3	2	9	6	7	4
6	3	2	8	5	7	4	1	9
9	5	8	4	1	2	7	6	3
7	4	1	9	3	6	2	8	5

Fearsome Five, p. 132

Champley "the Sausage-Maker" isn't the former embalmer (clue 6), the ex-horse-thief from Lhistz (clue 4) or the ex-soldier nicknamed "Stone Face" (clue 2), while Khirpon is the ex-gold miner (clue 1), so Champley must have been a farmer. Since Rampik's hometown starts with a letter in the second half of the alphabet (clue 3), he can't be the horse thief, nor the soldier (clue 2), so he must be the embalmer. So, from clue 6, Rampik isn't from Wolframberg, so he must be from Psephrok, and Rampik's nickname is therefore "Umbrolus" (clue 5). Neither Gortrach nor Khirpon are "Cudgels" (clue 1), so that must be Vulport's nickname. We know Khirpon's not "Stone Face," the ex-soldier, so he must be "the Rodent," and, by elimination, "Stone Face" must be Gortrach. Therefore, his hometown starts with a letter in the first half of the alphabet (clue 2). It isn't Kamanton (clue 2), or, from his former job, Lhistz, so it must be Chakitl. By elimination, Vulport must be the ex-horse thief. Champley isn't from Wolframberg (clue 6), so he must come from Kamanton, and Khirpon must come from Wolframberg.

Champley "the Sausage-Maker," Kamanton, farmer.
Gortrach "Stone Face," Chakitl, soldier.
Khirpon "the Rodent," Wolframberg, gold miner.
Rampik "Umbrolus," Psephrok, embalmer.
Vulport "Cudgels," Lhistz, horse thief.

Brewing Up, p. 134

Aggie's brew has a bit of a frog (line 2) and one cauldron has a tail of newt (line 1), so the liver in Sybil's brew (line 7), which isn't from a rat (line 8) or a shrew (line 11) must be from a vole. So, Sybil's potion doesn't cure warts (line 5). The flying potion has legs (line 6), Wanda's potion is to see the future (line 9) and the shrew brew will change your form (line 10), so Sybil's liver of vole must cause earthquakes. We know that the part of the shrew in the form-changing potion isn't its legs, liver, or tail. Nor is it its nose (lines 11 and 12), so it must be its ears. So, it's not part of Helga's brew (line 3) and its purpose rules out Wanda, so it must be in Winnie's potion. Helga's concoction doesn't shift warts (line 4), so she must have made the leg-based flying potion, leaving Aggie's frog froth as the wart remover. By final elimination, Aggie must have used nose of frog, Helga must have used leg of rat, and Wanda's future-seeing potion must have included the tail of newt.

Aggie, nose of frog, wart removal.
Helga, leg of rat, flying potion.
Sybil, liver of vole, cause earthquakes.
Wanda, tail of newt, see the future.
Winnie, ear of shrew, change form.

Drones on Charge, p. 136

Rupert de Grey was in court on Thursday (clue 5) and Montague Ffolliott was up before Simeon Silk (clue 3), so the Drone in court on Monday with Judge Barrington Beak (clue 6), who wasn't Gerald Huntingdon (clue 6) or Edward Tanqueray (clue 2), must have been Archie Fotheringhay on a charge of stealing Sergeant Sucker's bike (clue 1). Now, from clue 2, Edward Tanqueray can't have been in court on Friday or Tuesday and must have attended on Wednesday with, from the same clue, the concealing a suspect charge being answered on Tuesday and Judge Royston Robe presiding on Thursday in the case involving Rupert de Grey. Since the stolen bike charge was Monday's case, Montague Ffolliott couldn't have been in court on Tuesday (clue 3), so Montague and Judge Simeon Silk must have crossed paths on Friday. By elimination, Gerald Huntingdon must have been on trial on Tuesday. We now know either the judge or charge for four days, so Judge Wynford Wigge must have presided over the driving offense case (clue 4) on Wednesday and the driver must have been Edward Tanqueray, leaving the judge presiding over Gerald Huntingdon's suspect concealing case on Tuesday as Judge Benedict Bench. Finally, Montague Ffolliott wasn't charged with giving false information (clue 3) so he must have been charged, convicted, and fined for knocking off Sergeant Sucker's helmet, leaving Rupert de Grey as the Drone charged with sending Sergeant Sucker on a wild goose chase.

Monday, Archie Fotheringhay, Barrington Beak, stealing bike.
Tuesday, Gerald Huntingdon, Benedict Bench, concealing suspect.
Wednesday, Edward Tanqueray, Wynford Wigge, driving offense.
Thursday, Rupert de Grey, Royston Robe, false information.
Friday, Montague Ffolliott, Simeon Silk, dislodging helmet.

Plays for Today, p. 138

Airtight is at Rowse's (clue 5), Ross Lord's play is at the Hanover (clue 2) and the play at the St. Denis was called "unspeakable" (clue 3), so *Stooge* by Anthony Mark, which isn't "unspeakable" and isn't at the Imperial, must be at the Capital. *Watershed* isn't at the Imperial (clue 4) or the St. Denis (clue 3), so it must be Ross Lord's play at the Hanover. We now know the author or the review for three theaters, so John King's "extremely funny" tragedy (clue 5), which isn't *Airtight* at Rowse's (clue 5), must be at the Imperial. Henry Prince's play is not at the St. Denis (clue 3), so he must have written *Airtight* at Rowse's, leaving Siward Young as the author of the play at St. Denis. He didn't write *Geneva* (clue 6), so he must have penned *Lockyer* and received the "unspeakable" review, leaving John King's "extremely funny" tragedy at the Imperial as *Geneva*. Anthony Mark's *Stooge* at the Capital wasn't descried as "total trash" (clue 1) or rubbish (clue 7) so it must have been called "very poor." Nor was Ross Lord's *Watershed* at the Hanover called "rubbish," so it must have been "total trash," leaving *Airtight* by Henry Prince at Rowse's theater (all tickets still available) as "rubbish."

Airtight, Henry Prince, Rowse's, "rubbish."
Geneva, John King, Imperial, "extremely funny."
Lockyer, Siward Young, St. Denis, "unspeakable."
Stooge, Anthony Mark, Capital, "very poor."
Watershed, Ross Lord, Hanover, "total trash."

Highway Robbery, p. 140

One day's haul was a diamond ring and $11 (clue 6), and the $15 cash was extracted from a couple (clue 2), so the cash Lord Fullbank handed over along with his watch that wasn't $5 or $8 (clue 3) must have been $18. So, from clue 4, this wasn't on Thursday or Friday. Monday's item was the gold pendant (clue 1) and Tuesday was the day Sir Hugo Cashe was robbed (clue 2), so Lord Fullbank must have been relieved of his watch and $18 on Wednesday and, from clue 4, the clock must have been purloined on Friday. Earl Richies wasn't robbed on Monday (clue 1) or on Thursday, when a couple lost $15 (clue 2), so he must have been robbed of his clock

on Friday. We now know either the item or the cash stolen on four days, so the ring and $11 must have belonged to Sir Hugo Cashe, Tuesday's victim, and by elimination, the bracelet must have been taken along with the $15 on Thursday. It didn't belong to the Bundells (clue 5) and must have been stolen from the Tidisomes, leaving Monday's theft of the pendant from Lord and Lady Bundell. So, they didn't lose $8 (clue 1) and must have handed over $5, leaving Earl Richies being robbed of a clock and $8 on Friday.

Monday, Lord and Lady Bundell, pendant, $5.
Tuesday, Sir Hugo Cashe, ring, $11.
Wednesday, Lord Fullbank, watch, $18.
Thursday, Lord and Lady Tidisome, bracelet, $15.
Friday, Earl Richies, clock, $8.

Delivery Duty, p. 142

Ricky Wrench was told to make the delivery at 2:00 p.m. (clue 2) and the 1:00 p.m. delivery was an envelope (clue 3), so Mike Mallet, who was told to deliver a cigar box but not at either 10:00 a.m. or 3:00 p.m. (clue 6), must have been instructed to deliver at 11:00 a.m. by Amanda Anderson (clue 3). So, from clue 6, the 10:00 a.m. delivery must have been at the behest of Carl Cooper, and the female client of Dick Drill (clue 1) must have been Esther Erikson. She didn't request the 3:00 p.m. delivery and we know either the client or the detective for three other times, so Dick Drill must have been instructed by Esther Erikson to deliver the envelope at 1:00 p.m. The wallet was to be delivered before noon (clue 4), so it must have been Carl Cooper's wallet to be delivered at 10:00 a.m. Spike Spanner wasn't detailed to make the 3:00 p.m. delivery (clue 5), so he must have been told by Carl Cooper to deliver the wallet at 10:00 a.m., leaving Nicky Nail as the detective told to deliver at 3:00 p.m. Ricky Wrench wasn't detailed to deliver the leather pouch (clue 2), so he must have been told to deliver the briefcase. So, his client wasn't Donald Davis (clue 5) and must have been Boris Bailey, leaving Nicky Nail's client as Donald Davis and his task as the delivery of the leather pouch at 3:00 p.m.

Dick Drill, Esther Erikson, envelope, 1:00 p.m.

Mike Mallet, Amanda Anderson, cigar box, 11:00 a.m.

Nicky Nail, Donald Davis, leather pouch, 3:00 p.m.

Ricky Wrench, Boris Bailey, briefcase, 2:00 p.m.

Spike Spanner, Carl Cooper, wallet, 10:00 a.m.

Return Message, p. 144

Ricky Wrench, instructed by Boris Bailey, was given the message "The morgue" (clue 3) and Spike Spanner's wallet was empty (clue 1), so the detective who delivered the small rock and was given the message "Tell him, 'I love you'" (clue 2) (and so must have been instructed by a male client), must have been sent by Donald Davis to deliver the rock in the leather pouch. Mike Mallet's cigar box was delivered in the Honolulu Bar (clue 4), the recipient at the train station replied "Humph!" (clue 5), and the one-dollar bill was taken to the bus station (clue 5), so the Nicky Nail, rock in a pouch, "I love you" incident, which wasn't at the news stand must have been in McGinty's Bar. Mike Mallet's cigar box didn't contain the photo (clue 4), so it must have contained the key blank. The detective sent to the train station wasn't Dick Drill (clue 6) or, from his message, Ricky Wrench, so it must have been Spike Spanner who took the empty wallet to the train station only to receive the message "Humph!" By elimination, the photo must have been delivered at the news stand. Dick Drill didn't go to the bus station (clue 6), so it must have been he who took the photo, in the envelope, to the news stand, leaving Ricky Wrench's briefcase containing a single dollar being delivered to the bus station. Finally, Dick Drill didn't receive the message "Tuesday" (clue 6), so he must have been told "It's on" when he handed over the photo in

the envelope at the news stand, leaving Mike Mallet delivering the key blank in the cigar box to the Honolulu Bar and being given the message "Tuesday."

Dick Drill, photograph, news stand, "It's on."

Mike Mallet, key blank, Honolulu Bar, "Tuesday."

Nicky Nail, small rock, McGinty's Bar, "I love you."

Ricky Wrench, one dollar, bus station, "The morgue."

Spike Spanner, nothing, train station, "Humph!"

Sickies, p. 146

The road worker was third into the surgery (clue 4) and Norm Shirker is a truck driver (clue 6), so Colin Ilmore, who was seen fourth but isn't the factory worker (clue 3) and can't be the builder (clue 2) must be the window cleaner with the drinker's elbow (clue 1). So, from clue 2, the man with tweeter's thumb can't have been seen first, second, or fifth, and must have been the road worker seen third. Again, from clue 2, Guy Slacking must have been second in the line, and the builder must have been first with the outgrowing hair (clue 5). It doesn't belong to Ed Downe (clue 5) and must be Ivor Dodge's hopeful dodge. By elimination, Ed Downe must be the road worker with the tweeter's thumb who was third on the list, fifth in line must have been truck driver Norm Shirker, and Guy Slacking, second in line, must be the factory worker. So, he hasn't got the unflattened foot (clue 3) and must be suffering from sleeper's shoulder, leaving Norm Shirker as the man with the unflattened foot, and everyone knows it's dangerous to drive a truck with an unflattened foot.

First, Ivor Dodge, builder, outgrowing hair.
Second, Guy Slacking, factory worker, sleeper's shoulder.
Third, Ed Downe, road worker, tweeter's thumb.

Fourth, Colin Ilmore, window cleaner, drinker's elbow.
Fifth, Norm Shirker, truck driver, unflattened foot.

Blind Dates, p. 148

The problem with the companion in April wasn't an obsession with sports (clue 1), poor table manners (clue 2), rampant egocentricity (clue 3), or lack of dress sense (clue 5) and so it must have been a lack of conversation. So, from clue 4, the date with Hugh must have been on May 23. The snag in August wasn't table manners (clue 2), sartorial mismanagement (clue 5), or an egocentric nature (clue 3), so it must have been the sporting obsession. The man wasn't Timothy (clue 1) or Martin (clue 2), and the date in the month rules out David (clue 6), so Carinthia's date on August 19 must have been with Monty. The badly-dressed man was not the companion for July 3 (clue 5), nor was it the man with poor table manners (clue 2) so it must have been the egocentric man. The meal on this occasion wasn't Indian (clue 1), Italian (clue 3), Chinese (clue 5), or, from its date number, Thai (clue 6), so it must have been Greek. August's restaurant wasn't Indian (clue 1), Chinese (clue 5), or Italian (clue 3), and so it must have been Thai. From clue 2, Martin can't have met Carinthia in June, and so he must have been her date in April, and Hugh, the May companion, must have displayed poor table manners. By elimination, Carinthia's companion must have turned up badly dressed in June. So, from clue 5, Hugh's poor table manners must have been displayed in May at the Chinese restaurant. From clue 1, the Indian restaurant date couldn't have been in June, and must have been Martin's date with no conversation in April, leaving the June date with the badly-dressed man in an Italian restaurant, of all places. Finally, from clue 3, this wasn't with David, so it must be Timothy who needs some new attire, leaving Carinthia's companion in July as David who exhibited egocentricity at a Greek restaurant.

April 16, Martin, Indian, no conversation.
May 23, Hugh, Chinese, poor table manners.
June 4, Timothy, Italian, badly-dressed.
July 3, David, Greek, egocentric.
August 19, Monty, Thai, obsessed with sports.

Logi-5, p. 150

E	D	B	A	C
A	E	C	B	D
C	B	A	D	E
B	C	D	E	A
D	A	E	C	B

Killer Sudoku, p. 150

7	9	2	5	1	6	8	4	3
4	5	3	9	8	2	1	6	7
6	8	1	7	3	4	5	2	9
3	2	5	8	6	1	9	7	4
9	4	7	3	2	5	6	1	8
1	6	8	4	7	9	3	5	2
8	7	4	6	5	3	2	9	1
2	3	6	1	9	7	4	8	5
5	1	9	2	4	8	7	3	6

Battleships, p. 151

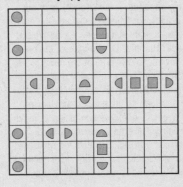

Wayne in the East, p. 152

Wayne's at St. Martin's Church on Wednesday (clue 3) and in Luckstowe on Thursday (clue 5), so, from clue 1, he'll be in Gippswick, at Grummitt House, on either Monday or Tuesday. So, it can't be the location of Wayne's award reception on Friday (clue 4), nor of his presenting an award (clue 1). The AGM is in Woolmarket (clue 6) and the book signing is at Elzevir Brothers (clue 7), so the Gippswick event must be the schools talk. This isn't on Tuesday (clue 2), so it must be on Monday. So, from clue 1, on Tuesday Wayne will present an award. From what we now know, the book signing at Elzevir Brothers must be on Thursday, in Luckstowe. By elimination, St. Martin's Church must be the venue for the AGM and is therefore in Woolmarket. From clue 6, the Tuesday event must be in Storbury, leaving Friday as the day Wayne's in Redewich. The Storbury venue is not Eastshire College (clue 6), so it must be the Windmill Hall, leaving Eastshire College in Redewich.

Monday, Gippswick, Grummitt House, schools talk.
Tuesday, Storbury, Windmill Hall, present award.
Wednesday, Woolmarket, St Martin's Church, AGM.
Thursday, Luckstowe, Elzevir Brothers, book signing.
Friday, Redewich, Eastshire College, receive award.

Terminally Terminal, p. 154

Emily Edinburgh is going to a job interview, the person going to a sales conference has been delayed by a computer crash (clue 5), the person flying to Rome is attending a wedding (clue 4), and a man is going on vacation (clue 5), so Rebecca Rome, who is delayed by the late arrival of her plane (clue 2) but who isn't going to Rome (clue 1), must be going shopping, leaving the woman going to the sales conference as Pauline Paris. The person going to Rome for a wedding isn't Bartholomew Berlin (clue 4), so it must be Lawrence Lisbon, and so, from clue 4, Bartholomew Berlin must be going to Lisbon. Now, from clue 6, Rome is not the airport closed by fog. Berlin airport has snow trouble (clue 3), so Lawrence Lisbon traveling to Rome must be delayed because of a baggage mix-up. By elimination, Bartholomew Berlin must be traveling to Lisbon for a vacation but must be delayed because of fog at Lisbon. Pauline Paris isn't going to Paris (clue 1) and her plane's computer problem rules out Berlin, so she must be going to a sales conference in Edinburgh. Finally, Rebecca Rome, delayed by a late arrival, isn't going to snowy Berlin, so she must be going to Paris for a weekend of shopping, leaving Emily Edinburgh's flight to Berlin for a job interview delayed until the snow is cleared.

Bartholomew Berlin, Lisbon, vacation, fog at destination.
Emily Edinburgh, Berlin, job interview, snow at destination.
Lawrence Lisbon, Rome, wedding, baggage mix-up.
Pauline Paris, Edinburgh, sales conference, computer crash.
Rebecca Rome, Paris, shopping, late arrival.

Native Germans, p. 156

The man in position 3 is a computer programmer (clue 6). Ludwig Haber is in position 1 (clue 4), so clue 3 rules out the man in position 2 as the auto mechanic and clue 1 rules him out as the TV cameraman, who is next clockwise to Karl Brandt, alias Blue Cloud. So, the man in position 2 must be the airline pilot, and so, from clue 5, Red Owl must be in position 4. Since the computer programmer is in position 3, clue 1 rules out Blue Cloud for position 2, so he must be in position 3. So, from clue 1, Red Owl in position 4 must be the TV cameraman, leaving Ludwig Haber in position 1 as the auto mechanic. So, from clue 3, Erich Spitz must be Red Owl, leaving Wilhelm Klein in position

2. He isn't Fire Hawk (clue 2), so he must be Running Elk, leaving Fire Hawk in position 1.

1, Fire Hawk, Ludwig Haber, auto mechanic.

2, Running Elk, Wilhelm Klein, airline pilot.

3, Blue Cloud, Karl Brandt, computer programmer.

4, Red Owl, Erich Spitz, TV cameraman.

Variations on a Raid, p. 158

The 1938 movie, set in World War I, doesn't feature Sarah Ryder as its heroine (clue 3), nor Barbara Adams (clue 1), while Greta Fermi is in the 1995 version (clue 6) and Mary Liston is in the movie with the Spanish Civil War setting (clue 4), so the 1938 heroine must be Jane Irwell, and its hero is therefore David Ellery (clue 5). The hero in the 2014 version isn't Tom Walker (clue 1), Gavin Hart (clue 2), or Brian Croft (clue 4), and so the 2014 hero must actually be heroine Nadia Oswald. The 1995 heroine is Greta Fermi, clue 4 rules out the 1976 hero as Brian Croft, and clue 1 rules out 1976 for Tom Walker and his American Civil War background, so the 1976 hero must be Gavin Hart. Clue 1 rules out Barbara Adams for 1957 and clue 4 rules out Mary Liston, so the 1957 heroine must be Sarah Ryder. So, the 1957 background is not the Crimean War (clue 3), nor can it be World War II (clue 2), so it must be the American Civil War and the 1957 hero is therefore Tom Walker. So, from clue 1, Barbara Adams must be in the 1976 movie and, by elimination, Mary Liston must be in the Spanish Civil War version with Nadia Oswald released in 2014. From clue 4, the 1995 hero must be Brian Croft, and, from clue 2, the 1995 setting must be World War II, leaving the Crimean War as the background for the 1976 movie.

1938, David Ellery, Jane Irwell, World War I.

1957, Tom Walker, Sarah Ryder, American Civil War.

1976, Gavin Hart, Barbara Adams, Crimean War.

1995, Brian Croft, Greta Fermi, World War II.

2014, Nadia Oswald, Mary Liston, Spanish Civil War.

Way Downstream, p. 160

Paul was in boat 2 (clue 3), so, from clue 2, the inflatable can't have been boat 1. Nor can boat 1 have been the punt containing Penny and her boyfriend (clue 1) or the canoe (clue 5), so boat 1 must have been the rowboat. Clue 6 now tells us that Paul must have been Graves; Nick is Mr. Dale (clue 2), so Mr. Moody, who wasn't Lloyd (clue 4), must be Bruce Moody, leaving Lloyd as Lloyd Kirby, who was with Anne (clue 5). Lucy was in boat 3 (clue 7), and clue 5 tells us Anne wasn't in boat 4, so she and Lloyd must have been in boat 1. From clue 2, Sandra wasn't in the inflatable, so she must have been in the canoe and, by elimination, Lucy's boat 3 must have been the inflatable. So, from clue 2, Nick Dale must have been in boat 4, leaving Lucy's companion as Bruce Moody. Neither he, Lloyd, nor Nick were with Miss Gray (clue 4), so her companion must have been Paul Graves on boat 2. Bruce's companion Lucy wasn't Miss Smith (clue 3) or Miss Lee (clue 7), so she must have been Lucy Hanson. So, from clue 1, Penny must have been with Nick Dale in boat 4, leaving Paul Graves with Sandra Gray in the canoe. Miss Smith can't have been in boat 4 (clue 3), so she must be Anne Smith in boat 1, the rowboat, leaving Miss Lee as Penny Lee, accompanying Nick Dale in boat 4, the punt.

1, Lloyd Kirby, Anne Smith, rowboat.

2, Paul Graves, Sandra Gray, canoe.

3, Bruce Moody, Lucy Hanson, inflatable.

4, Nick Dale, Penny Lee, punt.

The Eighth, p. 162

The fort built in 1877 has become Los Pinons (clue 1) and the one in Rodelo Hills was built in 1874 (clue 4), so the fort at Silver Butte that is now Swainson (clue 2), which can't have been set up in 1868 or 1871 (clue 2), must have dated from 1880. So, from clue 2, Fort Nelson must be the 1874 fort. San Bernardo isn't on the site of the 1868 fort (clue 5) and the town that was Fort Lowell, built in 1871, has a one-word name (clue 6), so San Bernardo must be on the site of Fort Nelson, built in 1874. So, from clue 5, the fort in Dyer's Canyon must have been Fort Lowell. It hasn't become Guthrie (clue 5), so it must now be Tornillo, and Guthrie must be on the site of the 1868 fort. It can't have been in the Redstone Pass (clue 3), so it must have been on the Arrow River, leaving the Redstone Pass as the site of Los Pinons, the 1877 fort site. Fort Dohenny wasn't built in 1868 or 1877(clue 1), so in 1880, by Silver Butte. Finally, from clue 3, Fort Bullen, which isn't in the Redstone Pass, must have been at the Arrow River, leaving the Redstone Pass fort as Fort Hutton.

Fort Bullen, 1868, Arrow River, Guthrie.
Fort Dohenny, 1880, Silver Butte, Swainson.
Fort Hutton, 1877, Redstone Pass, Los Pinons.
Fort Lowell, 1871, Dyer's Canyon, Tornillo.
Fort Nelson, 1874, Rodelo Hills, San Bernardo.

Around Lyonesse, p. 164

Ship C is registered on Rubicon Prime (clue 3), so it can't be the *Black Opal* or the *Silver Fox* (clue 2). From clue 2, ship D must be the *Black Opal* or the *Silver Fox* and must be registered on either Cingraike or New Georgia. Ship B is registered on either Luna or Terra Nova, so ship C can't be the *Nomad* (clue 2), and, since ship D isn't registered on Terra Nova (clue 2), ship C can't be the *Argosy* (clue 1) and must be the *Wotan*. From clue 3, ship E, like ship D, must be either the *Black Opal* or the *Silver Fox*. Ship B can't be the *Argosy* (clue 1), so it must be the *Nomad*, and the *Argosy* must be ship A. So, the *Nomad* is registered on Terra Nova (clue 1) and, by elimination, ship E must be registered on Luna. Neither ship A nor ship C is registered on Luna or Terra Nova (clue 2), so ship A, like ship D, must be registered on either Cingraik or New Georgia. Since ship B isn't the *Black Opal*, ship A can't be registered

on New Georgia and must be registered on Cingraik, leaving ship D registered on New Georgia. Also from clue 5, ship E must be the *Black Opal*, so ship D must be the *Silver Fox*, Captain Shamoun's ship (clue 3). Now, from clue 4, ship E must be carrying emergency ration packs and, from clue 5, the farming equipment must be on ship A, the *Argosy*, and the mining equipment on ship C, the *Wotan*. Captain Kimball's ship isn't carrying emergency rations or luxury foods (clue 4), so it must be ship A, the *Argosy*, and ship B must be Captain Garlock's ship. Captain Kirk's ship isn't the *Wotan* (clue 1), so it must be the *Black Opal*, ship E. Finally, from clue 1, the luxury foods must be on ship B, the *Nomad*, Captain Tarl must command the *Wotan*, and, by elimination, the industrial equipment is the *Silver Fox*'s cargo.

A, *Argosy*, Kimball, Cingraik, farming equipment.
B, *Nomad*, Garlock, Terra Nova, luxury foods.
C, *Wotan,* Tarl, Rubicon Prime, mining equipment.
D, *Silver Fox*, Shamoun, New Georgia, industrial equipment.
E, *Black Opal*, Kirk, Luna, emergency ration packs.

Lifestory, p. 166

The 7:30 p.m. movie's female star is Meg Awatt (clue 5); the woman in the 1:00 a.m. movie can't be Ruth Less (clue 1), nor, as Tom Morrow is in the 11:30 p.m. movie (clue 6), can Hazel Nutt be in the 1:00 a.m. movie (clue 4), and clue 7 rules out Annie Moore, so the final movie of the night must star Kerry Blue. So, clue 2 rules out 8:30 p.m. and 1:00 a.m. for Lance Korpral. He's in *The Roman and the Rebel* (clue 2), so he can't be in the 10:00 p.m. movie, *Mr. and Mrs. Chaplin* (clue 3), so Lance Korpral must star in *The Roman and the Rebel* at 7:30 p.m. Clue 1 now rules out 8:30 p.m. and 10:00 p.m. for *Your Money or Your Wife!*, so it must be on at 1:00 a.m. Clue 7 now rules out *Tony and Cherie* for the

8:30 p.m. movie, so it must be coming on at 11:30 p.m., leaving *Caesar and Cleo* as the 8:30 p.m. movie. Now, from clue 7, Mack Numbre must be Dick Turpin in the 1:00 a.m. movie. Clue 6 rules out Guy Sospittle for the 8:30 p.m. movie, so he must be in the 10:00 p.m. one, leaving Percy Vere in the 8:30 p.m. movie. So, from clue 4, Hazel Nutt must be in the 11:30 p.m. movie, and the woman in *Tony and Cherie*, who isn't Annie Moore (clue 7), must be Ruth Less, leaving Annie Moore in the 8:30 p.m. movie, *Caesar and Cleo*.

7:00 p.m., Lance Korpral, Meg Awatt, *The Roman and the Rebel*.

8:30 p.m., Percy Vere, Annie Moore, *Caesar and Cleo*.

10:00 p.m., Guy Sospittle, Hazel Nutt, *Mr. and Mrs. Chaplin*.

11:30 p.m., Tom Morrow, Ruth Less, *Tony and Cherie*.

1:00 a.m., Mack Numbre, Kerry Blue, *Your Money or Your Wife!*

Crème de la . . ., p. 168

The crème de carrot costs $15 (clue 3), so the most expensive liqueur, which isn't crème de cucumber (clue 1), crème de cheese (clue 2), crème de peanut (clue 5), or crème de olive (clue 6) must be crème de rice. Bottle 1, the crème de olive, isn't priced at $20 (clue 6) and we know it's not $15 or $25. It can't be $23 (clue 5) and, since Danebury's liqueur costs $20 (clue 3), the crème de olive can't cost $18 and so it must cost $21, and, from clue 6, Warton's drink must cost $23. From clue 5, Barton's crème de peanut can't cost $25, $20, or $15, and its brand or type rules out $21 and $23, so it must cost $18 and bottle 3 must be the $20 offering from Danebury's (clue 3). So Bartlet's $18 crème de peanut, immediately left of the $23 bottle, must be on the bottom row, either bottle 4 or 5, with the $23 bottle as bottle 5 or 6. If bottle 5 were the $23 bottle, there would be nowhere for the crème de cucumber on the top row (clue 1)—if it were bottle 2, it would have to be priced at $20, which we

have already allocated to bottle 3, and if it were bottle 3, the $23 bottle would have to be bottle 6. So, Warton's $23 bottle must be bottle 6, the crème de cucumber must be Danebury's crème de cucumber in bottle 3 at $20, and Bartlets's $18 crème de peanut must be bottle 5. From clue 1, bottle 2 must be Haskill's drink. We now know that the crème de cheese isn't priced at $15, $18, $21, or $25. Since Tingle's drink isn't $18, the crème de cheese can't be $20, and so it must be Warton's $23 bottle of crème de cheese in position 6. So, from clue 2, Tingle's drink must be Tingle's crème de olive priced at $21 in position 1. The two triangular bottles, 1 and 5, total $39, so the second circular bottle, bottle 2, to go with the $23 bottle 6 can't be $15 (clue 4) and must be the $25 Haskill's crème de rice. By elimination, bottle 4 must be Jasper's crème de carrot at $15 a bottle.

1, Tingle's crème de olive, $21.
2, Haskill's crème de rice $25.
3, Danebury's, crème de cucumber, $20.
4, Jasper's crème de carrot, $15.
5, Bartlet's crème de peanut, $18.
6, Warton's crème de cheese, $23.

Domino Search, p. 170

1	3	0	6	5	5	1	5
6	1	3	6	6	2	5	0
3	2	5	0	0	1	1	2
3	4	6	0	3	4	5	4
5	6	4	4	4	2	2	1
0	1	2	1	3	5	6	6
2	3	6	4	0	0	2	4

Sign In, p. 171

2	3	5	4	1
5	2	1	3	4
1	4	3	5	2
3	1	4	2	5
4	5	2	1	3

Sudoku, p. 171

8	3	7	9	6	4	1	5	2
4	5	6	8	2	1	3	7	9
2	9	1	7	5	3	8	4	6
9	1	2	4	8	7	6	3	5
7	4	5	3	9	6	2	1	8
6	8	3	2	1	5	4	9	7
5	6	8	1	4	9	7	2	3
3	2	4	5	7	8	9	6	1
1	7	9	6	3	2	5	8	4

Cooped Up, p. 172

Dolly is hen 2 (clue 4), so hen 5, who isn't Loretta (clue 1), Shania (clue 2), Tammy (clue 3), or Emmylou (clue 5), must be Tanya. Hen 1, who likes a handful of mealworms, laid two more eggs than hen 3 (clue 6), so didn't lay 2 or 3 eggs. Since Dolly is hen 2, hen 1 can't have laid 5 eggs (clue 2), and hen 4 laid 6 eggs (clue 4). Since hen 3 can't have laid 5 eggs (clue 2), hen 1 can't have laid 7 eggs (clue 6), so she must have laid 4 eggs, and hen 3 must have laid 2 eggs. Dolly laid one more egg than the hen who likes wheat (clue 4), so since the mealworm eater laid 4, Dolly can't have laid 5. So, from clue 2, Shania can't be hen 1. Nor can she be hen 6, opposite hen 4 who has laid 6 eggs, so she must be hen 4 and hen 6 must have laid 5 eggs. From clue 3, the hen that laid 3 eggs can't be number 2 and must be number 5, with corn-loving Tammy is position 3, laying 2 eggs. By elimination, Dolly must have laid 7 eggs

last week. So, from clue 4, the hen that likes wheat must be Shania in position 4 with her 6 eggs. Now, from clue 5, Emmylou must be hen 6 and Tanya, on the same level but closer to the door, must like eating rice and, from clue 1, Loretta must be hen 1, like mealworms, and laid 4 eggs last week. Also from clue 1, Dolly in roost 2 must like millet, leaving Emmylou in roost 6 as the hen who chooses barley.

Hen 1, Loretta, mealworms, 4 eggs.
Hen 2, Dolly, millet, 7 eggs.
Hen 3, Tammy, corn, 2 eggs.
Hen 4, Shania, wheat, 6 eggs.
Hen 5, Tanya, rice, 3 eggs.
Hen 6, Emmylou, barley, 5 eggs.

Chortle's Weekly, p. 174

The trendy schoolteacher was in the third sketch (clue 3) and Kate Franklin appeared in the typewriter repairman sketch (clue 5), so the first sketch, featuring Pete Brennan (clue 1), which wasn't about the gardening presenter (clue 2) or the Bronx boy (clue 4), must have been about the high school student. Nor could the gardening presenter appear in the second sketch (clue 2) and since Pete Brennan was in the first the second could not have been about the Bronx boy clue 4), so it must have feature Kate Franklin and the typewriter repairman. The guest in the last sketch wasn't Lucy Marsh (clue 2) or Dave Cooke (clue 4), so it must have been Ian Palmer and the sketch therefore featured the character Graham (clue 6). The high school student in the first sketch isn't Dennis Digby (clue 1), Hugo (clue 2), or E.R. Girles (clue 4), and so it must be Toby. Now, Bronx boy E.R. Girles (clue 4) can't have been the character in sketch 2 or 3, and so it must have been in sketch 4; so, from clue 4, Dave Cooke must have been in sketch 3, leaving Lucy Marsh in sketch 4. So, from clue 2, the trendy schoolteacher in sketch 3 must be Hugo, and Graham must be the gardening presenter in sketch 5, leaving sketch 2 as the one featuring typewriter repairman Dennis Digby and guest actress Kate Franklin.

First, Toby, high school student, Pete Brennan.
Second, Dennis Digby, typewriter repairman, Kate Franklin.
Third, Hugo, trendy schoolteacher, Dave Cooke.
Fourth, E.R. Girles, Bronx boy, Lucy Marsh.
Fifth, Graham, gardening presenter, Ian Palmer.

What in the Trash, p. 176

Junk Junction was featured in Thursday's strip (clue 3), so Monday's location, which wasn't Detritus Drive (clue 1), Litter Lane (clue 2), or Pulp Parade (clue 4), must have been Waste Way. So, from clue 6, Caroline Carrott must have sweetened the deal in Tuesday's paper. From clue 1, Barry Bakander couldn't have been in Thursday or Friday's strip, and since Thursday's was set in Junk Junction, it couldn't have been Wednesday, so Barry Bakander must have been in Monday's strip. So, from clue 1, Detritus Drive must have featured in Tuesday's strip with Caroline Carrott, and the rain barrel must have been whisked away on Wednesday. So, this wasn't the day that featured Briony Brybe, who was getting rid of a garden chair (clue 2) and nor could Briony have been in Friday's strip (clue 2), so she must have been disposing of the lawn chair in Thursday's strip set in Junk Junction. Also from clue 2, Litter Lane must have been Friday's setting, leaving Wednesday's strip set in Pulp Parade and featuring Graham Grease (clue 4) getting rid of his rain barrel. By elimination, Sophie Sweetener must have been the character in Friday's Litter Lane strip. She didn't bribe Larry to cart off a cold frame (clue 5) and couldn't have been disposing of a lawn mower (clue 4), so Sophie must have asked Larry to take away a lawn roller. Finally, the cold frame wasn't in Monday's strip (clue 5), so it must have been what Caroline Carrott needed taking away from Detritus Drive on Tuesday, leaving Monday's strip showing Barry Bakander of Waste Way greasing Larry's palm to take away his old lawn mower.

Monday, Waste Way, Barry Bakander, lawn mower.
Tuesday, Detritus Drive, Caroline Carrott, cold frame.
Wednesday, Pulp Parade, Graham Grease, rain barrel.
Thursday, Junk Junction, Briony Brybe, chair.
Friday, Litter Lane, Sophie Sweetener, roller.

Takeout Cena, p. 178

Euselus was sent to Quindecim (clue 2) and Delius runs the Tiberside Inn (clue 5), so the tavern owned by Nigelus and visited by Branelus (clue 4), which wasn't the IV Seasons or the Labyrinth (clue 4), must have been the Fat Dormouse. The IV Seasons sells the meat parcel (clue 4), Cluelus bought the fish 'n' turnips (clue 1), and Pruus developed the chicken in a bucket (clue 2), so the Fat Dormouse must have created the beef patty between two halves of a mini loaf (and usually cooked by the tavern's oversized under-chef Big Maccius). From her dish, Pruus doesn't own the IV Seasons, so she must cook at the Labyrinth. We now know either the chef or the patronizing slave for four taverns, so Cluelus must have bought the fish 'n' turnips from Delius's Tiberside Inn, leaving the dough disk as the innovation at the Quindecim. It wasn't invented by Fanius so it must have been created by Clarissus, leaving Fanius's new dish as the drunkards' favorite meat parcels at the IV Seasons. Finally, this wasn't the tavern visited by Hopelus (clue 4) so it must have been where Gormlus was sent, leaving Hopelus visiting Pruus's Labyrinth and taking home a chicken in a bucket.

Branelus, Fat Dormouse, Nigelus, beef patty.
Cluelus, Tiberside Inn, Delius, fish cena.
Euselus, Quindecim, Clarissus, dough disk.
Gormlus, IV Seasons, Fanius, meat parcels.
Hopelus, Labyrinth, Pruus, fowl.

Bargain Board, p. 180

The 20% savings is not on the Value Ticket (clue 1), the Super Saver or the Mega Coupon (clue 2), or the Diamond Token (clue 4), so it must be the Bumper Voucher. The 25% offer is not on the Value Ticket (clue 1) or the Super Saver or Mega Coupon (clue 2), so it must be the Diamond Token. From clue 2, it must be on the top row, so, from clue 3, the 20% Bumper Voucher must be on the bottom row in position 4, and the 25% Diamond Token must be number 1. So, from clue 2, the Super Saver must be number 3. The Value Ticket isn't number 5 (clue 1), so it must be number 2, leaving number 5 as the Mega Coupon. From clue 1, the Value Ticket must offer 35% savings. Finally, the Super Saver doesn't offer a 40% savings (clue 2), so it must offer 30%, leaving the Mega Coupon in position 5 offering 40% off.

1, Diamond Token, 25%.
2, Value Ticket, 35%.
3, Super Saver, 30%.
4, Bumper Voucher, 20%.
5, Mega Coupon, 40%.

Mrs. Robinson, p. 181

The Finance worker is the Finance Director (clue 2), so Jocelyn Robinson, who is a Manager but not in Personnel (clue 1), must be in the Parks Department. She hasn't been there for three years (clue 1) and Katrina Robinson has been with the Council for four years (clue 3), so Mrs. Jocelyn Robinson must have been a Parks Department Manager for five years. The Finance Director hasn't been at the Council for three years, so Mrs. Katrina Robinson must have been the Finance Director for four years, leaving Mrs. Lucille Robinson as the Personnel Department Secretary with three years of service.

Jocelyn, Parks, Manager, 5 years.
Katrina, Finance, Director, 4 years.
Lucille, Personnel, Secretary, 3 years.

Homeward Bound, p. 182

The train journey takes fifty minutes (clue 4), so Mrs. Lucille Robinson, whose journey is ten minutes shorter than that on the bus, must take thirty minutes, and the bus journey must take forty minutes. So, by elimination, Mrs. Lucille Robinson must walk home to her house in Netherlipp (clue 3). So, Mrs. Katrina Robinson's journey, longer than that to Lower Crispin (clue 2), must be the fifty-minute train commute to Stonekeigh, leaving Mrs. Jocelyn Robinson making the forty-minute bus journey to Lower Crispin.

Jocelyn, bus, Lower Crispin, 40 mins.
Katrina, train, Stonekeigh, 50 mins.
Lucille, walk, Netherlipp, 30 mins.

Battleships, p. 183

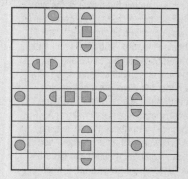

String Stuff, p. 184

Bertram Bowman is a fiddler (clue 1) and Keith Kord is playing *Streets of Netherlipp* (clue 2), so the banjo picker picking *Wallingfen Lineman*, who isn't Stella Strummet (clue 3), must be Penny Picker. Stella Strummet is playing in the Mall (clue 3), so the guitarist playing in the bus station (clue 4) must be Keith Kord playing *Streets of Netherlipp*, leaving the mandolin player as Stella Strummet. Penny Picker isn't in the Town Square (clue 5), so she must be playing *Wallingfen Lineman* on her banjo on Main Street, leaving Bertram Bowman fiddling in the Town Square. So, he's not playing *24*

Hours from Keighshire (clue 5) and must be playing *I Belong to Stonekeigh*, leaving Stella Strummet playing *24 Hours from Keighshire* on her mandolin in the Mall.

Bertram Bowman, *I Belong to Stonekeigh*, fiddle, Town Square.

Keith Kord, *Streets of Netherlipp*, guitar, bus station.

Penny Picker, *Wallingfen Lineman*, banjo, Main Street.

Stella Strummet, *24 Hours from Keighshire*, mandolin, Mall.

Strong Stuff, p. 186

Pamela Plonque's wine was called "ruthless" (clue 2) and Hortense Hooch added brandy (clue 4), so the person who added vodka to make a "brutal" drink (clue 1) must have been male, as must the maker of the gin and rhubarb brew (clue 1). The gooseberry wine was described as "barbaric" (clue 3), so Pamela Plonque's "ruthless" wine must have been based on beetroots and, by elimination, laced with schnapps. We now know either the description or the wine to go with three spirits, so the "barbaric" gooseberry wine must have been spiked with brandy by Hortense Hooch, leaving the elderflower wine as the "brutal" vodka concoction, and the rhubarb and gin drink as the "uncompromising" draft. It wasn't made by Gordon Grogue (clue 5), so it must have been the work of Larry Likka, leaving Gordon Grogue as the brewer of the "brutal" elderflower and vodka beverage.

Gordon Grogue, elderflower and vodka, "brutal."

Hortense Hooch, gooseberry and brandy, "barbaric."

Larry Likka, rhubarb and gin, "uncompromising."

Pamela Plonque, beetroot and schnapps, "ruthless."

Range of Interests, p. 188

Ken Lee wrote about Yeovil (clue 6), so the surname of the jazz band leader who wrote about Chinese coinage, which must have three or four letters (clue 2), must be Rosie Swan, whose book came out in 2013 (clue 1). The painter, whose book came out in 2011, isn't Ken Lee or Lucy Merritt (clue 1), or Alan Blake, who's a soccer player (clue 5), so it must be Emma Foley. Lucy Merritt isn't the TV chef (clue 4), so she must be the novelist, leaving Ken Lee as the TV chef. Lucy Merritt didn't write about Easter Island (clue 4) or London ghosts (clue 3), so she must have written the book on Captain Kidd that came out in 2010 (clue 2). The 2012 book's author must have had a five-letter surname (clue 2), so it must be Alan Blake, leaving Ken Lee's book published in 2014. Finally, as Emma Foley didn't write about London ghosts (clue 3), she must have written about Easter Island, leaving Alan Blake's subject as London ghosts.

Alan Blake, soccer player, London ghosts, 2012.

Emma Foley, painter, Easter Island, 2011.

Ken Lee, TV chef, Yeovil, 2014.

Lucy Merritt, novelist, Captain Kidd, 2010.

Rosie Swan, jazz band leader, Chinese coinage, 2013.

Battleships, p. 190

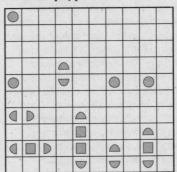

Logi-5, p. 191

B	C	D	E	A
E	D	A	C	B
A	E	C	B	D
C	A	B	D	E
D	B	E	A	C

Killer Sudoku, p. 191

7	9	2	5	1	6	8	4	3
4	5	3	9	8	2	1	6	7
6	8	1	7	3	4	5	2	9
3	2	5	8	6	1	9	7	4
9	4	7	3	2	5	6	1	8
1	6	8	4	7	9	3	5	2
8	7	4	6	5	3	2	9	1
2	3	6	1	9	7	4	8	5
5	1	9	2	4	8	7	3	6

Five Macs, p. 192

McCardle's nickname is "Skip" (clue 3), and Maclean is from Aberdeen (clue 5), so, from clue 1, "Sparks" from Glasgow, who isn't McSorley or Macleod, must be "Sparks" Mackamotzi. Ulysses Macleod isn't "Tiny" (clue 2) and Eddie is "Cat" (clue 5), so Ulysses must be "Lucky" Macleod. Eddie isn't Maclean (clue 5), so he must be Eddie McSorley. By elimination, Maclean must be "Tiny" Maclean and Arnold from Edinburgh (clue 6) must be Arnold "Skip" McCardle. Ian isn't Mackamotzi (clue 4), so he must be Ian "Tiny" Maclean from Aberdeen, leaving Mackamotzi as Oscar "Sparks" Mackamotzi from Glasgow. Finally, from clue 2, Ulysses "Lucky" Macleod isn't from New York City, so he must be from Dundee, and New York City must be Eddie "Cat" McSorley's home.

Arnold McCardle, Edinburgh, "Skip."
Eddie McSorley, New York City, "Cat."
Ian Maclean, Aberdeen, "Tiny."

Oscar Mackamotzi, Glasgow, "Sparks."
Ulysses Macleod, Dundee, "Lucky."

Crispin in Bloom, p. 194

The second person up before the committee was Lawrence Lax (clue 1) and the third was charged with careless hedging (clue 3), so, from clue 2, Simon Slappe-Dasche, charged with reckless planting, must have been fourth with the third-up careless hedger sentenced to trash collection and Roberta Remisce fifth and sentenced to fence painting. Sylvia Slack will spend some time edging the town square (clue 5) and the under-weeder will atone for their crime by weeding the town curbs (clue 4), so Simon Slappe-Dasche will pay for his reckless planting with a period of watering the easements. From her punishment, Sylvia Slack wasn't third up before the committee, so she must have been first, leaving Sheryl Shoddy as third to be tried, charged with careless hedging and sentenced to trash collection. Sylvia Slack wasn't charged with miserly mulching (clue 5), so she must have been charged with negligent mowing. Finally, Roberta Remisce's punishment rules her out as the under-weeder, so she must have been charged with miserly mulching and sentenced to fence painting, leaving Lawrence Lax, second to have his case considered, as the under-weeder who will be weeding curbs for a while.

First, Sylvia Slack, negligent mowing, square edging.
Second, Lawrence Lax, under-weeding, curb weeding.
Third, Sheryl Shoddy, careless hedging, trash collection.
Fourth, Simon Slappe-Dasche, reckless planting, easement watering.
Fifth, Roberta Remisce, miserly mulching, fence painting.

Second-Hand Siblings, p. 196

Lily has been brought a wooden train (clue 2), so Chloe, who has brought a rag doll to the hospital for a baby with a four- or five-letter name (clue 4), must be visiting Simon Little (clue 6). Mark has a new brother called Daniel (clue 1), so Charlotte Newcome, who has also come to visit a baby boy (clue 1), must be visiting George. Alexandra is not Harry's sister (clue 2), so she must be Joshua's sibling, leaving Harry as Lily's big brother. Alexandra's present is neither the rattle (clue 2) nor the teddy (clue 3), so it must be the musical toy and her surname must therefore be Goodchild (clue 5). Mrs. Bourne's son has a six-letter name (clue 4), so it must be Daniel, leaving Lily as Lily Young. Finally, as baby George has not been brought a teddy (clue 3), it must be the rattle, leaving Daniel as the recipient of the new teddy bear.

Alexandra Goodchild, Joshua, musical toy.
Daniel Bourne, Mark, teddy.
George Newcome, Charlotte, rattle.
Lily Young, Harry, wooden train.
Simon Little, Chloe, rag doll.

Scent to Your Room, p. 198

The Dusty Lane air freshener has so far lasted for thirty-two days (clue 1) and the item in the kitchen has lasted for thirty-four days (clue 2), so the Baker's Parlor, which is not in the kitchen (clue 2) and has not lasted for thirty-six or forty days (also clue 2), must have lasted for thirty-eight days. The Waftair product has lasted for forty days (clue 3), but the fragrance is not Coffee House Blues (also clue 3), or Odor Killer, which is made by Zephyr (clue 6), so it must be the Strawbale in the bedroom (clue 4). The Freshayr product is in the hall (clue 5), so the air freshener in the dining room, which is not made by Aromist or Atmosfear (clue 1), must be Zephyr's Odor Killer. By elimination, this air freshener must have lasted thirty-six days and the fragrance in the kitchen must be Coffee House Blues. The Aromist fragrance is not the thirty-eight-day lasting Baker's Parlor or Dusty Lane (clue 1), so it must be the Coffee House Blues in the kitchen. Baker's Parlor is not made by Atmosfear (clue 2), so it must be the Freshayr fragrance in the hall, and, by elimination, the

Atmosfear air freshener must be Dusty Lane and must be in use in the sitting room.

Bedroom, Waftair, Strawbale, 40 days.
Dining room, Zephyr, Odor Killer, 36 days.
Hall, Freshayr, Baker's Parlor, 38 days.
Kitchen, Aromist, Coffee House Blues, 34 days.
Sitting room, Atmosfear, Dusty Lane, 32 days.

Action and Reaction, p. 200

Friday's target store wasn't Harry Spencers (clue 1), Mark Rods (clue 2), Debbie Nicks (clue 3), or Harvey's (clue 4), so it must have been Selfenhams. Fay's action on Monday wasn't fainting (clue 1), stealing (clue 2), being drunk (clue 3), or dropping her bags (clue 4), so it must have been going into labor. This wasn't at Harry Spencers (clue 1), Debbie Nicks (clue 3), or Harvey's (clue 4), so it must have been at Mark Rods. So, from clue 2, Fay must have feigned stealing on Tuesday and was completely ignored on Wednesday. So, this wasn't the day Fay pretended to faint and was covered with a blanket (clue 1), nor did Fay faint on Friday, since she fainted two days after she left Old Mr. Withers screaming (clue 1), so she must have fainted and been covered over on Thursday, Harry Spencers must have been targeted on Wednesday, and the screaming Mr. Withers must have witnessed the stealing on Tuesday. The call to 911 wasn't on Friday (clue 3), so it must have been on Monday in Mark Rods after Fay pretended to go into labor. From clue 3, Debbie Nicks must have been the store where Fay shoplifted and was screamed at on Tuesday, and Wednesday's ignored episode in Harry Spencers must have been the Oscar-winning drunk act. By elimination Thursday's fainting and covering must have taken part in the bed department of Harvey's, and Friday's events must have been the dropped bags over the floor of Selfenhams, leaving the staff in fits of laughter.

Monday, Mark Rods, in labor, call 911.
Tuesday, Debbie Nicks, stealing, scream.

Wednesday, Harry Spencers, appear drunk, ignore.
Thursday, Harvey's, faint, cover.
Friday, Selfenhams, drop bags, laugh.

Diggers, p. 202

The pond is being cleared in Blackfriars (clue 2), so the digger in The Croft, who isn't repairing a drain or doing archaeology (clue 3), or a community project—Una's activity (clue 4)—must be digging the garden. Quarry is repairing a drain but not on Molford Road or Plough Lane, where Burrows is digging (clue 6), so it must be hacking away at the ground in Friars Meadow and is therefore Alan (clue 5). Edna is Edna Pitt (clue 5) so Ian, who isn't Delve or Wells (clue 1), must be Ian Burrows digging on Plough Lane. By elimination, he must be the archaeologist, and Molford Road must be where Una is turning over the earth in her community project. Wells isn't the gardener in The Croft and isn't the Blackfriars digger (clue 2), so it must be Una Wells the community project digger on Molford Road. Delve isn't digging in The Croft (clue 3), so that must be Edna Pitt's garden location. By elimination, Delve must be Oliver Delve, and must be pond-clearing in Blackfriars.

Alan Quarry, Friars Meadow, repairing drain.
Edna Pitt, The Croft, digging garden.
Ian Burrows, Plough Lane, archaeology.
Oliver Delve, Blackfriars, clearing pond.
Una Wells, Molford Road, community project.

Noah Trouble, p. 204

The water was three feet deep on Wharf Road (clue 4) and the cats were plucked from a five-feet-deep street (clue 5), so the guinea pigs picked up on Weir Street, where the water was neither six nor seven feet deep (clue 6), must have been saved from a flood of four feet. On the third street that Noah visited, the water was seven feet deep (clue 2), so, from clue 3, Southbank Road was not the first on his itinerary, from where he collected two

ducks. The first street was also not Bridge Street (clue 1) or, from the animals collected, Weir Street (clue 6), so it must have been Mill Road. By elimination, the depth of water here must have been six feet. Wharf Road was not where the rabbits came from (clue 4) or, from the water's depth, the cats, so it must have been where Mr. Arkwright collected the goats, leaving the pair of rabbits as the animals found in the seven-foot flood. Now, from clue 3, the goats could not have been the second collection, so they must have been his fourth acquisition, and he must have paddled down Southbank Road third and taken the guinea pigs on board fifth (clue 3). By elimination, the cats must have been on Bridge Street, down which Noah must have floated second.

First, Mill Road, 6 feet, ducks.
Second, Bridge Street, 5 feet, cats.
Third, Southbank Road, 7 feet, rabbits.
Fourth, Wharf Road, 3 feet, goats.
Fifth, Weir Street, 4 feet, guinea pigs.

Dawdling Duos, p. 206

Billy and his companion were four minutes late (clue 2) so Rory and his friend, who were an even number of minutes late but a minute earlier than the duo playing Power Rangers (clue 4), and so cannot have been ten minutes late, must have been six minutes late, and therefore Rory's partner in crime must have been Shaun (clue 5). The Power Rangers duo must therefore have been seven minutes late arriving (clue 4). So, Henry and Sam, who were three minutes later at school than the pair swapping trading cards (clue 1), could not have been ten minutes late, and we know they were not six minutes late, so they must have been seven minutes late, and the pair swapping cards must have been four minutes late. James was playing football (clue 6) and Matthew hide-and-seek (clue 3), so Rory and Shaun must have been buying candy. Therefore, by elimination, Tom must have been playing football with James. Matthew and his friend were not five minutes late (clue 3), so they must have been ten minutes late, leaving the five-minute-late pair as Tom and James. Finally, Billy's friend was not Joe (clue 2), so it must have been Gareth, leaving Joe as Matthew's friend, playing hide-and-seek to delay their arrival at school.

Billy and Gareth, swapping cards, 4 minutes late.

Henry and Sam, playing Power Rangers, 7 minutes late.

Matthew and Joe, hide-and-seek, 10 minutes late.

Rory and Shaun, buying candy, 6 minutes late.

Tom and James, football, 5 minutes late.

Meet and Greet, p. 208

Seventeen of Cherilyn's clients were aboard the Humbergow plane (clue 4). The largest group of twenty-eight cannot have flown from Glaston (clue 2), Stanwick (clue 5), or Heathsted (clue 7), so they must have been on the Plainair flight from Gatside (clue 1). This had an afternoon arrival time (clue 1), but the 1:35 arrival had only fourteen of Cherilyn's clients aboard (clue 6) and clue 5 rules out 3:45, so the flight from Gatside must have landed at 2:55. Therefore, from clue 5, the flight from Stanwick must have landed at 3:45. The plane from which Cherilyn had to meet only six passengers cannot have been operated by Cloudbase (clue 2), Jetaway (clue 3), or FlyOff (clue 7), and we know it was not the Plainair flight, so the operator must have been Skyways. The 10:15 arrival cannot have been the Cloudbase flight (clue 2), nor was it operated by Jetaway (clue 3) or FlyOff (clue 7), and we know it was not the Plainair plane, so it must have been the Skyways flight. We have now matched four numbers of tourists with an airport or a time, so, by elimination, the 3:45 arrival from Stanwick must have had sixteen of Cherilyn's clients aboard. The Skyways flight was not the one from Heathsted (clue 7), so the latter did not have six aboard, and we know the number aboard the planes from Humbergow, Gatside, and Stanwick, so it must be the plane with

fourteen people aboard for Cherilyn to meet, which arrived at 1:35, leaving the Skyways flight arriving at 10:15 as the one which set off from Glaston. Clue 7 now reveals the FlyOff flight as the one that landed at 3:45 from Stanwick, and, by elimination, the plane from Humbergow must have landed at 11:00. This was not operated by Jetaway (clue 3), so it must have been the Cloudbase flight, and the Jetaway plane must have been the one from Heathsted, which arrived at 1:35.

10:15, Glaston, Skyways, 6.
11:00, Humbergow, Cloudbase, 17.
1:35, Heathsted, Jetaway, 14.
2:55, Gatside, Plainair, 28.
3:45, Stanwick, FlyOff, 16.

First Jobs, p. 210

The village where the tradesman arrived at 9:45 a.m. cannot be Dun Planking (clue 3), Higher Poynting (clue 4), Lower Stipple (clue 5), or Much Flushing (clue 6), so it must be Little Hynge. The tradesman concerned cannot be Smiley (clue 2), Jolly (clue 4), or Potts (clue 6), so it must be either Joynson or Rafter. Joynson is not a plasterer (clue 4) and Rafter cannot be one (clue 1), so the Little Hynge job needed a different tradesman. But not a joiner (clue 2), roofer (clue 3), or painter (clue 4), so it must have been a plumber. He cannot be Joynson (clue 1), so it must be Rafter. The plasterer's name must therefore be Smiley (clue 1). The tradesman who arrived at 11:00 a.m. cannot be the joiner (clue 2), roofer (clue 3), or painter (clue 4), so it must be the plasterer. The joiner's time of arrival cannot be 10:45 a.m. (clue 2), nor can that be the time of the painter (clue 4), so it must be the roofer who got to his destination at that time. Jolly cannot be the painter (clue 4) or the joiner (clue 1), so they must be the roofer. Joynson, who also cannot be the joiner (clue 1), must be the painter, and Potts, by elimination, the joiner. Joynson must have arrived at 10:30 a.m. (clue 4), and Potts, by elimination, at 10:15 a.m. It must be Jolly therefore who went to Higher Poynting (clue 4). Smiley cannot have been called to Dun Planking (clue 3) or Much Flushing, where Joynson must have turned up (clue 6), so they must have been called to Lower Stipple, with Dun Planking receiving the joiner at 10:15 a.m.

Dun Planking, Potts, joiner, 10:15 a.m.
Higher Poynting, Jolly, Roofer 10:45 a.m.
Little Hynge, Rafter, plumber, 9:45 a.m.
Lower Stipple, Smiley, plasterer, 11:00 a.m.
Much Flushing, Joynson, painter, 10:30 a.m.

Logi-5, p. 212

A	D	B	E	C
C	E	A	B	D
D	B	C	A	E
B	C	E	D	A
E	A	D	C	B

Killer Sudoku, p. 212

2	9	3	5	4	6	8	7	1
8	4	1	9	7	2	3	6	5
6	5	7	1	8	3	2	4	9
1	2	4	8	3	5	6	9	7
5	7	9	2	6	1	4	3	8
3	8	6	7	9	4	1	5	2
7	6	8	3	2	9	5	1	4
4	1	2	6	5	7	9	8	3
9	3	5	4	1	8	7	2	6

Battleships, p. 213

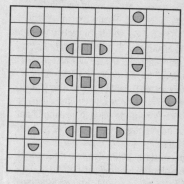

Spy Catcher, p. 214

Wintersky was based in Miami (clue 2) and the FBI operation in San Diego was Grizzly (clue 6), so Stormcloud, dealt with by Operation Fox, which wasn't based in New Orleans or New York (clue 5), must have worked in Dayton. The New York group was dealt with in 1943 (clue 4), so Cabaret was not the group dealt with by Operation Puma in 1941 (clue 3), nor was that Windmill (clue 1), so it must have been Oaktree, and, by elimination, it must have been based in New Orleans. The Miami operation against Wintersky wasn't Coyote (clue 2), so it must have been Operation Tiger, leaving Coyote as the 1943 New York operation. Now, from clue 3, Tiger must have been the 1944 operation, with Cabaret the 1943 target and Stormcloud the spy ring broken in 1945. So, Cabaret was the target of Operation Coyote and, by elimination, the San Diego group must have been Windmill, dealt with in 1942.

1941, Oaktree, New Orleans, Puma.
1942, Windmill, San Diego, Grizzly.
1943, Cabaret, New York, Coyote.
1944, Wintersky, Miami, Tiger.
1945, Stormcloud, Dayton, Fox.

Poster Palace, p. 216

Poster B is for *Snowbird* (clue 4), so, since the posters for *Gunpowder* and *Home Ground* are side by side (clue 3), poster A must be for

White Dragon. So, from clue 2, Dean Morley must be the star of *Snowbird* and poster C must be in Spanish. Poster D is in German (clue 1), so the Susan Starr movie advertised in Hindustani (clue 3) must be *White Dragon* on poster A and the poster for Dean Morley's movie must be in French. The star on the German poster D isn't Chuck McRay (clue 1), so it must be Jayne Busby and the movie is therefore *Gunpowder* (clue 3), leaving Chuck McRay as the star of *Home Ground*, featured on poster C.

A, Susan Starr, *White Dragon*, Hindustani.
B, Dean Morley, *Snowbird*, French.
C, Chuck McRay, *Home Ground*, Spanish.
D, Jayne Busby, *Gunpowder*, German.

Battleships, p. 217

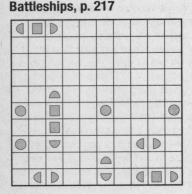

Mysterious Flatland, p. 218

Rusty and Olive Brown went to the Red Pavilion (clue 6) and Charlie Chan's cuisine is Anglo-Chinese (clue 1), so Lewis and Bren Gunn's Cantonese meal, which wasn't at the Jade Dragon (clue 3) or the Lantern, where $40 was spent (clues 3 and 7), must have been at Wong Ping's. Now, Matt and Pat Ernal's $72 meal (clue 5), which wasn't at the Jade Dragon (clue 3), must have been at Charlie Chan's Anglo-Chinese restaurant. The Szechuan-style meal cost $56 (clue 2). Since the bill at the Lantern was $40, from clue 3, Lewis and Bren Gunn's meal can't have cost $48, so it must have cost $64, and so the bill

at the Jade Dragon was $56 (clue 3). Now, by elimination, Rusty and Olive Brown must have spent $48. So, they didn't eat Pekingese cuisine (clue 4) and must have had Shanghai cuisine, leaving the Pekingese restaurant as the Lantern. The couple who ate there weren't Lennox and Beverley Hills (clue 7), so they must have been Tom and Kit Katt, leaving Lennox and Beverley Hills as the couple who spent $56 at the Jade Dragon.

Brown, Red Pavilion, Shanghai, $48.
Ernal, Charlie Chan's, Anglo-Chinese, $72.
Gunn, Wong Ping's, Cantonese, $64.
Hills, Jade Dragon, Szechuan, $56.
Katt, Lantern, Pekingese, $40.

Fathom It Out, p. 220

The 2013 case was not based in Misselton (clue 3). Clue 1 rules out Crowhampton and clue 7 rules out the Pridewell murder, which was committed by Gerry Savage, while the 2012 investigation took place in Hambury (clue 4), so, by elimination, Fathom must have worked in Littlechurch in 2013 on a case depending on a soil sample (clue 2). The 2009 murderer was Leslie Baddey (clue 5). His conviction cannot have been based on fingerprints (clue 7) and the vital witness was tracked down in 2011 (clue 6). We know 2009 was not the year of the soil sample and Karl Crooke confessed to his crime (clue 1), so Leslie Baddey must have been convicted by a DNA sample. We now know Gerry Savage's Pridewell crime was not detected in 2009, 2012, or 2013, and clue 7 also rules out 2010, so it must have been the 2011 case, in which the vital witness was located. So, from clue 7, the fingerprint evidence was used against the Hambury murderer in 2012, which, by elimination, leaves 2010 as the year Karl Crooke's confession was made. So, from clue 1, the Crowhampton crime was the 2009 one for which Leslie Baddey was arrested, leaving the location of the 2010 murder as Misselton. The guilty party in the 2013 case was not Anthony Black (clue 3), so he must have been Marlon Hood, leaving Anthony Black as the man who left his fingerprints at the scene of the 2012 crime in Hambury.

2009, Crowhampton, Leslie Baddey, DNA sample.

2010, Misselton, Karl Crooke, confession.

2011, Pridewell, Gerry Savage, vital witness.

2012, Hambury, Anthony Black, fingerprints.

2013, Littlechurch, Marlon Hood, soil sample.

Les Autres Reliques, p. 222

Marc Vaurien in St. Malo isn't selling an item which belonged to Uramis (clue 1), Maximos, whose item is offered by Jules Sangsue (clue 4), Silvis (clue 5), or Archamos, whose item is for sale in Grenoble (clue 6), so he must be selling Damos's dice box (clue 5). The item Jean Bourricot is selling isn't an item from Archamos or Uramis (clue 6), so it must have belonged to Silvis, probably. It's not the belt buckle, which belonged to Archamos or Uramis (clue 2), the crucifix, which Raoul Dingue is selling (clue 3), or the powder horn (clue 5), so it must be the spurs, on sale in Toulon (clue 2). The Maximos item isn't the belt buckle or the crucifix (clue 3), so it must be the powder horn. It's not for sale in Nice (clue 3), so it must be being sold from Dijon, and, by elimination, Uramis's item must be on sale in Nice. The seller there isn't Louis Poisseux (clue 3), so it must be Raoul Dingue and the item is therefore the crucifix. Finally, by elimination, Archamos's item must be the belt buckle, and its seller must be Louis Poisseux.

Archamos, belt buckle, Louis Poisseux, Grenoble.

Damos, dice box, Marc Vaurien, St. Malo.

Maximos, powder horn, Jules Sangsue, Dijon.

Silvis, spurs, Jean Bouricot, Toulon.

Uramis, crucifix, Raoul Dingue, Nice.

Dear Sir, p. 224

The Monday letter was about the cost of trash disposal (clue 3), and Miss Sharp wrote the Tuesday letter (clue 5). The *Churchminster Sentinel* reader's letter was printed on Thursday (clue 4), so Colonel Crusty's letter to the *Wallingfen Recorder*, which was not about television and which cannot have appeared on Friday (clue 1), must have been in Wednesday's paper. So, from clue 1, the Thursday letter in the *Churchminster Sentinel* must have complained about the quality of television programs. We know that the letter to the *Crispin Tribune* was not printed on Wednesday or Thursday. Clue 6 rules out both Friday and Tuesday, when Miss Sharp's letter appeared, so it must have been Monday's missive about trash disposal charges. Since Mrs. Short complained about government policies (clue 6), hers was not the Monday or Thursday letter, and we know it was not printed on Tuesday or Wednesday, so it must have been in Friday's paper. From clue 2, it must have been Miss Sharp's Tuesday letter that went to the *Netherlipp Courier*, which leaves Mrs. Short as the writer to the *Stonekeigh Advertiser*. Clue 2 also reveals young men's fashion as the topic raised in the Wednesday letter from Colonel Crusty, so, by elimination, Miss Sharp must have written about inconsiderate cyclists. Finally, from clue 4, it was not Mr. Cross who wrote to the *Churchminster Sentinel*, so it must have been Major Quarrell, leaving Mr. Cross as the writer of Monday's letter to the *Crispin Tribune*.

Monday, Mr. Cross, *Crispin Tribune*, trash disposal.

Tuesday, Miss Sharp, *Netherlipp Courier*, cyclists.

Wednesday, Colonel Crusty, *Wallingfen Recorder*, men's fashion.

Thursday, Major Quarrell, *Churchminster Sentinel*, TV programs.

Friday, Mrs. Short, *Stonekeigh Advertiser*, government policies.

Classic B and Ps, p. 226

The touring car dates from 1949 (clue 3). The 1960 car can't be the sportscar (clue 1) or the Beaufort limousine (clue 4), so it must be the Grand Prix car, vehicle 1 (clue 2). It can't be the Bulldog or the Blenheim (clue 3), so it must be the Baltimore. The Blenheim isn't the sportscar (clue 1), so it must be the touring car, leaving the sportscar as the Bulldog. Since the Blenheim is the touring car, clue 1 now tells us the 1938 car was the Bulldog sportscar, which leaves the Beaufort limousine as the 1927 car. So, from clue 4, vehicle 2 is the Bulldog. The touring car isn't vehicle 3 (clue 3), so it must be vehicle 4, leaving vehicle 3 as the Beaufort.

1, Baltimore, Grand Prix car, 1960.
2, Bulldog, sportscar, 1938.
3, Beaufort, limousine, 1927.
4, Blenheim, touring car, 1949.

Chase the Ace, p. 227

The card on the left is a face card (clue 2), so, from clue 3, the Jack must be one of the four right-most cards. The second from the right is the 10 (clue 2), so since no adjacent cards are of adjacent value (clue 1), the Jack can't be first or third from the right and must be fourth from the right. So, from clue 3, the 8 must be fifth from the left and the 2 must be second from the left. The Queen is immediately left of an odd-numbered card (clue 3), so it isn't the leftmost face card, which must therefore be the King (clue 2). The only run of three unallocated cards for the 7, 4, and 9 is now the sixth, seventh, and eighth from the left, and so the 7 must be seventh from the left. From clue 1, the sixth from the left can't be the 9 and must be the 4, with the 9 as the eighth from the left. The Queen, being immediately left of an odd card (clue 3), can't be first or third from the right or fourth from the left, so it must be third from the left. So, the 6 can't be fourth from the left (clue 3) and isn't the furthest right (clue 2), so it must be third from the right. Finally, the 3 is further right than the 5 so it must be the rightmost card, with the 5 as the fourth from the left. The sharp-eyed will have noticed that only twelve cards are laid out and that twelve cards are mentioned in the clues, so the answer to the question, "Can you find the Ace?" is "No." He is a card shark after all, and, if you're interested, it's up his right sleeve.

King, 2, Queen, 5, 8, 4, 7, 9, Jack, 6, 10, 3

Person of the Year, p. 228

The surname of the thirty-six-year-old winner cannot be Bland (clue 1), Rooney (clue 2), Mills (clue 3), or Parker (clue 5), so it must be Doherty. That of the person of sixty-four cannot be Rooney (clue 2), Mills (clue 3), or Parker (clue 5), so it must be Bland. This person's occupation cannot be window cleaner (clue 1), bar attendant (clue 3), mailman (clue 4), or lunch lady (clue 5), so it must be stallholder. The occupation of the person aged fifty-two cannot be window cleaner (clue 1), bar attendant (clue 3), or lunch lady (clue 5), so it must be the male mailman (clue 4). So, since Kath cannot be fifty-two, the window cleaner cannot be forty-nine, so they must be either thirty-six or thirty-seven. From clue 2, the winner aged thirty-seven must have the surname Mills, so the thirty-six-year-old winner must be the bar attendant (clue 3), surnamed, as we know, Doherty. The window cleaner must therefore be Mills, aged thirty-seven. Kath is too old to be the bar attendant or window cleaner and too young to be the stallholder (clue 1), so she must be the lunch lady, aged, by elimination, forty-nine. The two youngest winners cannot include Reg (clue 3) or Jim (clue 5), so they must be Anne and Gordon. Gordon is too young to be Parker (clue 5), so the mailman's surname cannot be Rooney, so it must be Parker and Gordon must be Mills (clue 4). From clue 2, Rooney must be Kath's surname, Parker's age must be fifty-two, and his first name must be Reg (clue 5), with Jim being the first name of Bland. Finally, by elimination, Anne's surname must be Doherty.

Bar attendant, Anne Doherty, 36.
Lunch lady, Kath Rooney, 49.
Mailman, Reg Parker, 52.
Stallholder, Jim Bland, 64.
Window cleaner, Gordon Mills, 37.

Barbies, p. 230

Buchanan is an astropolitics researcher (clue 4), so Brian, who researches biogeology (clue 3) but whose surname isn't Birkenshaw (clue 3) or Browning (clue 5), must be Brian Battersby. So, he doesn't work on Saturday (clue 2) or Sunday (clue 3), so he must work on Friday evening. So, from clue 5, Miss Browning must work on Saturday evening and Bruce must take the Saturday lunch shift. Bettina works the day after the chemohistorian (clue 1), so she can't work on Saturday and must run the bar on Sunday lunchtimes. So, Ms. Browning must be Bridget Browning and Bettina must be Bettina Buchanan, the astropolitical researcher. By elimination, Bruce must be Bruce Birkenshaw. He doesn't research medicoliterature (clue 3), so he must be the chemohistorian, leaving Bridget Browning as the medicoliterature researcher.

Bettina Buchanan, astropolitics, Sunday lunch.
Brian Battersby, biogeology, Friday evening.
Bridget Browning, medicoliterature, Saturday evening.
Bruce Birkenshaw, chemohistory, Saturday lunch.

Queue, p. 232

The Lynes are heading for Shingle Head (clue 3) and the family going to Rock Banks are passing the time playing consequences (clue 4), so the Kews, who are playing I-Spy (clue 1) but who aren't going to Sandy Cove (clue 1) must be heading for Pebble Bay. The family going to Rock Banks isn't the Oldupps (clue 4), so it must be the Jammes, leaving the Oldupps on their way to Sandy Cove but held up at Macaroni Junction. So, they're not playing Botticelli (clue 2) and must be playing charades, leaving the Lynes on their way to Shingle Head playing Botticelli at the Crispin Bottleneck (clue 2). Finally, the Jammes aren't at the Moorland Cutting and must be stuck playing consequences on the Stonekeigh Bypass on their way to Rock Banks, leaving the Kews playing I-Spy and stuck on the Moorland Cutting on their way to Pebble Bay.

Crispin Bottleneck, Lyne, Botticelli, Shingle Head.
Macaroni Junction, Oldupp, charades, Sandy Cove.
Moorland Cutting, Kew, I-Spy, Pebble Bay.
Stonekeigh Bypass, Jamme, consequences, Rock Banks.

Logi-5, p. 234

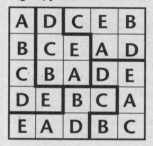

A	D	C	E	B
B	C	E	A	D
C	B	A	D	E
D	E	B	C	A
E	A	D	B	C

Killer Sudoku, p. 234

8	7	3	2	6	4	9	5	1
4	5	6	9	7	1	2	8	3
1	9	2	8	5	3	6	4	7
3	2	1	4	8	6	5	7	9
5	4	7	1	9	2	8	3	6
9	6	8	5	3	7	1	2	4
7	8	5	3	1	9	4	6	2
6	1	4	7	2	5	3	9	8
2	3	9	6	4	8	7	1	5

Domino Search, p. 235

3	2	2	6	6	6	4	6
3	5	1	2	5	5	2	5
1	1	2	3	6	2	0	6
4	0	2	3	4	5	4	0
4	1	6	6	4	0	1	5
4	1	2	1	1	3	5	0
5	4	3	0	3	0	0	3

The Bodyguard, p. 236

The court appearance is on the 9th (clue 2), so, from clue 4, Stuart Temple must be the client on the 24th and the wedding must be on the 14th. So, Stuart Temple isn't the pop singer visiting the hospital (clue 3), nor is he going to the prize-giving, where Gary Horton will be the client (clue 5), so his event must be the literary lunch, leaving the novelist's event on the 11th (clue 1) as the prize-giving and the novelist as Gary Horton. By elimination, the pop singer must have booked Tommy for the 19th. The singer isn't Donald Ellis (clue 3) or Ray Sellars, who is the racing driver (clue 6), so it must be Carolyn Dunne. The journalist hasn't booked Tommy for the 9th or the 14th (clue 2), so they must have secured Tommy's services for the 24th and is therefore Stuart Temple. By elimination, Donald Ellis must be the media tycoon. He hasn't booked Tommy for the 9th (clue 5), so he must have done so for the wedding on the 14th, leaving Ray Sellars making a court appearance on the 9th.

9th, Ray Sellars, racing driver, court appearance.
12th, Gary Horton, novelist, prize-giving.
14th, Donald Ellis, media tycoon, wedding.
19th, Carolyn Dunne, pop singer, hospital visit.
24th, Stuart Temple, journalist, literary lunch.

Number Series, p. 238

Two puppies featured in one title (clue 7), and the group of three was having a party (clue 5), so, from clue 1, the number of lambs feeling sad must have been four, and, also from that clue, six kittens must have appeared in another story. We now know that the little mice (clue 6) did not number two, four, or six, and the five creatures were described as itsy-bitsy (clue 3), so there must have been three little mice who were having a party. Now, by elimination, the five itsy-bitsy creatures must have been ducklings. The creatures who came to play cannot have been the two puppies (clue 4), and, since they were described as wee (clue 4), they cannot have numbered three or five, and we know the four lambs were feeling sad, so the wee creatures who came to play must have been the six kittens. So, from clue 4, it must have been the five itsy-bitsy ducklings who ran away. Now, by elimination, the two puppies must have had friends. Finally, from clue 2, the four lambs, who were not tiny, must have been young, leaving *Two Tiny Puppies and their Friends* as the full remaining title.

Two Tiny Puppies and Their Friends.
Three Little Mice Have a Party.
Four Young Lambs Feeling Sad.
Five Itsy-Bitsy Ducklings Run Away.
Six Wee Kittens Come to Play.

Grove Wood, p. 240

Store 1 can't have sold the rosewood dice box (clue 1), nor can the item bought there have been made of mahogany (clue 2) or bamboo (clue 4), so it must have been made of pear wood. The rocking horse came from store 3 (clue 3), so Relics, which sold the jewel box and must have an odd number (clue 4), must be store 1. So, from clue 4, the bamboo item came from store 2 and must have been the bedside table. By elimination, the rocking horse must have been made of mahogany, and so, from clue 2, store 2 must be Darby and Jones. Also by elimination, store 4 must have sold the rosewood dice box. It isn't

Cobwebs (clue 1), so it must have been Father Time, leaving Cobwebs as store 3.

1, Relics, jewel box, pear wood.
2, Darby and Jones, bedside table, bamboo.
3, Cobwebs, rocking horse, mahogany.
4, Father Time, dice box, rosewood.

Coolers, p. 241

Since each jug has a different combination of two juices (intro), each juice must appear in two different jugs. From clue 1, none of jugs A, B, or E contains mango juice, so that must be in both jug C and jug D. From clue 2, neither jug A nor jug D contain coconut, which also isn't in jug C (clue 3), so jugs B and E must both have coconut. Jug A can't have banana (clue 4) and we know it doesn't have coconut or mango, so it must have pineapple and orange. So, from clue 2, jug D must have mango and banana. So, from clue 4, jug B must have banana along with its coconut, and jug C must have orange to accompany its mango. By elimination, jug E's mixture must be coconut and pineapple.

A, orange and pineapple.
B, banana and coconut.
C, mango and orange.
D, banana and mango.
E, coconut and pineapple.

Mentioned in Dispatches, p. 242

The appliance to be found in bay 15 of one of the rows is used for washing (clue 1), but it is not the dishwasher, which is in an even-numbered bay (clue 2), so it must be the washing machine. One of the appliances is in bay 3 of row 2 (clue 5), while the television is in bay 6 of one of the rows (clue 3), so the oven in row 1, which is not in bay 12 (clue 3), must be in bay 4 and is therefore on level 5 (clue 4). The dishwasher is not in bay 3 (clue 2), so it must be bay 12, leaving the fridge, stacked on level 2 (clue 2), as the appliance in bay 3/row 2. We know that the item on level 3/row 3 (clue 1) is not in bays 3 or 4, nor is it in bays 12 or 15 (clue 1), so it must be bay 6 and must therefore be the television.

The dishwasher is not on level 1 (clue 2), so it must be on level 4, leaving the appliance on level 1 as the washing machine in bay 15. Finally, the dishwasher on level 4 is not in row 4 (clue 6), so it must be in row 5, leaving the washing machine in row 4.

Oven, row 1, bay 4, level 5.
Dishwasher, row 5, bay 12, level 4.
Fridge, row 2, bay 3, level 2.
Television, row 3, bay 6, level 3.
Washing machine, row 4, bay 15, level 1.

Night Duty, p. 244

Luke Mason's partner isn't Diane Ellis (clue 1), Vicky Wills (clue 5), Kay Lovell, who is teamed with Brian Cook (clue 2), or Jim Kelly (clue 3), so it must be Alec Brown. They aren't dressed as Goths or bikers, which is the disguise of Diane Ellis and her partner (clue 1), nor as cyclists, the disguise of Grace Hall and her partner (clue 4), nor students (clue 5), so they must be dressed as bar staff and are therefore at the Plum and Peacock (clue 6). Peter Quinn is at the Spider's Web (clue 3), and the woman at Area 51 (clue 3) must be either Grace Hall or Tina Stone, so Brian Cook and Kay Lovell, who aren't at Number 99 (clue 2), must be at the Lotus Eater. Therefore, they're not dressed as students (clue 5), so they must be parading as Goths. The students aren't Vicky Wills and her partner (clue 5), so they must be Jim Kelly and his female partner at Area 51 (clue 3), and Vicky Wills's partner must be Grace Hall, leaving the woman at Area 51 as Tina Stone. By elimination, Peter Quinn's partner must be Diane Ellis, and Grace Hall and Vicky Wills must be at Number 99.

Brian Cook, Kay Lovell, Lotus Eater, Goths.
Grace Hall, Vicky Wills, Number 99, cyclists.
Luke Mason, Alec Brown, Plum and Peacock, bar staff.
Peter Quinn, Diane Ellis, Spider's Web, bikers.
Tina Stone, Jim Kelly, Area 51, students.

Critter's Creatures, p. 246

Kate's home has a playroom (clue 5), so the resident of home 1 with its gallery (clue 4), who isn't Benedict (clue 1), Beatrice (clue 2), Cleopatra (clue 4), Antony (clue 4), Hamlet (clue 6), or Juliet (clue 6), must be Romeo. Kate's home is on the top shelf (clue 5), so the resident of number 8, who can't be Beatrice (clue 2), Cleopatra (clue 4), or Juliet (clue 6), must be male. So, from clue 3, the home with the penthouse can't be number 7 and must be number 2. So, Kate's top shelf house with a playroom must be number 3. Now, from clue 1, Benedict's house must be number 6 or 7. As we have seen, the resident of number 8 is male, so Benedict can't have number 7 and must live in number 6. So, from clue 1, home number 4 must have the loft storage and, from clue 7, Benedict's number 6 must have the observatory. Residence 4 can't be occupied by Beatrice (clue 2), Cleopatra (clue 4), Hamlet (clue 6), or Juliet (clue 6), so it must be home to Antony. So, Cleopatra doesn't have home 5 and must have home 7. Hamlet can't be in residence 1 or 5 (clue 6) so he must have home 8 and, also from clue 6, Cleopatra's home 7 must have the attic bedroom. So, Beatrice doesn't have residence 5 and must have residence 2 with the penthouse, and residence 5 must have the garret. By elimination, Hamlet's upper floor at number 8 must be the studio space and Juliet must occupy number 5 with its top-floor garret.

1, Romeo, gallery.
2, Beatrice, penthouse.
3, Kate, playroom.
4, Antony, loft storage.
5, Juliet, garret.
6, Benedict, observatory.
7, Cleopatra, attic bedroom.
8, Hamlet, studio space.

Dysart Five, p. 248

Irene's appointment was at 11:00 a.m. (clue 4) and Mrs. Clarke's was at 11:30 a.m. (clue 7), so, Ellen's appointment, from clue 6, can't have been at 12:00 noon or 10:00 a.m. Since she was seeing Mr. Tobias (clue 6), she can't have had the 10:30 a.m. appointment with Mr. Ronald (clue 5), and so Ellen must have had the 11:30 a.m. appointment and is therefore Ellen Clarke. So, from clue 6, Irene must be Irene Ward. Ursula is Ursula Lambert (clue 3), so Alice, who isn't Mrs. Naylor (clue 5), must be Alice Jones and therefore met with Mr. Godfrey (clue 1). That wasn't at 10:00 a.m. (clue 5), so it must have been at 12:00 noon. The 10:00 a.m. client wasn't Olivia (clue 2), so her appointment must have been at 10:30 a.m., leaving the 10:00 a.m. client as Ursula Lambert. By elimination, Olivia must be Olivia Naylor. Finally, from clue 4, Irene Ward didn't see Mr. Monty and must have seen Young Mr. Godfrey, leaving Ursula Lambert as Mr. Monty's client with the 10:00 a.m. appointment.

Alice Jones, 12:00 noon, Mr. Godfrey.
Ellen Clarke, 11:30 a.m., Mr. Tobias.
Irene Ward, 11:00 a.m., Young Mr. Godfrey.
Olivia Naylor, 10:30 a.m., Mr. Ronald.
Ursula Lambert, 10:00 a.m., Mr. Monty.

Vacation Homes, p. 250

The former net store, building 5, doesn't have a leaking roof (clue 6) or rotting floors (clue 1). The ex-beer store is haunted (clue 2) and the building with no heating is number 4 (clue 3), which also tells us that rat-infested Benbow Villa can't be building 5 (clue 4). So, building 5 must be the multiple death scene and, from clue 4, rat-infested Benbow Villa must be number 6. Crow's Nest Cottage, the ex-cart shed, can't be building 1 or 2 (clue 1). Building 3 is Nelson House (clue 7), so Crow's Nest Cottage must be building 4 with the rotten floors at building 1. Clue 5 rules out the ex-shanty as building 1, 2, or 6, so it must be building 3. By elimination, it must have a leaking roof, and the haunted ex-beer store must be building 1. So, Fisherman's Cottage must be building 5 (clue 5). The ex-beer store isn't Neptune's Nook (clue 2), so it must be Safe Harbor, leaving Neptune's Nook as building 2. Finally, Benbow Villa wasn't originally a trawler (clue 4), so it must have been a stable, leaving the former trawler as building 2.

1, Safe Harbor, beer store, haunted.
2, Neptune's Nook, trawler, rotten floor.
3, Nelson House, shanty, leaking roof.
4, Crow's Nest Cottage, cart shed, no heating.
5, Fisherman's Cottage, net store, death scene.
6, Benbow Villa, stable, rats.

Water Nymphs, p. 252

Ms. Herring's boat is the *Seagull* (clue 7) and *Bluebell* is a catamaran (clue 4), so Ms. Claymore's sailing dinghy, which isn't Trudy's *Swordfish* (clue 6), or the *Cutlass* (clue 1), must be the *Diamond*. Pauline Rose's (clue 3) boat can't be the catamaran *Bluebell* (clue 1), so it must be the *Cutlass*. It isn't the rowboat (clue 3) and the motorboat is Brenda's vessel (clue 2), so Pauline Rose's boat must be an inflatable. Ms. Claymore's boat type tells us she's not Brenda, nor is she Laura (clue 5), so she must be Edna Claymore. Brenda's boat type rules out three names for it, and we know it isn't the *Swordfish*, so it must be the *Seagull* and she must be Ms. Herring. By elimination, Laura's boat must be the *Bluebell*, and Trudy's must be a rowboat. Finally, from clue 5, Laura isn't Ms. Flint, so she must be Laura Pigeon, leaving Ms. Flint as Trudy Flint.

Brenda Herring, *Seagull*, motorboat.
Edna Claymore, *Diamond*, sailing dinghy.
Laura Pigeon, *Bluebell*, catamaran.
Pauline Rose, *Cutlass*, inflatable.
Trudy Flint, *Swordfish*, rowboat.

In the Aria, p. 254

I Monna Mobile is from an 1839 work (clue 4) and *Topo Gigio* is in *Carmenda* (clue 5), so the 1841 opera, *Cosi Fan Belt* (clue 1), which does not include the aria *Uno Cornetto* (clue 1), or *Nissan Dormobile* (clue 2) must contain *Pizza di Actione*, sung by Lancia Ferrari (clue 6). The character of Fiatuno

does not appear in the 1835 or 1837 operas (clue 2) or, from clue 2, the 1843 work, so he must be in the 1839 opera, singing *I Monna Mobile*. Therefore, *Rigomortis* must have been written in 1837 and the opera featuring the aria *Nissan Dormobile* in 1835 (clue 2). By elimination, *Rigomortis* must include the aria *Uno Cornetto*, and *Carmenda* must have been composed in 1843. The 1835 opera including *Nissan Dormobile* is not *Don Johnsoni* (clue 3), so it must be *La Travesti*, featuring the character of Figarol (clue 3). This leaves *I Monna Mobile* as the popular aria from *Don Johnsoni*. Finally, Grandebusti is not a character in *Rigomortis* (clue 1), so it must be in *Carmenda,* leaving *Rigomortis* as the opera featuring Alf Aromeo.

1835, *La Travesti, Nissan Dormobile*, Figarol.
1837, *Rigomortis, Uno Cornetto*, Alf Aromeo.
1839, *Don Johnsoni, I Monna Mobile*, Fiatuno.
1841, *Cosi Fan Belt, Pizza di Actione*, Lancia Ferrari.
1843, *Carmenda, Topo Gigio*, Grandebusti.

Sign In, p. 256

1	4	5	2	3
3	2	1	4	5
4	5	2	3	1
2	1	3	5	4
5	3	4	1	2

Sudoku, p. 256

8	3	7	9	6	4	1	5	2
4	5	6	8	2	1	3	7	9
2	9	1	7	5	3	8	4	6
9	1	2	4	8	7	6	3	5
7	4	5	3	9	6	2	1	8
6	8	3	2	1	5	4	9	7
5	6	8	1	4	9	7	2	3
3	2	4	5	7	8	9	6	1
1	7	9	6	3	2	5	8	4

Battleships, p. 257

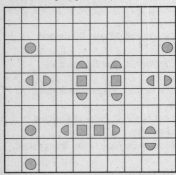

Sweet Charity, p. 258

Mrs. Price-Lowe must have paid either $1 or $2 for her item (clue 2), but she did not spend $1 (clue 1) and must have spent $2 on the jigsaw (clue 6), so the person who has brought in the CDs and is purchasing the lampshade must be paying $4 for it (clue 2). From clue 1, Mrs. Barginn, who brought in the blouses (clue 1), must have been making a purchase for $1 (clue 1). She is not buying the jacket, as that costs more than the tie (clue 5), or the tie itself, as that is Mr. Sayle's purchase (clue 4), so it must be the set of plates. The jacket costs more than the tie (clue 5), so it must be $5, and the tie must be $3. The person who's brought the CDs and paid $4 for the lampshade isn't Mr. Steele (clue 3), Mr. Sayle, or Mrs. Pryce-Lowe, so it must be

Miss Snipp, and, by elimination, the person who has bought the jacket for $5 must be Mr. Steele. The person who has donated the baby clothes has not purchased the jigsaw or jacket, so it must be Mr. Sayle, who has bought the tie. Finally, the person who has brought in the toys is spending more than the person who has donated the coat (clue 2), so the former must be Mr. Steele with his $5 jacket, and the latter Mrs. Pryce-Lowe with her $2 jigsaw.

Mrs. Barginn, blouses, set of plates, $1.
Mrs. Pryce-Lowe, coat, jigsaw, $2.
Mr. Sayle, baby clothes, tie, $3.
Miss Snipp, CDs, lampshade, $4.
Mr. Steele, toys, jacket, $5.

Courier Favor, p. 260

The package containing the spare parts weighs 2.5lbs (clue 6), so the 0.5lb package, which is on its way to Milan and does not contain books or computer software (clue 3), or fashion samples (clue 4), must contain documents and therefore is being consigned via Rapidispatch (clue 1). So, from clue 4, the fashion samples must weigh 2lbs and the package for New York, 1lb. The latter is not books (clue 3), so it must be the computer software and, by elimination, Parcelprompt's 1.5lb package (clue 5) must contain the books. They are not being sent to Frankfurt (clue 3) or Paris, which is the destination of Speedway's parcel (clue 1), so it must be Madrid. The Interswift package does not contain computer software (clue 2), so it does not weigh 1lb, and as it weighs less than the Speedway consignment (also clue 2), it is not 2.5lbs, so it must be 2lbs of fashion samples. Therefore, Speedway's package must be the 2.5lb one for Paris (clue 2), containing the spare parts. By elimination, the computer software must be being collected by Fastline, and Interswift must be taking the 2lb package of fashion samples to Frankfurt.

Fastline, computer software, 1lb, New York.
Interswift, fashion samples, 2lbs, Frankfurt.
Parcelprompt, books, 1.5lbs, Madrid.

Rapidispatch, documents, 0.5lb, Milan.
Speedway, spare parts, 2.5lbs, Paris.

Muddelle's Muddle, p. 262

Monday's object was discovered in the laundry basket (clue 3) and the kebab was half-eaten on Wednesday (clue 2), so the strange item in the fridge which, from clue 1, couldn't have been found on Friday, Thursday, or Tuesday, must have been found on Wednesday. So, also from clue 1, the remnants of the Chinese meal must have been on Thursday and the carton of milk must have been discovered in an odd place on Friday. The item left in the laundry basket on Monday wasn't the book (clue 3) and couldn't have been the old socks (clue 4). The dirty mug was found in the washing machine (clue 2), so Monday's discovery must have been the laptop in the laundry basket. The curry wasn't eaten on Friday (clue 4), or, since we have now placed the misplaced laptop on Monday, Tuesday (clue 4), so curry must have been Monday's lunch. Pizza wasn't Friday's lunch (clue 5), so it must have been partly eaten on Tuesday, leaving fish and fries as Friday's midday meal. So that wasn't the day the professor left something in the pantry (clue 3), and his mislaid object on Friday, the milk carton, rules out the washing machine, so he must have eaten fish and fries and left a milk carton in the linen closet on Friday. The mug-in-the-washing-machine incident wasn't on Thursday (clue 2), so it must have been on Tuesday after the pizza lunch. From clue 3, the book wasn't found on Thursday, so it must have been discovered in the fridge on Wednesday, leaving the pair of old socks being found in the pantry on Thursday.

Monday, Indian curry, laptop in the laundry basket.
Tuesday, pizza, dirty mug in the washing machine.
Wednesday, kebab, book in the fridge.
Thursday, Chinese, old socks in the pantry.
Friday, fish and fries, milk carton in the linen closet.

Great Non-Escape, p. 264

The 2013 arrest was in Bangkok (clue 2), and Insp. Bell made the arrest in Maputo (clue 5), so the person arrested in 2010 by Insp. Heddlu (clue 1), who wasn't arrested in Quito (clue 4) or Southend (clue 1), must have been arrested in Nassau, and was therefore Peter Head (clue 6). Don Caster was caught in 2011 (clue 1), so Joan Town, Insp. Mouchard's prisoner (clue 4), must have been arrested in 2012 at the earliest, and thus the Quito arrest must have been in either 2013 or 2014; it wasn't in 2013 (clue 2), so it must have been in 2014. The Quito arrest wasn't made by Insp. Vigilis (clue 4), so the detective must have been Insp. Jager. Don Caster wasn't arrested by Insp. Vigilis (clue 1), so he must have been Insp. Bell's prisoner from Maputo. By elimination, the 2012 arrest must have been in Southend. Mary Kirk wasn't Insp. Vigilis' prisoner (clue 3), so she must have been Insp. Jager's. Finally, Ken Ilworth wasn't caught in 2012 (clue 2), so he must have been arrested in 2013, in Bangkok by (by elimination) Insp. Vigilis, leaving Joan Town as the 2012 Southend arrestee.

Don Caster, 2011, Maputo, Inspector Bell.
Joan Town, 2012, Southend, Inspector Mouchard.
Ken Ilworth, 2013, Bangkok, Inspector Vigilis.
Mary Kirk, 2014, Quito, Inspector Jager.
Peter Head, 2010, Nassau, Inspector Heddlu.

Address Unknown, p. 266

Both Gormlus and Euselus took an hour longer than someone else (clues 3 and 6), so both must have each taken two-and-a-half or three-and-a-half hours. The house by the three-mile marker took four hours to find (clue 4), so Branelus, who was looking for the house near the olive grove but didn't take two hours to find it (clue 2), must have taken one-and-a-half hours. Cluelus was sent to find the oak door (clue 1), so, as we have seen, he didn't take three-and-a-half hours. Nor was three-and-a-half hours the time taken to find the house behind the wall (clue 3), the house with no garden (clue 5), or the big villa (clue 6), so it must have been the house by the pear tree. One address was behind the wall beside the Tiber (clue 3), so Branelus' one-and-a-half-hour search for the location near the olive grove, which couldn't have been for the house with no garden (clue 5), must have been for the big villa. So, from clue 6, Gormlus must have hunted for two-and-a-half hours and Euselus must have hunted for the house by the pear tree for three-and-a-half hours and, from clue 4, Gormlus' two-and-a-half-hour search must have been for the house behind the wall beside the Tiber. By elimination, Hopelus must have been sent to deliver a message to the house with no garden. It's not on the Caelian Hill (clue 5) or in the cobblers' quarter (clue 1), so he must have found it at the third milestone after four hours. So, from clue 5, the search on the Caelian Hill must have been Euselus' three-and-a-half-hour hunt for the house by the pear tree. By final elimination, Cluelus must have found the oak door in the cobblers' quarter after two hours.

Branelus, the big villa near the olive grove, 1½ hours.

Cluelus, the oak door in the cobblers' quarters, 2 hours.

Euselus, near the pear tree on Caelian Hill, 3½ hours.

Gormlus, behind the wall beside the Tiber, 2½ hours.

Hopelus, house with no garden at third milestone, 4 hours.

Address: John Underhill, Andover, Massachusetts.

Imaginary Memoirs, p. 268

Michael Warden's pen name is Geoff Lester (clue 3) and George Gordon's book is about a cage fighter (clue 1), so the man who, as Austin Caxton, has written about a London gang boss (clue 2), must be John Dawkins. *Hellbender* is about the Spitfire pilot (clue 5),

so Edith Granger's *Dark City*, which isn't about a Mafia hitman (clue 4), must be about a Cold War spy. Belinda Waters's book isn't about the Spitfire pilot either (clue 5), so *Hellbender* must be Michael Warden's Geoff Lester book, leaving Belinda Waters's book as the story of the Mafia hitman. *No Way Back*, written under the pen name Guy Darrell (clue 1), isn't George Gordon's book (clue 1), so it must be by Belinda Waters. George Gordon's pen name isn't Marc le Roux (clue 2), so it must be Frank Vance, and Marc le Roux must be Edith Granger's pen name. Finally, the book by John Dawkins, alias Austin Caxton, isn't *Bad Medicine* (clue 2), so it must be *The Seesaw*, leaving *Bad Medicine* as George Gordon's cage-fighter book.

Belinda Waters, Guy Darrell, *No Way Back*, Mafia hitman.

Edith Granger, Marc le Roux, *Dark City*, Cold War spy.

George Gordon, Frank Vance, *Bad Medicine*, cage fighter.

John Dawkins, Austin Caxton, *The Seesaw*, London crime boss.

Michael Warden, Geoff Lester, *Hellbender*, Spitfire pilot.

West End Girls, p. 270

From clue 4, Selina Rolf didn't spend $280 or $320 and, since it was the swimsuit that cost $360 (clue 2), clue 4 also rules out $440. Leah Maxim spent $400 (clue 6), so Selina Rolf must have spent $360 on a swimsuit. Therefore, from clue 4, the jacket must have cost $280. We know that its purchaser wasn't Selina Rolf or Leah Maxim, nor can she have been Donna Essex (clue 1). Alison Bolt bought a dress (clue 5), so it must have been Verity Wild, the model (clue 3), who bought the jacket. Now, Donna Essex can't have spent $320 (clue 1), so she must have spent $440, leaving Alison Bolt as the actress who spent $320 (clue 7). From clue 1, the baseball player's wife who bought the underwear must have been Leah Maxim, who spent $400, and Donna Essex must have bought the shoes. She isn't the TV presenter (clue 8), so she must be the pop singer, leaving the TV presenter as Selina Rolf, who bought the swimsuit.

Alison Bolt, actress, dress, $320.
Donna Essex, pop singer, shoes, $440.
Leah Maxim, baseball player's wife, underwear, $400.
Selina Rolf, TV presenter, swimsuit, $360.
Verity Wild, model, jacket, $280.

Identifying the Unidentified, p. 272

Brad's using room 1 (clue 3), so Ross, who can't be using room 4, 7, or 2 (all clue 2), must be in room 3 and is therefore the UFO contactee (clue 5). So, Mr. La Rue is in room 4 (clue 2). Clue 1 now tells us that Toby, the film actor, isn't using room 7, so he must be in room 4, and Brad's surname must be Munro. Ross isn't Wasson the science fiction writer (clue 6), nor Conrad, who is Floyd (clue 4), so his surname must be Brady. By elimination, Wasson must be Jonah. Floyd won't be using room 2 (clue 4), so he must be in room 7, leaving room 2 for Jonah. Brad isn't the journalist (clue 3), so he must be the UFO researcher, leaving Floyd Conrad as the journalist.

Brad Munro, UFO researcher, 1.
Floyd Conrad, journalist, 7.
Jonah Wasson, science fiction writer, 2.
Ross Brady, UFO contactee, 3.
Toby La Rue, film actor, 4.

Battleships, p. 274

Sign In, p. 275

5	4	3	1	2
1	3	2	5	4
4	2	5	3	1
2	5	1	4	3
3	1	4	2	5

Sudoku, p. 275

8	3	1	4	5	2	7	6	9
2	9	7	8	1	6	4	5	3
5	4	6	3	9	7	8	2	1
3	1	5	2	7	8	6	9	4
9	8	4	1	6	5	2	3	7
6	7	2	9	4	3	5	1	8
7	2	3	5	8	9	1	4	6
1	6	9	7	2	4	3	8	5
4	5	8	6	3	1	9	7	2

Vacation Reading, p. 276

Book 4 is about wildlife (clue 3). Book 1, *Warriors*, isn't fantasy fiction (clue 6), nor can it be crime fiction (clue 1), true crime (clue 2), or science fiction (clue 4), so it must be history and is therefore by James Portman (clue 5). As the writer of book 6 is male (clue

6), clue 1 now rules out books 2, 5, and 6 as crime fiction, so by elimination that must be the genre of book 3, and, from clue 1, Carol Kaine must have written book 2. Its genre can't be science fiction (clue 4) or true crime (clue 2), so it must be fantasy fiction. Nor can the true crime book be book 6 (clue 2), so it must be book 5, leaving book 6 as science fiction, and, from clue 2, its author is Steven Bauer. The book's title can't be *The Road* (clue 4) or *Private Lives* (clue 7), nor is it *Grand Tour* (clue 2), while *Shadows of Blood* is by Tricia Lane (clue 1), so Steven Bauer's book must be *Treasure*, and from clue 7, *Private Lives* must be book 4. So, *Shadows of Blood* by Tricia Lane must be book 5, the true crime. So, from clue 2, Grand Tour must be by a man and Carol Kaine's fantasy fiction must be *The Road*. So, *Grand Tour* must be the crime fiction in position 3 and, by elimination, its male author must be Bernard Joyner. Finally, Victoria Ray must have written *Private Lives*, the wildlife book in position 4.

1, *Warriors*, James Portman, history.
2, *The Road*, Carol Kaine, fantasy fiction.
3, *Grand Tour*, Bernard Joyner, crime fiction.
4, *Private Lives*, Victoria Ray, wildlife.
5, *Shadows of Blood*, Tricia Lane, true crime.
6, *Treasure*, Steven Bauer, science fiction.

Paragon in Europe, p. 278

The burglar was Helen Marcus (clue 2) and the Oporto villain was Chick Lumsky (clue 4), so the smuggler in Danzig, who wasn't Stella Piper (clue 3) or Zebedee Wyatt (clue 5), must have been Enzo Dragoti. The kidnapping is in *The Paragon and the Red Roadhouse* (clue 4), so *The Paragon and the Poisoned Patriot*, in which the villain is Zebedee Wyatt, which doesn't involve a murder (clue 5), must feature the crime of fraud. The Danzig story isn't *The Paragon and the Ghostly Galleon* (clue 3), and *The Paragon and the Diamond Dragon* is set in Antwerp (clue 5), so the Danzig story must be *The Paragon and the*

Angry Archer. From clue 5, *The Paragon and the Diamond Dragon* isn't about a murder, so it must be the burglary story. There's a male villain in Budapest (clue 1), so it can't be Stella Piper and must be Zebedee Wyatt, and Stella Piper must be the villain in Corunna. *The Paragon and the Red Roadhouse* isn't set in Oporto (clue 4), so it must be set in Corunna and, by elimination, the Oporto story must be *The Paragon and the Ghostly Galleon*, and must be about a murder.

The Paragon and the Angry Archer, Danzig, smuggling, Enzo Dragoti.
The Paragon and the Diamond Dragon, Antwerp, burglary, Helen Marcus.
The Paragon and the Ghostly Galleon, Oporto, murder, Chick Lumsky.
The Paragon and the Poisoned Patriot, Budapest, fraud, Zebedee Wyatt.
The Paragon and the Red Roadhouse, Corunna, kidnapping, Stella Piper.

Music and Words, p. 280

Berry Likely was named as lyricist in June (clue 2). The December lyricist can't be Piers Send (clue 1) or Jack Hammer, whose show is *The Fountain* (clue 4). Clue 6 rules out Roy De France, whose show is about the Battle of Narvik, so the December lyricist must be Mack Iavelli. The Dr. Crippen show was announced in April (clue 5), so clue 4 rules out Jack Hammer as the January lyricist, and clue 1 rules out Piers Send, so he must have been Roy De France. His show about the Battle of Narvik isn't *Werewolves*, which is about werewolves (clue 1). Clue 3 rules out *Celebration* and clue 6 rules out *Early to Bed*, so the January show must be *Next Day*. Clues 1 and 2 rule out September for the werewolf show, and clues 2 and 4 rule out the Great Depression one, so the September show must be about pool. Its lyricist isn't Jack Hammer (clue 4) and the date rules out Berry Likely and Mack Iavelli, so he must be Piers Send. So, from clue 1, the December show must be *Werewolves*. By elimination, Jack Hammer must be the April lyricist writing about Dr. Crippen and, from clue 4, the Great Depression is the theme of the June show. Finally, from clue 6, *Early to Bed* must be Piers Send's September show, leaving Berry Likely's show as *Celebration*, about the Great Depression.

January, Roy De France, *Next Day*, Battle of Narvik.
April, Jack Hammer, *The Fountain*, Dr. Crippen.
June, Berry Likely, *Celebration*, Great Depression.
September, Piers Send, *Early to Bed*, pool.
December, Mack Iavelli, *Werewolves*, werewolves.

Old-Time Horrors, p. 282

Kurt Vorster, who worked on the 1933 movie, was not the scriptwriter (clue 6), nor can he have been the producer of *The Faceless Killer*, which came out the year before Wilbur Francke's movie (clue 2), while the costume designer was Freeman McMichael (clue 4) and the makeup artist's big movie came out in 1932 (clue 5), so Kurt must have been the stop-motion animator. So, from clue 3, Benedict De Forest's *House of the Hell Maiden* must have come out in 1932, and he was the makeup artist. Since the 1929 movie was *The Crawling Horror* (clue 1), clue 2 tells us that Wilbur's movie can't date from 1929 or 1930, so, by elimination, it must have come out in 1931 and, from clue 2, *The Faceless Killer* must date from 1930. By elimination, the man who worked on it must have been Randall Bancroft, and Freeman McMichael must have worked on *The Crawling Horror*. Also by elimination, the 1931 movie must have had Wilbur Franke as scriptwriter. Clue 6 tells us Wilbur worked on *Food for the Ghoul Woman*, leaving Kurt Vorster's movie as *Day of the Death Bat*.

Benedict De Forest, makeup artist, *House of the Hell Maiden*, 1932.
Freeman McMichael, costume designer, *The Crawling Horror*, 1929.
Kurt Vorster, stop-motion animator, *Day of the Death Bat*, 1933.
Randall Bancroft, producer, *The Faceless Killer*, 1930.
Wilbur Francke, scriptwriter, *Food for the Ghoul Woman*, 1931.

Trail Drive, p. 284

Ranch D sent 650 cows on the drive (clue 2). The ranch owner can't have been Jack Nelson (clue 3) and Dan Addison's Rocking A can't have sent 650 cows (clue 4). Clue 5 rules out Slim Leamas, so ranch D must have been Mack McLean's. So, ranch D wasn't the Lazy K (clue 4) or the Box M (clue 1), so it must have been the Flying H. Now clue 1 tells us that the 750 cows can't have come from the Box M, and clue 4 rules out the Rocking A, so they must have come from the Lazy K. So, from clue 4, the Rocking A must have sent 850 cows, leaving the Box M sending 950. The latter can't be ranch A (clue 1), and neither can the Rocking A, which sent 850 cows (clue 3), so ranch A must have been Lazy K. So, from clue 4, the Rocking A must have been ranch B, leaving the Box M as ranch C. From clue 3, Jack Nelson owned the Lazy K, leaving Slim Leamas as owner of the Box M.

A, Lazy K, 750, Jack Nelson.
B, Rocking A, 850, Dan Addison.
C, Box M, 950, Slim Leamas.
D, Flying H, 650, Mack McLean.

Circuit Training, p. 285

Component 3 is the Preregulator (clue 2). From clue 2, the Expeller must be either component 5 or component 6. From clue 3, it can't have only two connections so it can't be number 5, and therefore must be number 6 with the Disaccumulator being component 5. So, from clue 3, the Upsweller must have two direct connections. It's on the lower row (clue 3), so it must be component 8. The Redischarger has an even number (clue 4), but since the Upsweller is number 8 and is not connected to the Redischarger, the latter can't be number 4 and must be component 2. Now, from clue 1, the Loss Collector must be either component 4 or 7, and the Antisender must be either 1 or 4. So either way one of them is number 4. So, the Undirector, which isn't component 7 (clue 4) must be component 1. Finally, from clue 1, component 4 must be the Antisender and component 7 must be the Loss Collector.

1, Undirector; 2, Redischarger; 3, Preregulator; 4, Antisender; 5, Disaccumulator; 6, Expeller; 7, Loss Collector; 8, Upsweller.

Bloop Bloop, p. 286

Dr. Adam Baxter is in the scene where Kelly is shot and Pete Ramsey in the scene at police HQ (all clue 1), so the chase scene in Chinatown, which involves a man (clue 4) must involve Teller, who is therefore male. The meeting with Sean includes a changing hairstyle (clue 1), so it isn't Lara Mazova's, whose blooper was a camera in shot, and who isn't in the bomb-defusing scene (clue 2) and must therefore have had breakfast with Sean. Since Pete Ramsey isn't the one who meets with Sean (clue 1), he must be involved with defusing the bomb, and Gail Hadley must meet Sean and so have a changing hairstyle. This leaves Dr. Adam Baxter in the airport lounge with a vanishing jacket (clue 5). Lara Mazova isn't in the coffee shop scene (clue 6), so she must be in Joe's Diner, and the coffee shop must be where Gail Hadley meets Sean with a variable hairstyle. Finally, Teller's Chinatown chase didn't involve reappearing beer (clue 3), so he must have a color-changing shirt, and Pete Ramsey must have the reappearing beer while the bomb's being defused at police HQ.

Dr. Adam Baxter, death of Kelly, airport lounge, vanishing jacket.
Gail Hadley, meeting with Sean, coffee shop, changing hairstyle.
Lara Mazova, breakfast with Sean, Joe's Diner, camera in shot.
Pete Ramsey, defusing bomb, police HQ, reappearing beer.
Teller, chase scene, Chinatown, color-changing shirt.

To All in Tents, p. 288

The family booked for twelve nights wasn't from Bellford (clue 1), Ridgewood (clue 3), or Framebury (clue 4), so it must have come from Domecaster. The family booked for fourteen nights wasn't from Ridgewood (clue 3) or Framebury (clue 4), so it must have come from Bellford. The family booked for six nights can't have been the Fawcetts (clue 3), the Doughtys (clue 4), or the Wilkinses (clue 5), so it must have been the McClures. The family from Bellford can't have been the Doughtys (clue 4) or the Wilkinses (clue 5), so it must have been the Fawcetts. The Tent 4 family can't have been the Fawcetts (clue 1), the McClures (clue 2), or the Wilkinses (clue 5), so it must have been the Doughtys. The Tent 3 family wasn't the Fawcetts (clue 3) or the McClures (clue 2), so it must have been the Wilkins family. From clue 5, the Wilkins family must have booked for twelve nights and the Doughtys in Tent 4 for nine nights. The Fawcetts from Bellford were next left to the family booked for twelve nights (clue 1), so it must have been in Tent 2. By elimination, the McClures, booked for six nights, must have been in Tent 1. The family from Framebury wasn't the Doughtys (clue 4), so it must have been the McClures, leaving the Doughtys' hometown as Ridgewood.

1, McClure, Framebury, 6 nights.
2, Fawcett, Bellford, 14 nights.
3, Wilkins, Domecaster, 12 nights.
4, Doughty, Ridgewood, 9 nights.

Domino Search, p. 289

6	0	2	4	4	0	2	4
5	5	1	4	3	6	5	4
6	1	1	0	0	6	3	5
2	6	2	2	1	5	4	5
3	5	6	4	5	0	2	0
6	1	2	0	2	1	6	4
3	1	3	3	3	3	0	1

Careering Along, p. 290

The insurance brokers cannot have had Mr. Archer or Mr. Bellamy as a partner (clue 1), nor can they be Duncan and Jackson (clues 1 and 4), while Mr. Tomkins is a real estate agent (clue 6), so Mr. Rumford must have been a partner in the insurance brokerage firm. By similar reasoning, from clue 1, Walter cannot have worked for Mr. Archer, Mr. Bellamy, or Mr. Duncan, and Mr. Rumford employed John (clue 3), so Walter must have worked for Mr. Tomkins, the real estate agent. We know the partner of Mr. Stokes, who was a lawyer (clue 5), was not Mr. Duncan, Mr. Rumford, or Mr. Tomkins, and clue 5 rules out Mr. Archer, so he must have been Mr. Bellamy. We have now matched four firms' first partners' names with either an employee or a second partner, so Harold, who worked for Mr. Devonish (clue 2) cannot have also been employed by any of Messrs. Bellamy, Duncan, Rumford, or Tomkins. Therefore, Mr. Devonish's partner must have been Mr. Archer. We can rule out three descriptions for this firm, and they were not the investment advisers (clue 2), so they must have been the accountants. Now, by elimination, the investment advisers must have been Duncan and Jackson. Arthur was not their employee (clue 4), so Norman must have been, and Arthur must have worked for Bellamy and Stokes. Finally, from clue 6, Mr. Bates must have been the partner of Mr. Rumford in the insurance brokers' business, leaving Mr.

Tomkins's real estate agent partner as Mr. Russell.

Arthur, Bellamy and Stokes, lawyers.
Harold, Archer and Devonish, accountants.
John, Rumford and Bates, insurance brokers.
Norman, Duncan and Jackson, investment advisers.
Walter, Tomkins and Russell, real estate agents.

Surfing, p. 292

The "Last chance" item cost $5.99 (clue 5), so the $7.99 one, which wasn't advertised with "Don't miss out" (clue 4) or "Limited offer" (clue 6) must have been "Only a few left," and so it must have been the knee pillow. The sock presser is priced at $6.99 (clue 2), so the kettle lock, which isn't the cheapest item (clue 4) must be priced at $5.99 and, from clue 4, the "Don't miss out" offer must be at $4.99. By elimination, the "Limited offer" must be the $6.99 sock presser and, from clue 6, Bruce Bucks must have spent $7.99 on the knee pillow because there were "Only a few left." Boris Brass bought the wine prop (clue 1), so Delia Dosh, who hasn't just bought the sock presser (clue 2), must have fallen for the "Last chance" to buy the kettle lock for $5.99, leaving Bridget Bread as the purchaser of the "Limited offer" sock presser at $6.99. By final elimination, Boris Brass's new wine prop must have been the "Don't miss out" item priced at $4.99.

Boris Brass, wine prop, Don't miss out, $4.99.
Bridget Bread, sock presser, Limited offer, $6.99.
Bruce Bucks, knee pillow, Only a few left, $7.99.
Delia Dosh, kettle lock, Last chance, $5.99.

You Essay, p. 294

Jeremy Jotter wrote *Thank Hugh* (clue 2) and Norman Noat's story was set in an art gallery (clue 3). *After U*, set in a 1960s university but not written by Sophie Scribel (clue 1), must have been by Deirdre Dashov. *Bless Shoes* is about a blizzard (clue 1) and the riot was in the casino (clue 4), so Deirdre's *After U*, which wasn't about a fire (clue 5), must have been about a concert at a university in the sixties. The riot in the casino isn't the story of *Good for Ewe* (clue 4), so it must be Jeremy Jotter's *Thank Hugh*. Finally, the market wasn't on fire (clue 5), so it must have been the art gallery that was ablaze with, by elimination, the story being *Good for Ewe*, leaving Sophie Scribel's story as *Bless Shoes* about a blizzard in an eighteenth-century market.

Deirdre Dashov, *After U*, university, concert.
Jeremy Jotter, *Thank Hugh*, casino, riot.
Norman Noat, *Good for Ewe*, art gallery, fire.
Sophie Scribel, *Bless shoes*, market, blizzard.

Ars Pro Gloria Artis, p. 296

The acrylic piece was placed sixth (clue 1), so the medium used for the seventh-placed entry, which wasn't oils (clue 3), pastel (clue 4), or crayon (clue 5), must have been the pink watercolor canvas (clue 6). Now, from clue 5, the black canvas must have been placed either eighth or ninth. The green canvas was ninth (clue 2), so the black canvas must have been eighth. Delia Dye's red effort wasn't sixth, so it must have been tenth, leaving the sixth-placed acrylic as the white painting. So, from clue 3, Horace Hue must have painted the pink watercolor placed seventh, and the eighth-placed entry must have been in black oils. We now know either the artist or the medium for four placings, so William Wash's watercolor must be the green lawn in ninth place, leaving Delia Dye's tenth-place red ketchup in crayon. Finally, from clue 5, Sheryl Shade didn't create the black canvas, so she must have painted the bear's eye view in white acrylics placed sixth, leaving the unlit black panther on a black background in black oils as the painting by Theresa Tint that finished in eighth place.

Delia Dye, crayon, red, 10th.

Horace Hue, watercolors, pink, 7th.
Sheryl Shade, acrylic paint, white, 6th.
Theresa Tint, oil paint, black, 8th.
William Wash, pastel, green, 9th.

Crazy Games, p. 298

The waterwheel is at the ice cream parlor (clue 3), and crazy bocce is played in the parking lot at the Pirate's Parrot bar (clue 2), so crazy billiards, which involves a model of King Kong but isn't at either of the diners (clue 1), must be at the Sunken Wreck bar. The game at Pebble Bay is crazy croquet (clue 5), so the game at Coral Dunes, which includes the dragon obstacle (clue 6) and which, being a ball game (clue 6), isn't chess or darts, must be bocce at the Pirate's Parrot bar. We know either the location or business for three of the game obstacles, so the Beach Diner at Shingle Head (clue 4), which doesn't have the lighthouse (clue 4), must have the windmill, leaving the Promenade Diner as the location of the game with the lighthouse. The crazy game played there isn't crazy darts (clue 4), so it must be crazy chess. By elimination, the game at the Beach Diner in Shingle Head must be crazy darts through the windmill, and the crazy croquet in Pebble Bay must be played at the ice cream parlor and involve negotiating the revolving waterwheel. Finally, crazy chess with the lighthouse obstacle at the Promenade Diner isn't in Sandy Cove (clue 2), so it must be in Rock Banks, leaving Sandy Cove as the location of the Sunken Wreck bar with its crazy billiards and flailing King Kong.

Coral Dunes, Pirate's Parrot bar, crazy bocce, dragon.
Pebble Bay, ice cream parlor, crazy croquet, waterwheel.
Rock Banks, Promenade Diner, crazy chess, lighthouse.
Sandy Cove, Sunken Wreck bar, crazy billiards, King Kong.
Shingle Head, Beach Diner, crazy darts, windmill.

Disaster TV, p. 300

I watched *Eastdale* on Wednesday evening (clue 6). The Monday show was not *Home Affairs* (clue 2), *Farmside* (clue 4), or *Jubilee Square* (clue 1), so it must have been *Brook Street*, featuring Annie Moane, and *Jubilee Square* must have been on Tuesday (clue 1). The character in Thursday's soap had a drinking problem (clue 3), so *Farmside's* discovery of an affair (clue 4) must have been on Friday. By elimination, Thursday's soap must have been *Home Affairs*, and I must have watched Dan Hartid's business fail on Wednesday (clue 2). Damon Gloom was not in Tuesday's *Jubilee Square* or Thursday's *Home Affairs* (clue 2), so it must have been his affair that was discovered on Friday. The Thursday character with the drinking problem was not Taylor Woe (clue 3), so it must have been Ed Hunglow, leaving Taylor Woe as the character who appeared in Tuesday's *Jubilee Square*. He had not lost his job (clue 5), so his marriage must have been breaking up, leaving the jobless soap character as Annie Moane.

Monday, *Brook Street*, Annie Moane, lost job.
Tuesday, *Jubilee Square*, Taylor Woe, marriage failing.
Wednesday, *Eastdale*, Dan Hartid, business failing.
Thursday, *Home Affairs*, Ed Hunglow, drinking problem.
Friday, *Farmside*, Damon Gloom, affair discovered.

Women's Writes, p. 302

Peggy O'Dwyer's story is science fiction (clue 2) and Laura Bell's took first prize (clue 6), so the third-placed crime story, which isn't by Helena Flower (clue 5) or Emily Blades (clue 7), must be Selina Stokes's story, *Shadow of Doubt* (clue 1). Now, from clue 2, Peggy O'Dwyer's story can't have won second or fifth prize, so it must have come fourth, and therefore fifth prize must have gone to *City Lights* (clue 2). From what we now know, the fifth-placed story, which isn't by Emily Blades (clue 7), must be by Helene Flower, and second prize must have gone to Emily Blades's story, *Green Shoes* (clue 3). It's not the fantasy (clue 3) or the war story (clue 4), so it must have been about vampires and, by elimination, the war story, *A Bargain* (clue 4), must have been Laura Bell's first-prize winner. Also by elimination, the fantasy must be Helena Blades's fifth-placed story and Peggy O'Dwyer's fourth-placed story must have been the *Sun Rise*.

First, Laura Bell, *A Bargain*, war.
Second, Emily Blades, *Green Shoes*, vampire.
Third, Selina Stokes, *Shadow of Doubt*, crime.
Fourth, Peggy O'Dwyer, *Sun Rise*, science fiction.
Fifth, Helena Flower, *City Lights*, fantasy.

On Your Medal, p. 304

Gold medal number 1 is for a female competitor (clue 2), medal 2 is for Stan Swain (clue 5), and medal 8 for the winner of the Top Plowman cooking competition (clue 1), so the medal for Cow Wrestling to be awarded to Rosebud the cow (clue 3), which is directly below that which has been won by Horace Hick and which isn't number 6 (clue 3), must be medal 7, and Horace Hick's name must be on medal 4. Now, from clue 6, Yasmin Yoakel's medal can't be any of medals 1, 3, 6, or 8, and must be medal 5 with the 4x4 Relay medal as medal 6. The woman who has won medal 1 isn't Theresa Tyke (clue 4), so it must be Sylvia Serff, leaving Theresa Tyke as the winner of medal 6 for the 4x4 Relay and, from clue 4, Stan Swain's medal 2 must be for Rowing. So, the woman who has won the 100m Butterfly must be Yasmin Yoakel winning medal 5. Peter Pessant didn't win the Top Plowman medal 8, so he must have won medal 3, leaving the winner of the Top Plowman medal as Ricky Rube. From clue 1, Sylvia Serff must have won medal 1 for Boxing. Finally, Peter Pessant hasn't won the Archery radio soap opera quiz, so he must have won medal 3 for Welly

Throwing, leaving Horace Hick winning medal 4 for his unmatchable knowledge of all things Ambridge.

1, Boxing, Sylvia Serff.
2, Rowing, Stan Swain.
3, Welly Throwing, Peter Pessant.
4, Archery, Horace Hick.
5, 100m Butterfly, Yasmin Yoakel.
6, 4x4 Relay, Theresa Tyke.
7, Cow Wrestling, Rosebud.
8, Top Plowman, Ricky Rube.

Cocktails and Crimes, p. 306

Judith McVitie offended in Shanghai (clue 2) and the Moscow Mule drinker was in Cairo (clue 1), so Diana Flambard, who drank the Earthquake (clue 3) but didn't offend in Warsaw or Oporto (clue 3), must have done so in Leipzig. The Warsaw crime was smuggling (clue 3), so Sally Van Der Waal, who was drunk and disorderly but not in Cairo (clue 1), must have offended in Oporto. The Zombie drinker, who was accused of burglary (clue 5), didn't offend in Warsaw (clue 3) or Cairo (clue 1), so she must have been arrested in Shanghai and was therefore Judith McVitie (clue 2). The espionage accusation wasn't in Cairo (clue 1), so it must have occurred in Leipzig to Diana Flambard. Patricia Paolucci's offense wasn't assault (clue 4), so she must have been charged with smuggling in Warsaw (clue 3). So, by elimination, Colette Barwick must have committed assault in Cairo, and, from clue 1, must have drunk a Moscow Mule. Patricia Paolucci didn't drink the Bellini (clue 4), so she must have had the Gimlet, leaving Sally Van Der Waal as the Bellini drinker.

Colette Barwick, Moscow Mule, Cairo, assault.
Diana Flambard, Earthquake, Leipzig, espionage.
Judith McVitie, Zombie, Shanghai, burglary.
Patricia Paolucci, Gimlet, Warsaw, smuggling.
Sally Van Der Waal, Bellini, Oporto, drunk and disorderly.

Lesson Notes, p. 308

Mr. Griffiths teaches the violin (clue 6), Mr. Manning must be due at Northfield School later than 11:00 a.m. (clue 4), and Miss Morgan is teaching after midday (clue 3), so the trumpet lesson at 11:00 a.m., which is not being given by Mrs. Gifford (clue 1), must be given by Mr. Adley. The piano lesson at Round Hill School is more than seventy minutes earlier than Mr. Manning's lesson at Northfield (clue 4), so it cannot be by Miss Morgan (clue 3) and must be by Mrs. Gifford. She is not teaching at 10:00 a.m. (clue 1), so she must be due in class at Round Hill at 11:20 a.m. So, from clue 4, Mr. Manning's lesson at Northfield must be starting at 12:50 p.m. So, Miss Morgan's lesson must be at 12:30 p.m. (clue 3) and, by elimination, Mr. Griffiths's lesson must be at 10:00 a.m. The lesson at King John is before Mrs. Gifford's (clue 1). The teacher is not Mr. Adley (clue 2), so it must be Mr. Griffiths. Miss Morgan is not teaching at St. Edward's School (clue 3), so that must be Mr. Adley, leaving Bishop Sutton as Miss Morgan's destination. She will not be teaching clarinet there (clue 5), so it must be cello, leaving the clarinet teacher as Mr. Manning at Northfield.

10:00 a.m., Mr. Griffiths, King John, violin.
11:00 a.m., Mr. Adley, St. Edward's, trumpet.
11:20 a.m., Mrs. Gifford, Round Hill, piano.
12:30 p.m., Miss Morgan, Bishop Sutton, cello.
12:50 p.m., Mr. Manning, Northfield, clarinet.

First Things First, p. 310

Mr. Kayos is organized by Miss Chewsday (clue 5) and the PAs of both Mr. Avock and Mr. DeSarray sent flowers (clue 6), so Miss Mundy, who sent malt whiskey (clue 4), but doesn't work for Mr. Mayhemme (clue 4) must be Mr. Termoyle's PA, and so she must have apologized for his forgetting the charity golf game. Mr. Kayos's PA didn't send the chocolates (clue 5), so they must have been sent by Mr. Mayhemme's PA. The roses were sent as an apology for forgetting the anniversary (clue 1), so Mr. DeSarray's PA's sunflower apology, which weren't for missing a meal (clue 6), must have been for forgetting the birthday, and so his PA must be Miss Frydeigh. So, Mr. Avock's non-meal mess-up (clue 6) must have been his forgetting the anniversary. His PA isn't Miss Wensdee (clue 6), so it must have been Miss Thirsdie who sent the roses on behalf of Mr. Avock, leaving Miss Wensdee looking after Mr. Mayhemme, and Miss Chewsday sending chrysanthemums to say sorry for what Mr. Kayos did. Finally, Mr. Mayhemme didn't forget to turn up for Sunday lunch, so he must have forgotten about a Saturday dinner arrangement, leaving Mr. Kayos forgetting to go to Sunday lunch.

Mr. Avock, Miss Thirsdie, anniversary, red roses.

Mr. DeSarray, Miss Frydeigh, birthday, sunflowers.

Mr. Kayos, Miss Chewsday, Sunday lunch, chrysanthemums.

Mr. Mayhemme, Miss Wensdee, Saturday dinner, chocolates.

Mr. Termoyle, Miss Mundy, golf game, malt whiskey.

Gone to Market, p. 312

From clue 3, Sandy's stall, where the Belgian item was bought, must have been stall 7 or stall 8, so the item can't have been the silver hip flask (clue 4) or the porcelain vase (clue 3). The pewter jug came from Erroll's stall (clue 1) and the brass pillbox was of German origin (clue 7), while the gold etui was at stall 2 (clue 6), so Sandy must have sold Vic the earthenware pitcher. So, Sandy wasn't at stall 8 (clue 2) and must have run stall 7, and from clue 3, the porcelain vase must have been at stall 6, and was therefore a Dutch porcelain vase (clue 4). Steve ran stall 4 (clue 6) and we know Erroll's wasn't stall 2, 6, or 7. It wasn't stall 11 (clue 1), so Erroll's stall must have been stall 8, and the Italian item must have been bought from stall 11. So, from what we

already know, the Italian item must have been the silver hip flask, and, by elimination, the brass pillbox must have been on Steve's stall 4. Barney's stall wasn't stall 2 or stall 11 (clue 5), so he must have sold the Dutch porcelain vase from stall 6. The gold etui wasn't British (clue 6), so it must have been a French gold etui, leaving the British item as Erroll's pewter jug. Finally, from clue 5, Jane, who didn't sell the French etui at stall 2, must have sold the Italian hip flask at stall 11, leaving stall 2 as Kirk's.

2, Kirk, gold etui, French.

4, Steve, brass pill box, German.

6, Barney, porcelain vase, Dutch.

7, Sandy, earthenware pitcher, Belgian.

8, Erroll, pewter jug, British.

11, Jane, silver hip flask, Italian.

Rescue Party, p. 314

The dog was on Lindsay Street (clue 3), and Wharf Street was the site of the canal (clue 4), so the duck in the outhouse, which was not at Hopkins Farm or Burlington Road (clue 1), must have been on Alexandra Street. The rescue officer who dealt with it was not Clare (clue 2), Lenny, who went to Burlington Road (clue 1), Paul, who dealt with the animal stuck on the roof (clue 5), or Caroline, who helped rescue the cat (clue 6), so it must have been Bob. Lenny, on Burlington Road, didn't rescue the goat (clue 1), so it must have been the fox. It was not caught in a snare (clue 2), so it must have been knocked over. Clare's animal had also not been caught in a snare (clue 2), so it must have fallen into the canal on Wharf Street. By elimination, the animal caught in the snare must have been Caroline's cat. This was not on Lindsay Street, which was the dog, so it must have been at Hopkins Farm. By elimination, the Lindsay Street dog must have been up on the woof, sorry, roof and rescued by Paul, and Clare's animal that had fallen into the canal must have been the goat.

Bob, Alexandra Street, duck, trapped in outhouse.

Caroline, Hopkins Farm, cat, caught in snare.
Clare, Wharf Street, goat, fallen in canal.
Lenny, Burlington Road, fox, knocked over.
Paul, Lindsay Street, dog, stuck on the roof.

Love and Death, p. 316

The City Guard officer who died in an accident was either Aeric Ormson or Van the Axeman (clue 5). Van was killed trying to kill Shee-La (clue 1), so the City Guard must have been Aeric. The man from Eurali who died saving Shee-La wasn't Donal the Red (clue 3) or Mordok the Shark, who came from Kuhhrl (clue 4), so it must have been Garin of the Hills. He wasn't the pirate captain (clue 2) and can't have been the pit-fighter (clue 3) or the mercenary, who came from Ogravar (clue 4), so he must have been an outlaw leader. Donal the Red wasn't murdered (clue 3), so he must have died in battle. So, he can't have been the mercenary (clue 3) or the pit-fighter (clue 3) and must have been the pirate captain. So, he was not from Kroprom (clue 3) and must have been from Phoeba. By elimination, Mordok the Shark must have been murdered. He can't have been the mercenary (clue 4), so he must have been the pit-fighter. By elimination, the mercenary must have tried to kill Shee-La and was therefore Van the Axeman, and Aeric Ormson the City Guard must have been from Kroprom.

Aeric Ormson, City Guard officer, Kroprom, accident.
Donal the Red, pirate captain, Phoeba, in battle.
Garin of the Hills, outlaw leader, Eurali, saving Shee-La.
Mordok the Shark, pit-fighter, Kuhhrl, murdered.
Van the Axeman, mercenary, Ogravar, trying to kill Shee-La.

Bertram's Hotel, p. 318

The guest from Sydney in room 35 was male (clue 2). Frank Glen was in room 42 (clue 5) and Andy Brock was from Kingston (clue 6), so the man from Sydney must have been Jack King. He didn't complain about poor food (clue 6), Susan Terry complained about the faulty shower (clue 1), the New Yorker complained about the wrong paper (clue 3), and the guest in room 35 complained about not being able to sleep (clue 4), so Jack's complaint must have been about his passport being stolen. Susan's complaint rules her out for room 35, nor can she have been in room 05 (clue 1), so she must have been in room 51. From her complaint, she's not from New York and she can't be from Calgary (clue 1), so her home must be Dunedin, New Zealand. As Jack was in room 26, Andy Brock can't have been in room 35 (clue 6) and must have been in room 05. By elimination, the sleepless guest in room 35 must have been Pamela Quayle. From his or her complaint, the New Yorker can't be Pamela, who must thus be from Calgary, leaving Frank Glen as the New Yorker.

Andy Brock, Kingston, 05, poor food.
Frank Glen, New York City, 42, wrong paper.
Jack King, Sydney, 26, passport stolen.
Pamela Quayle, Calgary, 35, couldn't sleep.
Susan Terry, Dunedin, 51, faulty shower.

College Hall Saturday, p. 320

The Flab-Fighters meet at 9:45 a.m. (clue 6), so it's not the meeting in the Tower Room, which is at 9:15 a.m. (clue 4), or the Draw-Wing Room, where the meeting can't start later than 9:30 a.m. (clue 1). The Flab-Fighters don't meet in the Garde Room (clue 6) or the Sayle Room, used by the Writers' Circle (clue 3), so they must use the Bill Yard Room and are therefore led by Rose Garden (clue 7). From clue 1, the Crafters' Club can't meet in the Tower Room at 9:15 a.m., nor in the Draw-Wing Room, so they must be in the Garde Room. The Tower Room isn't used by the U3A (clue 4), which is led by Jean Poole (clue 2), so it must be used by the Dancercise group, and the U3A must meet in the Draw-Wing Room. Their meeting isn't at 9:30 a.m., when May Flower's group meets (clue 5), and clue 1 tells us it's not at 10:00 a.m., so it must be at 9:00 a.m. So, from clue 1, the 9:30 a.m. meeting must be the Crafters' Club's in the Garde Room. As Ruby Wryng's group meet earlier than Dawn Brakes's (clue 5), it must be the 9:15 a.m. one in the Tower Room, and Dawn's group must meet at 10:00 a.m. By elimination, this must be the Writers' Circle meeting in the Sayle Room.

Bill Yard Room, 9:45 a.m., Flab-Fighters, Rose Garden.
Draw-Wing Room, 9:00 a.m., U3A, Jean Poole.
Garde Room, 9:30 a.m., Crafters' Club, May Flower.
Sayle Room, 10:00 a.m., Writers' Circle, Dawn Brakes.
Tower Room, 9:15 a.m., Dancercise, Ruby Wryng.

Crème de la Crème, p. 322

Donalbain is figure 2 (clue 1) and Macbeth plays volleyball (clue 2), so figure 1, the rower (clue 8), who couldn't have been Third Witch (clue 3), must have been Lady Macduff. Figure 4 doesn't play tennis or hockey, the players of which both have other girls on their right (clues 3 and 4), so she must be the volleyball player who played Macbeth. The would-be President is right of the hockey player (clue 4), so she can't be the oarswoman, figure 1, or the hockey player. The tennis player wants to be a physicist (clue 3), so the would-be President must be the volleyball-playing figure 4. So, from clue 4, the hockey player must be figure 3 and the tennis-playing would-be physicist must be figure 2, Donalbain. By elimination, the hockey star must have been Third Witch. The tennis star's surname is either Polk or Sutton (clue 3), so Miss Cooper, who is either figure 1 or figure 2 (clue 2), must be figure 1, Lady Macduff the rower. So, from clue 3, the hockey player's surname must be Freeman. Miss Sutton is left of Judith (clue 7), so she can't be Macbeth and must be Donalbain, leaving Miss Polk, whose first name is Sonia (clue 6), as Macbeth, figure 4. By elimination, Miss Sutton must be figure 2, and, from

clue 7, figure 2 must be Judith. From clue 2, Miss Cooper isn't Helen and must be Angela, whose ambition is to be an army officer (clue 5), leaving Miss Sutton as Helen, and Judith Freeman's ambition as becoming a lawyer.

1, Angela Cooper, Lady Macduff, rowing, army officer.
2, Helen Sutton, Donalbain, tennis, physicist.
3, Judith Freeman, Third Witch, hockey, lawyer.
4, Sonia Polk, Macbeth, volleyball, President.

Wanted Men, p. 324

The Texas Ranger made the arrest in Belltower (clue 6). The State Sheriff's arrest in February wasn't in White Rock (clue 3) or in Eagle Creek, where Waco Shaw was caught (clue 1); the Fort Keppel arrest was in June (clue 5), so the February one must have been in San Pietro. Dan Griffin was caught in April (clue 4), Pat O'Kelly was shot by a bounty hunter (clue 1), and Joe Massey can't have been arrested in February (clue 6), so the State Sheriff must have arrested Buck Crane. The October capture wasn't by the bounty hunter (clue 1), the Pinkerton agent (clue 2), or the Texas Ranger (clue 6), so it must have been by the US Marshal. The bounty hunter didn't kill Pat O'Kelly in October or June (clue 1), so he must have done so in August, and Waco Shaw must have been caught in October. So, from clue 6, the Texas Ranger's arrest must have been in April, and his prisoner was therefore Dan Griffin, and Joe Massey was arrested in Fort Keppel in June. By elimination, Pat O'Kelly was shot in White Rock and Joe Massey must have been caught by the Pinkerton agent.

Buck Crane, February, San Pietro, State Sheriff.
Dan Griffin, April, Belltower, Texas Ranger.
Joe Massey, June, Fort Keppel, Pinkerton agent.
Pat O'Kelly, August, White Rock, bounty hunter.
Waco Shaw, October, Eagle Creek, US Marshal.

Play these other fun puzzle books by USA TODAY

USA TODAY Sudoku

USA TODAY Everyday Sudoku

USA TODAY Crossword

USA TODAY Logic

USA TODAY Mini Sudoku / Sudoku X

USA TODAY Word Roundup / Word Search

USA TODAY Word Play

USA TODAY Jumbo Puzzle Book

USA TODAY Picture Puzzles

USA TODAY Everyday Logic

USA TODAY Jumbo Puzzle Book 2

USA TODAY Don't Quote Me®

USA TODAY Txtpert™

USA TODAY Picture Puzzles Across America

USA TODAY Word Finding Frenzy

USA TODAY Sudoku 2

USA TODAY Crossword 2

USA TODAY Logic 2

USA TODAY Sudoku 3

USA TODAY Up & Down Words Infinity

USA TODAY Crossword 3

USA TODAY Sudoku Super Challenge

USA TODAY Crossword Super Challenge

USA TODAY Jumbo Puzzle Book Super Challenge